A Few NASCAR Records

Diehard NASCAR fans know their stats — here are a few to get you started:

- **NASCAR's winningest drivers:**
  - Richard Petty — 200
  - David Pearson — 105
  - Bobby Allison — 84
  - Darrell Waltrip — 84
  - Cale Yarborough — 83

- **NASCAR's top pole winners:**
  - Richard Petty — 126
  - David Pearson — 113
  - Cale Yarborough — 70
  - Darrell Waltrip — 59
  - Bobby Allison — 57

- **Multiple NASCAR Winston Cup Series Champions:**
  - Dale Earnhardt and Richard Petty — 7
  - Jeff Gordon, David Pearson, Lee Petty, Darrell Waltrip, and Cale Yarborough — 3
  - Buck Baker, Tim Flock, Ned Jarrett, Terry Labonte, Herb Thomas, and Joe Weatherly — 2

- Fastest lap of all-time: Bill Elliott — 212.809 mph (qualifying for the 1987 Winston 500 at Talladega Superspeedway in Alabama)

- Driver to top 200 mph more than anyone else: Cale Yarborough — 15 times in his career

- Most career race starts: Richard Petty — 1,177 (1958-92)

- Most career second-place finishes: Richard Petty — 158 (1958-92)

- Most consecutive top five finishes: David Pearson — 18 (1968)

- Most years leading the circuit in wins: Richard Petty — 7 (1958-92)

- Most consecutive years leading the circuit in wins: Jeff Gordon — 5 (1995-99)

- Most money won in a season: Jeff Gordon — $9,306,584 (1998)

- Most consecutive races started: Terry Labonte — 636 (1979-99)

- Most wins during a season in the modern era (1972 to present): Richard Petty and Jeff Gordon — 13

- Most consecutive wins in the modern era: 4 — Dale Earnhardt (1987), Bill Elliott (1992), Harry Gant (1991), Jeff Gordon (1998), Mark Martin (1993), Darrell Waltrip (1981), and Cale Yarborough (1976).

For Dummies™: Bestselling Book Series for Beginners

The Main Series

The three main NASCAR series are as follows:

- **NASCAR Winston Cup Series:** The NASCAR Winston Cup Series is where you can find NASCAR's superstars, including Jeff Gordon, Rusty Wallace, and Dale Earnhardt. NASCAR Winston Cup Series cars weigh 3,400 pounds without a driver and their engines produce about 750 horsepower, meaning the cars can reach speeds of 200 miles per hour at some tracks.

- **NASCAR Busch Series, Grand National Division:** Many drivers from the NASCAR Busch Series move to the NASCAR Winston Cup Series as they hone their driving skills, but some stay in this league because there's less pressure to perform. NASCAR Busch Series cars weigh 3,300 pounds without a driver and their engines produce about 550 horsepower, making the cars slower than their NASCAR Winston Cup Series counterparts.

- **NASCAR Craftsman Truck Series:** The NASCAR Craftsman Truck Series is the newest NASCAR series, beginning in 1995 with its inaugural season. It features souped-up pickup trucks with engines that produce about 710 horsepower. Trucks are capable of going about 190 miles per hour on certain tracks. This series is similar to the NASCAR Busch Series, because drivers are looking to advance to the NASCAR Winston Cup Series, but are happy making a living driving race trucks if no promotions pan out.

What the Flags Mean

During every NASCAR race, a NASCAR official (called the flagman) sits above the start/finish line, waving different colored flags at the competitors as they zoom by in their race cars. He's signaling them to slow down, speed up, move over, get off the track, or stop. Here's what his flags mean:

- **Green flag:** The flagman waves this flag to start a race or to restart a race. Green means "go," so when a driver sees this flag, he slams on the gas pedal and takes off.

- **Yellow flag:** A yellow flag means NASCAR officials have called a caution period because an accident or debris on the track makes driving conditions dangerous. When drivers see a yellow flag, they know they must slow down and drive cautiously around the track.

- **Red flag:** Drivers must stop on the racetrack — wherever they are — when they see the flagman wave a red flag. The red flag means it isn't safe for drivers to circle the track because of inclement weather or poor track conditions.

- **Black flag:** When the flagman waves a black flag at a driver, that driver must get off the track and go to the pits immediately. He did something wrong or his car isn't fit to be on the track.

- **Blue with diagonal yellow stripe:** This flag signifies to a driver that a faster, lead-lap car is about to pass him and he must yield to that car.

- **White flag:** This flag means that the race leader has one lap to go in the race.

- **Checkered flag:** When the checkered flag waves, a driver has crossed the finish line and won the race.

by Mark Martin

Hungry Minds™

HUNGRY MINDS, INC.

New York, NY ◆ Cleveland, OH ◆ Indianapolis, IN

NASCAR® For Dummies®

Published by
Hungry Minds, Inc.
909 Third Avenue
New York, NY 10022
www.hungryminds.com
www.dummies.com (Dummies Press Web site)

Library of Congress Catalog Card No.: 99-67176

ISBN: 0-7645-5219-8

Printed in the United States of America

10 9 8 7 6 5

1O/QV/QU/QR/IN

Distributed in the United States by Hungry Minds, Inc.

Distributed by CDG Books Canada Inc. for Canada; by Transworld Publishers Limited in the United Kingdom; by IDG Norge Books for Norway; by IDG Sweden Books for Sweden; by IDG Books Australia Publishing Corporation Pty. Ltd. for Australia and New Zealand; by TransQuest Publishers Pte Ltd. for Singapore, Malaysia, Thailand, Indonesia, and Hong Kong; by Gotop Information Inc. for Taiwan; by ICG Muse, Inc. for Japan; by Intersoft for South Africa; by Eyrolles for France; by International Thomson Publishing for Germany, Austria and Switzerland; by Distribuidora Cuspide for Argentina; by LR International for Brazil; by Galileo Libros for Chile; by Ediciones ZETA S.C.R. Ltda. for Peru; by WS Computer Publishing Corporation, Inc., for the Philippines; by Contemporanea de Ediciones for Venezuela; by Express Computer Distributors for the Caribbean and West Indies; by Micronesia Media Distributor, Inc. for Micronesia; by Chips Computadoras S.A. de C.V. for Mexico; by Editorial Norma de Panama S.A. for Panama; by American Bookshops for Finland.

For general information on Hungry Minds' products and services please contact our Customer Care Department within the U.S. at 800-762-2974, outside the U.S. at 317-572-3993 or fax 317-572-4002.

For sales inquiries and reseller information, including discounts, premium and bulk quantity sales, and foreign-language translations, please contact our Customer Care Department at 800-434-3422, fax 317-572-4002, or write to Hungry Minds, Inc., Attn: Customer Care Department, 10475 Crosspoint Boulevard, Indianapolis, IN 46256.

For information on licensing foreign or domestic rights, please contact our Sub-Rights Customer Care Department at 212-884-5000.

For information on using Hungry Minds' products and services in the classroom or for ordering examination copies, please contact our Educational Sales Department at 800-434-2086 or fax 317-572-4005.

Please contact our Public Relations Department at 212-884-5163 for press review copies or 212-884-5000 for author interviews and other publicity information or fax 212-884-5400.

For authorization to photocopy items for corporate, personal, or educational use, please contact Copyright Clearance Center, 222 Rosewood Drive, Danvers, MA 01923, or fax 978-750-4470.

Hungry Minds™ is a trademark of Hungry Minds, Inc.

About Mark Martin

photo: Steven Rose — Motorsports Memories

Mark Martin: Mark Martin has been racing all his life . . . well, practically. Mark began his professional racing career in the 1970s in the American Speed Association, where he was a four-time ASA champion. He successfully made the transition into the NASCAR Winston Cup Series scene in 1981, and has been racking up series points ever since. Since 1988, he has won 31 races in 12 full seasons and is considered by many to be the greatest active NASCAR Winston Cup Series driver without a championship. Over the last decade, he has finished in the top ten in the NASCAR Winston Cup Series annual point standings. Mark also has four IROC championships to his credit and is the winningest driver in the NASCAR Busch Series, with 38 wins.

He lives with his wife, Arlene, and son, Matt, in Florida.

About NASCAR

The National Association for Stock Car Auto Racing (NASCAR), organized in 1947 by Bill France, is America's premier motorsports and entertainment sanctioning body.

NASCAR's best known and most popular series is the NASCAR Winston Cup Series. Other top national series include the NASCAR Busch Series, Grand National Division and NASCAR Craftsman Truck Series. These marquee divisions are well-known to the millions of fans who attend these events and to the millions more who watch events on television. NASCAR also sanctions nine other regional touring series, as well as the NASCAR Weekly Racing Series.

To further benefit NASCAR's drivers, teams, tracks, and fans, the NASCAR lifestyle has become a recognized leader in the entertainment industry, including NASCAR Online (www.nascar.com), NASCAR Cafe restaurants, NASCAR Speed Parks, NASCAR Thunder retail stores, and NASCAR Silicon Motor Speedway. In February 2000, NASCAR also premiered its first animated children's television show, NASCAR Racers, on the Fox Kids Network.

Publisher's Acknowledgments

We're proud of this book; please send us your comments through our Online Registration Form located at www.dummies.com.

Some of the people who helped bring this book to market include the following:

Acquisitions and Editorial

Project Editor: Tere Drenth

Acquisitions Editor: Stacy S. Collins

General Reviewer: Bob Zeller

Acquisitions Coordinator: Lisa Roule

Editorial Director: Kristin A. Cocks

NASCAR Project Coordinator: Jennifer White

Special Help

Michelle Hacker, Wendy Lee, Jon Malysiak, Carol Strickland

Production

Project Coordinator: E. Shawn Aylsworth

Layout and Graphics: Elizabeth Brooks, Amy M. Adrian, Corey Bowen, Kelly Hardesty, Clint Lahnen, Barry Offringa, Tracy Oliver, Jill Piscitelli, Brent Savage, Jacque Schneider, Janet Seib, Brian Torwelle, Dan Whetstine

Special Art: Precision Graphics

Photography: Steven Rose — Motorsports Memories, David Schenk

Proofreaders: Laura Albert, Corey Bowen, John Greenough, Christine Pingelton, Marianne Santy

Indexer: Sherry Massey

General and Administrative

Hungry Minds, Inc.: John Kilcullen, CEO; Bill Barry, President and COO; John Ball, Executive VP, Operations & Administration; John Harris, CFO

Hungry Minds Consumer Reference Group

Business: Kathleen A. Welton, Vice President and Publisher; Kevin Thornton, Acquisitions Manager

Cooking/Gardening: Jennifer Feldman, Associate Vice President and Publisher

Education/Reference: Diane Graves Steele, Vice President and Publisher

Lifestyles: Kathleen Nebenhaus, Vice President and Publisher; Tracy Boggier, Managing Editor

Pets: Dominique De Vito, Associate Vice President and Publisher; Tracy Boggier, Managing Editor

Travel: Michael Spring, Vice President and Publisher; Suzanne Jannetta, Editorial Director; Brice Gosnell, Managing Editor

Hungry Minds Consumer Editorial Services: Kathleen Nebenhaus, Vice President and Publisher; Kristin A. Cocks, Editorial Director; Cindy Kitchel, Editorial Director

Hungry Minds Consumer Production: Debbie Stailey, Production Director

◆

The publisher would like to give special thanks to Patrick J. McGovern, without whom this book would not have been possible.

◆

Contents at a Glance

Cartoons at a Glance

By Rich Tennant

page 183

page 117

page 51

page 7

page 263

Fax: 978-546-7747
E-mail: richtennant@the5thwave.com
World Wide Web: www.the5thwave.com

Table of Contents

Introduction

· ·

Most of the time, people group NASCAR racing into one of two categories. It's a sport that's too simple because the cars just go around in circles. Or, it's a sport that's too technical because it's centered around engines, aerodynamics, and the physics of going fast. This book, however, shows you that NASCAR racing is really both of these things: It's simple in some ways, but complicated in others. That's what makes it so fun.

At first, the simplicity draws you in. You find that out when you go to a race — even if you close your eyes. When you sit in the grandstands, you can hear the cars roar by. You can feel the tremendous power of the engines when the stands shake, your seat vibrates, and your guts rumble. Then you can smell the distinct odor of burned rubber that hovers above the racetrack. NASCAR racing is a total body experience, you don't even have to see the cars — much less understand the inner workings of race cars — to get a thrill from racing.

If that's true, though, why read this book and find out all there is to know about NASCAR stock cars and NASCAR racing? Even though sitting in the stands with your eyes closed is entertaining, sitting there with an insider's view of the sport, including the technical side, enriches your experience so much more. You'll know what's going on when NASCAR officials give a driver a 15-second penalty. You won't be lost when the cars line up single file for a restart — and you'll know what a restart is! And a day later, you'll be able to hang out at the water cooler and talk to your co-workers with authority about the race. My job is to share with you all that a fan needs to know about NASCAR racing. That way, you can enjoy the sport as much as I do.

About This Book

I learned how to drive when I was just five years old, even before I could reach the pedals of a car. My dad propped me up in his lap, gave me the wheel, and then smashed his foot on the gas. From then on, I was hooked. I started to drive a race car at 15, even before I had a driver's license, and I woke up thinking about racing, and went to sleep dreaming about racing. And in all of my spare time, I worked on and raced cars. So it's no wonder the sport is such a big part of my life.

Sometimes, though, it's difficult to explain why NASCAR racing is so addictive, particularly to people who've never driven a race car and competed bumper-to-bumper at breakneck speeds. It's not like basketball, baseball, football, or other sports you play during recess in grade school.

I decided that the best way to explain my love for NASCAR racing wasn't by sticking fans in a race car and making them drive laps around Daytona International Speedway. It was by writing this book. If you can't discover the beauty of this sport by doing — and riding down the highway going 80 mph in your Honda Accord doesn't count — you may as well discover it by reading.

If you're a novice to NASCAR, I help you with the basics of the sport — the differences between the NASCAR Winston Cup Series and the NASCAR Busch Series, Grand National Division — so you can build upon your NASCAR knowledge from there. If you're more advanced, I share the subtleties of the sport so that you can sound like an old pro. No matter what level of NASCAR knowledge you have, you can find something new in the pages of this book — I believe it's the most comprehensive book available: I talk about NASCAR's origin, sponsors, engines, race teams, race strategies, pit stops, racetracks, and all you need to know if you want to be the quintessential NASCAR fan — and that's just the beginning. My goal is to get you to understand everything you see when you watch a race, and be able to converse and debate intelligently with the most ardent, well-informed NASCAR fans.

I hope that, in reading this book, you'll understand why NASCAR racing is my passion. Maybe it'll become your passion, too.

Foolish Assumptions

Even though this book is a ...For Dummies book, I don't assume that you're a fool. You're just trying to find out more about NASCAR racing so that you can enjoy the sport, as millions of people already do. Maybe you're a sports fan who's curious about racing. Maybe you're an avid race fan who wants to brush up on a few things. Maybe you're my mom who wants to read my book to boost my ego.

Maybe you just want the answers to these questions:

- Why does some guy stand above the track and wave all those flags? Is he telling the drivers something or part of an off-beat rhythmic gymnastics team?
- What is a restrictor-plate track and what's being restricted?
- Does it really matter where a driver qualifies for a race?
- Why do drivers have short tempers at short tracks?

✔ Are drivers athletes?

✔ Why are tires such a big deal during a race?

✔ Why does a regular Chevrolet Monte Carlo at a local dealership look nothing like the one Jeff Gordon drives?

✔ Who are the sponsors and why do race teams need them?

In this book, I answer these questions and more.

How This Book Is Organized

This book isn't just a few hundred pages of statistics and scintillating commentary. It's broken into five parts to be user-friendly. Each part deals with a major aspect of NASCAR racing and the parts are organized so you can find out more about the sport in a simple, painless manner. Each chapter within the part dissects a specific detail of the sport — such as qualifying, the racetracks, or different NASCAR series. Feel free to skip to the parts and chapters that interest you most.

Part I: NASCAR 101

If you've never seen NASCAR racing or only glanced at a race once or twice while flipping through the channels on your TV, you're probably wondering what all the hubbub is about. Why is NASCAR racing the nation's fastest growing sport? What is the allure? Why do I see the drivers on different cereal boxes or soda bottles every time I go to the supermarket? Is there a NASCAR invasion no one told me about? In this part, I reveal the mystery behind the boom of NASCAR racing.

Part II: What Makes It Stock-Car Racing?

I drive a Ford Taurus and make it go nearly 200 mph at some racetracks. I'm sure a few NASCAR fans wonder why their Taurus can't do the same thing. In this part, I tell you not only why your Taurus can't go that fast — besides the fact that the speed limits don't allow it — but also why yours has four doors while my Taurus doesn't have any. This is perhaps the most technical part of the book, detailing the race cars, the race teams, and many of the rules. It gets down to the nitty-gritty, which can help even the most avid NASCAR fan feel just a little more like a pro when tuning into a race or going to the racetrack.

Part III: What Happens On (And Off) the Track

Sometimes NASCAR drivers do strange things. They come in for pit stops and opt for just a splash-and-go. They draft behind other drivers on superspeed-ways with carburetor restrictor plates in their engines. They wear funny shoes. In this part, I decipher and explain racing itself, staying safe, and winning an event. No longer will you be perplexed when a driver talks about racing for championship points or doing the hat dance. The chapters in this part help you follow every word of racing jargon — and there's plenty of that to go around. NASCAR racing is its own world, and in this part, I invite you in and teach you about the native customs.

Part IV: Keeping Up with NASCAR Events

There's nothing worse than showing up at a NASCAR race in a hoop skirt and a bonnet. In this part, I tell you how to fit in at the racetrack by dressing like a NASCAR fan, talking like a NASCAR fan, watching a race like a NASCAR fan, and following NASCAR like a NASCAR fan.

Part V: The Part of Tens

If you don't have time to get drawn in by an entire chapter, the Part of Tens is perfect for you. In this part, you can find little morsels of information, pack-aged into neat, manageable (and short) chapters about NASCAR's all-time greatest drivers, the best NASCAR races, and future NASCAR stars. The lists aren't definitive so you can debate about it with your friends, but I picked my favorites.

Appendixes

In NASCAR racing, people talk in NASCAR language — which isn't at all simi-lar to the conversational French or obsolete Latin you studied in high school. It's a unique language used in racing circles and you can find a big chunk of it in Appendix A. They're all the racing terms you'll need to know.

Appendix B lists NASCAR's leading drivers in two major statistical categories, including NASCAR's winningest drivers. It's trivia you should know if you're planning to be a contestant on Jeopardy! some time soon.

Icons Used in This Book

To make things easier, I use icons — little pictures in the margins — throughout this book to highlight important information: giving you advice, a warning, or knowledge in order to impress friends at dinner parties.

This icon points out information that helps you save time, money, and effort.

If you know these words, you won't seem like an accountant among a group of rock stars when you're in a conversation with die-hard NASCAR fans.

Take heed when you see this caution flag. Its goal is to save you from losing money, getting hurt, or exposing yourself to other dangers.

When you see one of these icons, you'll know you're about to read a story from my years of NASCAR racing experience.

This information is for the real geeky fans who want to know all the details, no matter how complex. Non-geeks can skip these icons.

Where to Go from Here

You know when you're reading a great book and you're dying to get to the last chapter because you can't stand the suspense? Well, in this book you can. It won't ruin the story for you — because there is no story. There isn't a beginning, middle, or end, so just flip to the last chapter and read it first if you want. Go ahead. Your high school English teacher isn't looking. Actually, you can turn to any chapter and read it. There's nothing to be ashamed of because that's the way I've designed the book. Every chapter is written to stand alone and provide information about NASCAR's nuances. The Table of Contents and the Index list what's in this potpourri of NASCAR racing, so choose where you'd like to begin your journey — then have fun!

Part I
NASCAR 101

The 5th Wave   By Rich Tennant

"As a valued sponsor, sure, you can ride along during Happy Hour, but you'll have to leave your drink at the bar."

In this part . . .

NASCAR racing is everywhere nowadays: Races are on TV, racetracks are in nearly every part of the country, and drivers have their pictures on cereal boxes and billboards. If you're new to NASCAR, you may be perplexed by this invasion, so in this part, I reveal the mysteries of NASCAR racing and tell you why so many fans have been flocking to the sport in the recent years. I also answer all your questions about corporate involvement in the sport and why at times it seems as if NASCAR is one big, uninterrupted commercial for motor oil, beer, and laundry detergent.

In this part, I also describe each NASCAR series so that you can tell the difference between the NASCAR Winston Cup Series and the NASCAR Busch Series, Grand National Division — you'll also know that the Featherlite Southwest Series isn't racing's version of a featherweight boxing division.

If your dream is to be more than just a fan of the sport, I can help you out in that department, too. This part gives you a few hints on how to become a race car driver or get a job on a NASCAR crew.

Chapter 1

NASCAR Racing — The Best Sport Around

*N*ASCAR stands for the *National Association for Stock Car Auto Racing,* and it's the governing body for one of the most popular sports in the United States. NASCAR stages races and makes the rules for more than ten stock-car racing divisions that feature souped-up cousins to the passenger cars that you and I drive to the supermarket. Unlike your family sedan, however, stock cars can reach speeds of more than 200 miles per hour and have high-performance engines that make your car seem as if it's powered by two AA batteries.

The speed and power of NASCAR stock cars — and the people who drive those cars — have enticed millions of fans to the sport in recent years, making it the fastest-growing sport in the nation. In 1998, more than 6 million fans went to see NASCAR Winston Cup Series races. The NASCAR Winston Cup Series is the most watched and glitziest division of stock-car racing, with attendance quadrupling since 1980 and nearly doubling since 1990. NASCAR sanctions a dozen other series, including the NASCAR Busch Series and the NASCAR Craftsman Truck Series, discussed in Chapter 3.

With its phenomenal growth, NASCAR racing is outpacing every other major sport in the nation. Here's how some other pro sports grew since 1990, at the same time NASCAR's attendance rose 91 percent:

✔ National Hockey League (NHL) attendance was up 45.8 percent.

✔ Major League Baseball attendance increased by 28.4 percent.

✔ National Basketball Association (NBA) attendance grew 20.7 percent.

✔ National Football League (NFL) attendance rose 7.1 percent.

NASCAR racing's TV ratings have grown just as fast as its attendance has. Network ratings are up 19 percent, and cable ratings are up 33 percent since 1993. More than 180 million viewers tuned into NASCAR Winston Cup Series events in 1998. Those statistics make NASCAR Winston Cup Series racing one of the most popular sports to watch on TV, second only to NFL games.

Traditionally, stock-car racing has been known as a southern sport, with southern drivers and southern racetracks. But with increased TV coverage, media exposure, and new racetracks popping up from coast to coast — and in Alaska, too! — it has become a national sport. This chapter explains why NASCAR racing has spread so quickly with such fervor.

From Back Roads to the Big Time

Just a few decades ago, stock-car races weren't the professionally-run events that they are now, even though many organizations — including the United Stock Car Racing Association, the Stock Car Auto Racing Society, and the National Championship Stock Car Circuit — sanctioned the races. The schedule wasn't organized; instead, random races were held here and there, sprinkled throughout the southeastern United States wherever tracks were available (some were well-built but most were pretty shoddy). Some race promoters were less-than-honest, some even running off with the race purses and revenues, never to be seen again. Even worse, nobody — not even some of the less-observant drivers — knew who was in a race until the cars lined up for the start of the event.

Bill France Sr., a stock-car racer and race promoter, thought this was a silly way to run a sport, so he was determined to set a standard for drivers and track owners. He decided to devote his energy to promoting one main racing series — NASCAR. A *racing series* is similar to a baseball league, featuring a group of competitors who compete in a set number of events and follow a set of rules determined by the sanctioning body. At the end of the season, the sanctioning body in charge of making the rules, running the events, and making sure people follow the rules, names a series champion. That's exactly what France, who was also known as "Big Bill," wanted to create for stock-car racing. France had several goals:

- ✔ **Racetracks that were safe for the drivers, and track owners who repaired their facilities between races:** If a car crashed into or through a guardrail during one race weekend, under new rules, the track would have to be repaired by the next race.

- ✔ **Rules that wouldn't change from week-to-week or from race to race:** Before NASCAR was born, different tracks had different rules, and that drove racers crazy. Some even had quirky on-track rules, made up that morning by the race promoter to make things more fun. Because of these inconsistencies, drivers didn't know what to expect when they showed up at a racetrack.

- ✓ **A set schedule, to allow the same drivers to compete against each other each week:** This way, a national champion could be crowned at the end of the year.

- ✓ **A uniform point system to calculate which driver performed the best throughout the season:** Drivers could earn points according to how they finish in a race, with the winner receiving the most points and the last-place driver getting the least. With a points system like that, voilà!, the series could crown a definitive national champion, instead of having many "national champions" walking around after getting crowned at different tracks or in different, smaller series. Having just one national champion would make winning the title something special.

- ✓ **An insurance and benevolent fund:** This was meant to give the drivers something to fall back on in case they got hurt or couldn't drive anymore because of injuries.

MARK SAYS

The first NASCAR race

At NASCAR's debut, more than 14,000 people showed up at a track just south of Daytona Beach to see that race, making the first race a big hit. The 150-mile event was held on a unique track that was half on the beach and half on a local road, making it interesting for drivers, particularly when the tide was rushing in and the beach course narrowed. Red Byron, a driver from Anniston, Alabama, whose left leg was mangled when his bomber was shot down in World War II, won that first NASCAR race, enhancing his reputation as one of NASCAR's greatest early drivers. It also made him the answer to a common NASCAR trivia question: "Who won the first NASCAR-sanctioned race?"

Red Byron also won NASCAR's first Strictly Stock championship. The series debuted in 1949 and was limited to full-sized American stock cars only. The first Strictly Stock race was held in June 1949, when anyone with a car was eligible to race. And that was anyone — people who had never raced before made the trip to the ¾-mile dirt track in Charlotte, North Carolina, to see how they could do. All they needed was a car and a fair amount of guts.

The cars were plain vehicles like Buicks, Fords, and Lincolns, not like today's race cars, which are built from the ground up by multimillion-dollar teams and tuned specifically for racing (see Chapter 4). If drivers wanted to race back then, their family cars would turn into their race cars. That meant they drove their cars from home to the track — then onto the track! That also meant if a driver crashed and destroyed his car, he would be stranded. Hitchhiking home became an art.

At the first Strictly Stock races, drivers did modify their cars a little to compete in the race — that included smashing their headlights beforehand so that glass wouldn't land on the track after a head-on collision.

NASCAR has accomplished all of France's goals. Racetracks are safe and well-maintained. The annual racing schedule doesn't vary much from year-to-year. NASCAR tallies points earned at each race and at the end of the year, awards the series championship to the driver with the most points (see Chapter 8 for details).

What NASCAR Isn't

When people think of auto racing, the same image of a race car doesn't necessarily pop into their heads. That's because many different types of racecars and hundreds of different racing series, or racing leagues, exist throughout the world. Those series feature different types of cars — and stock cars are just one of them (see Figure 1-1).

Here are a few different race cars besides NASCAR stock cars:

✔ **Open-wheel cars:** The cars that run in the Indianapolis 500, perhaps the most famous car race in the world, are *open-wheel cars.* They're agile, lightweight racing cars with an *open cockpit,* which means they have no roofs. Open-wheel cars also have no fenders, so there's no sheet metal over the wheel area protecting the tires. With no fenders, they can't bump and bang as stock cars do, because they'll crash.

While NASCAR racing is exclusively a U.S.-based sport, you can find open-wheel racing on nearly every continent. It includes these prominent racing series:

- Formula One, which is arguably the world's most well-known open-wheel series.

- Championship Auto Racing Teams (CART), which races in various countries but mostly the United States on road courses and ovals.

- Indy Racing League (IRL), which races exclusively on oval tracks in the United States and has the Indy 500 on its yearly schedule.

✔ **Dragsters:** *Dragsters* are cars made to travel a short distance in a very short period of time. The fastest ones can go from zero to 100 mph in less than one second, reaching speeds of more than 320 mph. The top level dragsters are called *Top Fuel cars,* which are specialized cars that look more like rocket ships than anything else. They have long, tapered noses with two small tires at the front, then the driver sits in an open-topped cockpit about ten feet behind those wheels, with the engine behind him or her. Other dragsters look more like passenger cars: Funny cars are modified, jazzed-up stock cars, while Street Stock cars look like passenger cars.

✔ **Sports cars:** Most sports cars are just stock cars with highly specialized engines, but the fastest sports cars are open-cockpit cars that are close to the ground, like Ferraris, but without roofs. Those cars are prototypes, meaning they are built specifically for racing and aren't sold to the public.

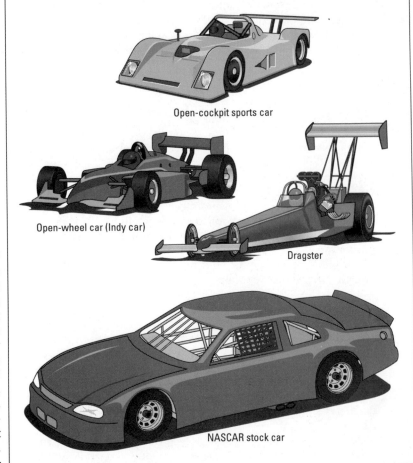

Open-cockpit sports car

Open-wheel car (Indy car)

Dragster

Figure 1-1: NASCAR stock cars look more like passenger cars than do open-wheel racecars, dragsters, or open-cockpit sports cars.

NASCAR stock car

Why NASCAR Racing Is So Popular

Many of today's NASCAR fans didn't grow up driving a race car or even going to stock-car races at their local track. Still, the sport is widely popular. The allure of NASCAR racing is multi-faceted, beginning with the colorful sights and the loud, resonating sounds of the sport. The other reasons are aplenty, including the tremendous exposure the sport gets on TV; drivers' accessibility to their fans; and close, competitive racing. It's addictive for a lot of reasons, but the bottom line is, people enjoy it because it's fun and exciting — for the competitors, too.

The need for speed

It's hard to explain the feeling a driver gets when he slides into a race car and takes hold of something so powerful. It's kind of like the feeling I get flying my private plane to races, something I started to do because of the strict time constraints on NASCAR drivers. At first, it was the only way I could get to testing sessions, practices, and races on time — because flying commercial airlines just didn't cut it. Soon after I began flying, though, I realized how awesome it is to soar through the air at 500 mph in a Learjet, with nothing to hinder me. It's unbelievable to be in control of something so powerful, which is the same feeling I get when driving a race car. I assume the feeling translates to fans when they watch races.

Watching a NASCAR race is a total-body experience: the earth-shattering sound of 750 horsepower engines roaring when drivers flip their ignition switches, the sound of the cars as they zoom by on the track — sort of like super-charged, giant-sized bees flying a million miles an hour — the feel of the grandstand vibrating as cars speed by, the undeniably gritty smell of burned rubber mixed in with gasoline and grease, and the huge assortment of colorful cars painted with all sorts of cool designs and logos. But speed is usually the first thing that lures fans to the sport.

Fans love to see cars go fast — maybe because they'd like to go fast themselves. It's sort of like driving down a secluded part of the highway at night knowing there are no cops around. Who wouldn't push the speed limit? That's what first attracted me to racing. I just wanted to go fast and think of ways to go faster.

While the adrenaline and the speed got me interested in racing, winning is what has kept me there. I wish I could describe the feeling of winning a race and pulling into Victory Lane with thousands of people cheering, and then having the car owner and crew there to celebrate the victory. It's just the most amazing feeling on earth — I wish everyone could experience it just once.

How I got started

Growing up in Batesville, Arkansas, I thought racing was the greatest thing in the world. My dad got me interested in it and, considering racing is for people who love taking risks, it was no wonder he liked it so much. My dad was the wildest, craziest, fastest-running guy around, and he wanted me to be the same way. As time went on, I began to love racing just as much as he did. And that played a big role in my wanting to drive cars for a living.

My dad used to prop me up in his lap while he was in the driver's seat of the car, and then, without taking no for an answer, would make me take the steering wheel. Then, he'd slam his foot on the accelerator and off we'd go. It scared me to death, but I was stuck steering that car sometimes at speeds over 80 mph on gravel roads around our hometown. But the more we drove, the more I got used to it — and the more I fell in love with the sensation of going fast and taking the car to the edge.

I started racing cars when I was 15, even before I had a driver's license. That's when I discovered everything about the sport of stock-car racing thrilled me. I became obsessed with the sounds and the speed — but mostly the prospect of becoming a successful driver someday. For me, there was nothing better than driving a race car, especially because I was good at it. I won my first race in only my second start at a local track in Arkansas.

The thrill of competition

Like other professional sports, NASCAR racing uses a rule book. Unlike other professional sports, that rule book changes during the season — and can even change from week to week. Even though that sounds annoying, it's beneficial for NASCAR racing in the long run. The good part about it is every team must follow the same set of rules, just as Bill France Sr. envisioned when he formed NASCAR, even if those rules frequently change. That's NASCAR's way of making sure that races are close and the competition is intense.

NASCAR officials tweak the rules throughout the year in order to make sure one car brand doesn't have a huge advantage on the track. The goal in NASCAR Winston Cup Series racing is to get all the competitors' cars as comparable as possible, so that one type of car doesn't have a distinct edge over any other. How fun would it be to watch races every week where the top ten cars were Pontiacs? Not much for the drivers and teams, either — especially for me, because I drive a Ford!

NASCAR's job isn't easy. Three brands of cars compete in the NASCAR Winston Cup Series — the Chevrolet Monte Carlo, the Ford Taurus, and the Pontiac Grand Prix. (The Dodge Intrepid makes its debut in the series in 2001.) These makes of cars are in the series because their manufacturers — General Motors, Ford, and DaimlerChrysler — want to market that specific brand of American-made passenger car to the public. If their brand of car wins a race on Sunday, car manufacturers believe consumers will be attracted to the car and want to buy one.

In NASCAR's rule book, it says the cars must be "American-made steel bodied passenger sedans," which is why Japanese car companies such as Honda and Toyota, who build engines for other racing series, aren't involved in NASCAR. That may change in the coming years, though, as more and more foreign cars are built in the United States — but only if NASCAR doesn't change or clarify its rules.

NASCAR racing is about much more than just making rules and sticking to them, though. Complicated strategies go into racing (see Chapter 9), which means that winning a race and becoming successful in NASCAR takes much more than just driving fast. It takes a savvy driver, a crew that works well together, a strong engine, and a sleek car. It takes fast pit stops and smooth moves on the track. It takes some luck, too.

Rules keep the fans happy

An example of the changing rules came at the beginning of the 1998 season, when the new Ford Taurus made its debut in the NASCAR Winston Cup Series. The car did quite well — too well as far as NASCAR was concerned. In the third race of the season at Las Vegas Motor Speedway, 13 of the top 14 finishers drove a Taurus. So to even things out among the Taurus, the Pontiac Grand Prix, and the Chevrolet Monte Carlo — which are the three car makes in the NASCAR Winston Cup Series — NASCAR changed the rules for the Taurus. The new rule mandated that Ford Taurus teams shave off a quarter inch from their cars' rear spoilers, the metal blade sticking up from the top of their trunk (see Chapters 4 and 13), which NASCAR thought would take away their aerodynamic advantage. Still, that rule change didn't do the trick. One week later at Atlanta Motor Speedway, eight of the top nine cars were Tauruses. NASCAR cut down the spoiler even more to even out the competition — and it worked.

To be honest, it can be frustrating to deal with a constantly changing rule book. For example, if a driver's team finds an edge over everybody else with the car's aerodynamics or in a particular part of the engine, NASCAR may change the rule regarding that area, which means that the car's advantage disappears. It's difficult to swallow at times, but I do appreciate how exciting those rule changes make the races for the fans. Without exciting races, there would be no fans. And without fans, I wouldn't be living my dream and racing for a living. So it's a necessary trade-off between the rules and success. And, unlike the rules changes before NASCAR was formed, at least we know our rule changes in advance. And at least we know there's a reason for all of it — to keep the competition even.

Mark Martin fans

It's hard to believe how many NASCAR fans buy racing paraphernalia to support their favorite drivers. Then again, as a driver it's even harder to believe how many fans root for me. I drove for a long time before that sunk in, but I'll never forget the moment it did. In 1990, a long seven years after my first NASCAR Winston Cup Series race, I was driving at North Wilkesboro Speedway in North Carolina, battling Dale Earnhardt for the lead. At that point, Earnhardt had won three of the seven NASCAR Winston Cup Series championships he has now, and my goal was to keep him from winning his fourth championship that year and to beat him in that race. It wasn't easy getting by Earnhardt, but when I finally passed him, the crowd went nuts.

Usually a driver doesn't see the fans because he's concentrating so much on the race. On that day, though, I could see the crowd out of the corner of my eye as soon as I began the pass. They were standing up, hooting and hollering as loud as they could as I pulled next to Earnhardt. They only got wilder as we raced side-by-side down the frontstretch, which is the straight section of racetrack between the first and last turns (see Chapter 8 for more details on the layout of racetracks). It created an even bigger stir when I passed Earnhardt for good and won the race that day. At that moment, standing there in Victory Lane and seeing all those fans, I realized that the crowd was rooting for me and that I had a pretty big following. Even though Earnhardt won the championship that year, with me finishing second, I still felt pretty good about that moment at North Wilkesboro. It was unforgettable.

Winning has become increasingly difficult as the sport has become more popular and more drivers enter races. That makes winning more special than it used to be. Don't get me wrong, it was special when I won my first NASCAR Winston Cup Series race in 1989, but today, there isn't as much disparity in equipment between first- and last-place teams. This is fine with me because it makes winning more satisfying.

Accessibility to drivers

The best part of racing is that drivers are regular people just like everybody else — and nearly as accessible. There are many ways to meet drivers, which is what many people think makes the sport special. NASCAR has no prima donnas, or at least not many, and for the most part everybody is humble about making it to the big time. Maybe that's because we still remember the days when we built, tuned, and fixed our own cars. Or maybe that's because we know how important the fans are to our sport — and without them we'd still be racing on some dirt track in Arkansas. Whatever the reason, it's not too difficult to meet a driver or get an autograph if you put some effort into it. It's not like the NBA or the NFL where you could wait years to meet your favorite athlete — or maybe never meet him at all.

Meeting Richard Petty

To give you an idea of how easy it was — and still is — to meet a driver, here's how I met Richard Petty, NASCAR's King. Petty is NASCAR's winningest driver, with 200 victories and seven NASCAR Winston Cup Series championships. He was just hanging out in his race shop when my dad and I went to visit. I was a teenager then and, of course, my jaw dropped when I saw him, but my dad was bold enough to approach him and introduce ourselves. Richard Petty was the most gracious guy I'd ever met and he talked to us for about ten minutes. Meeting Petty, who was, in my mind, the ultimate human being next to my dad, was one of the best things I'd ever experienced. There he was, the most famous stock-car driver in the world, just chatting with us about racing! To this day, that's one of the most memorable moments of my life.

People can relate to racing

Almost everyone knows what it's like to drive a car, but not everyone knows what it's like to dunk a basketball or hit a 100-mph fastball 500 feet for a homerun. People can relate to NASCAR racing because it seems so simple. That's why people, whether they admit it or not, speed down the highway and daydream about winning the Daytona 500. That daydreamer could be a 17-year-old high schooler who just got a driver's license, a 35-year-old orthodontist, or a 70-year-old retired school teacher. Driving, unlike other sports, is nearly universal. And people are drawn to it because they know how to do it.

In addition to being able to relate to driving the cars, fans also can relate to the drivers, perhaps more than they do to other athletes. Drivers don't just go from driving a stock car in high school to driving one for millions of dollars after signing a huge contract with a team. They must start at the bottom, many times building or working on their own equipment, proving their talent, and moving up the ranks in the sport. That makes even the best, most highly paid drivers in NASCAR more like your down-to-earth neighbor than like millionaires.

The sponsors

It costs millions of dollars to operate a NASCAR team each year, so team owners must get companies to sponsor their race teams to ease most of the financial burden. Those companies use NASCAR racing as a vehicle (no pun intended) for their marketing campaigns because their corporate logos are plastered on the car and on the drivers' uniforms. (See Chapter 2 for more on sponsors.) But it's a two-way street because NASCAR benefits, too. NASCAR's drivers aren't just identified with their sport, they're also identified with everyday products. When NASCAR fans see a box of Kellogg's Corn Flakes, they think of Terry Labonte, whose sponsor is Kellogg's. When they order a bottle of Miller Lite beer, they think of Rusty Wallace, who is sponsored by Miller. When they put a quart of STP oil in their car, they think of Richard Petty, NASCAR's winningest driver, whose sponsor was STP. So sponsors are integral in boosting NASCAR's popularity and helping the sport grow because they expose so many more people to the sport — even people who aren't necessarily sports fans. And, if it weren't for sponsors, teams wouldn't have enough money to travel to all the races so fans across the nation can see them compete in person.

Signing up the first sponsor

In 1970, Robert Glenn Johnson Jr., a legendary NASCAR driver and car owner who made his name as a bootlegger before racing in NASCAR, took a trip to Winston-Salem, North Carolina, and changed the sport of stock-car racing forever. Johnson, who goes by Junior instead of his given name, went to the town to talk to R.J. Reynolds Tobacco Company (RJR) executives and convince them to sponsor his race team. The meeting resulted in much more than anyone imagined. Instead of sponsoring Johnson's race team, RJR ended up sponsoring the entire series! Johnson's initial meeting with RJR executives prompted him to introduce those executives to NASCAR officials, which, in turn, began the relationship between NASCAR and RJR. That relationship still exists today. RJR decided to sponsor NASCAR's entire Grand National Series, which was NASCAR's top series at the time. That's how NASCAR's premier series became known as the NASCAR Winston Cup Series — Winston is one of RJR's main cigarette brands.

The sponsorship was the biggest thing to happen to the sport up to that point. RJR, with its power to promote and advertise, brought NASCAR racing into the mainstream. With the sponsorship, the schedule was reduced from more than 50 events each year to just about 30 — with no more than one race per week. The races that were eliminated were at small-town tracks, so only the bigger tracks — which could attract bigger crowds and make the series more professional — held races.

RJR's involvement in NASCAR paved the way for many other sponsors to get involved in the sport. They began sponsoring teams in order to get their products' names plastered on the sides of race cars — 200-mph billboards were born. Today, every team has a sponsor, including some of the U.S.'s biggest companies who produce some of the most popular products such as DuPont Automotive Finishes, Tide, Exide Batteries, and Kodak film. My team is sponsored by Valvoline, a motor oil company, and Cummins, an engine company. All sponsors have brought more exposure to the sport, too, through their commercials and magazine ads. (More about sponsorship in Chapter 2.)

Television time

When ESPN began broadcasting in 1979, it needed to fill up 24 hours each day with sports, sports, and sports of any kind. So broadcasting racing was an ideal way for them to fill up the hours. It was a perfect fit — you had a sports station that was looking for sports to televise and a sport that was looking to be on TV. TV rights to races were less expensive then, costing the networks about $50,000 per race. After the two came together, viewers stumbled upon racing, including NASCAR racing, whether they liked it or not because it was on so often. So television has helped the sport grow because so many people have become interested, perhaps after stumbling upon it while flipping through the channels.

The first NASCAR broadcast from beginning to end on TV was the 1979 Daytona 500, and that catapulted the sport into a new era. Now, nearly every major network and many cable stations can say they have broadcast a NASCAR race or have had some NASCAR coverage. That includes not only the major networks and ESPN, but also less sports-oriented stations such as The Nashville Network (TNN), which dedicates a lot of its time to NASCAR coverage.

It's a family affair

NASCAR promotes itself as a family sport and there's a lot of truth to that. It's a clean-cut sport filled with people who don't mind being role models and who (usually) don't get arrested, don't do drugs, and don't do shocking things that athletes from other sports may get caught doing. I think that it's rare to find a sport like that these days and I think that's partly why parents aren't afraid to bring their kids to the races.

Families interested in going to NASCAR races should keep the following points in mind, however:

- ✔ It's not the cheapest event that you can take your kids to, with tickets ranging from $25 to more than $250. Some tracks may have special, discounted tickets for younger children.
- ✔ It may not be a G-rated experience. Although some NASCAR fans are well behaved, some aren't.
- ✔ Drinking alcohol is allowed in the grandstands and in the infield, where fans have been known to carry coolers filled with alcohol and walk around somewhat less-than-clothed.

Not much of that gallivanting goes on during races, though. Much of it is contained to pre- and post-race activities, so if you want to protect your children from that hubbub, show up at the racetrack and head right for your seats.

Even though NASCAR racing is dangerous by nature and its fans may get out of hand at times, I think most of its athletes are special in the sports world — and that's what makes it appealing to families and children. Most racers are good, unspoiled guys who appreciate their families as much as they appreciate racing. In fact, many drivers bring their families to races because they are fortunate enough to have motorhomes parked at the racetrack so that families can stay together during race weekends. Many drivers attend a church service the morning of a race. We try to be as well-behaved as possible, because we realize that we are role models and that kids are watching our every move.

Racing started out as a family sport for me back in Arkansas, too. Even though my parents were divorced, racing was one way my family would get together and have fun. So, some of my best memories with my family were staged at the racetrack. Now I'm also creating some of those same memories for my 8-year-old son, Matt, who is starting to race quarter midgets at a small track near where I live in Florida. Quarter midgets are open-wheel cars small enough for young children to drive. My wife, Arlene, and I watch him race and always have a blast. It's just like old times.

NASCAR is like that, too — it's where families get together to watch their family members compete. What makes NASCAR especially family-oriented, though, is the many families who have been in the sport for generations — including the Frances who started NASCAR. Here are a few NASCAR racing families involved in the sport:

✔ **The Pettys:**

- Lee — winner of the first Daytona 500. Won NASCAR championships in 1954, '58, and '59.

- Richard (Lee's son) — holds the NASCAR record for career victories (200) and is tied with Dale Earnhardt for the most NASCAR Winston Cup Series championships (7).

- Kyle (Richard's son) — races in the NASCAR Winston Cup Series.

- Adam (Kyle's son) — raced in the NASCAR Busch Series, Grand National Division.

✔ **The Earnhardts:**

- Ralph — raced in NASCAR in the late 1950s and early '60s.

- Dale (Ralph's son) — shares the NASCAR record for most NASCAR Winston Cup Series titles (7) with Richard Petty. He raced in the NASCAR Winston Cup Series.

- Dale Jr. — won two consecutive NASCAR Busch Series championships, beginning in 1998, his first full season in the series. He will be a NASCAR Winston Cup Series rookie in 2000.

✔ **The Jarretts:**

- Ned — two-time NASCAR Winston Cup Series champion (1961 and '65).

- Dale (Ned's son) — won the 1999 NASCAR Winston Cup Series title.

- Jason (Dale's son) — races in the NASCAR Busch Series.

✔ **The Labontes:**

- Terry — two-time NASCAR Winston Cup Series champion who races in the series.

- Bobby (Terry's younger brother) — races in the NASCAR Winston Cup Series.

✔ **The Bodines:**

- Geoffrey — former Daytona 500 winner who still races in the NASCAR Winston Cup Series.

- Brett (Geoffrey's brother) — races in the NASCAR Winston Cup Series.

- Todd (Geoffrey's youngest brother) — races in the NASCAR Busch Series, and occasionally in the NASCAR Winston Cup Series.

✔ **The Wallaces:**

- Rusty — 1989 NASCAR Winston Cup Series champion.

- Mike — races in the NASCAR Craftsman Truck Series.

- Kenny — races in the NASCAR Winston Cup Series.

While plenty of family members have competed in NASCAR over the years, nobody beats the Pettys in longevity and racing lineage. Adam Petty was the fourth generation of the family to race in NASCAR — and no other pro sport can say that they had a fourth-generation athlete in their ranks. Maybe that's why people think NASCAR is so family-oriented — it's perfect for families because it's comprised of families. For me, it doesn't get any better than that.

MARK SAYS

Where are the women?

While NASCAR racing is family oriented, with many fathers, sons, and brothers in the sport, you won't see many mothers, daughters, or sisters on race teams. The truth is, there just aren't many women involved in NASCAR racing. As you may guess, stock-car racing started out as a male-dominated sport, and it hasn't changed much in image or in practice. Women have made only small advances in driving race cars, and nearly negligible advances in working as team mechanics or engineers. That's why I refer to drivers and team members as "he" throughout this book.

Even so, a few women drivers and women team members have made it at NASCAR's highest levels, such as NASCAR Winston Cup Series and NASCAR Busch Series racing. For example, Janet Guthrie raced in NASCAR Winston Cup Series in the mid-1970s, and competed in the 1977 Daytona 500, making her the only woman to compete in NASCAR's premier event. She finished 12th. More recently, Patty Moise raced a full season in the NASCAR Busch Series in 1998, but didn't return the next season. Also, Shawna Robinson, now a mother of two, became the only woman to win a pole position for a NASCAR Busch Series race, but took a hiatus from the sport in 1996 when she had difficulty securing a sponsor, and then decided to have children.

While not many women race, the ones who do aren't harassed or berated for getting involved in racing. Robinson, for example, says that people treat her just as they do the men drivers — and she prefers it that way because she would rather distinguish herself as a good driver than as a good *woman* driver.

Women have come a long way since the 1970's, when it was against most racetracks' rules for women to be in the pits because men thought it was inappropriate. (Stevie Waltrip, Darrell Waltrip's wife, got around those rules by listing herself as her husband's car owner so she could gain access to the pits. While women were banned, cars owners were not.)

Today, though, working in the NASCAR garage isn't that difficult — you can find women in the garage area on any given race weekend. Many women work as public relations representatives for drivers or race teams, journalists, and as car owners, who mostly own the team in name only while their husbands play an active role. (See Chapter 6 for more on team owners.) Some drivers' wives prefer to be more involved in the sport than others, including Jeff Burton's wife, Kim, who, like a few others, sits in the pits during a race and keeps a record of the pit stops and laps her husband has completed.

While the number of women working in the garage has grown only slowly over the years, the number of female fans recently has rocketed. Today, nearly 50 percent of fans who attend races are women, which is a tremendous gain from 1975 when just 15 percent of attendees were women. That growth is part of the overall growth of NASCAR. When men go to races, they figure why not bring their wives, girlfriends, or daughters along? That demystifies the sport for women, while getting them addicted to the sport at the same time.

Chapter 2

The Big Business of NASCAR

*I*f you think NASCAR racing is just a bunch of rednecks driving souped-up cars, you're mistaken. It takes much more than a guy working on his granddad's old Plymouth — no matter how powerful the engine — to race in NASCAR today. And the money invested and reaped is pretty hefty, too.

You can see evidence of NASCAR's growth everywhere you look. While you may expect to find life-sized cutouts of Dale Earnhardt (the seven-time NASCAR Winston Cup Series champion) greeting you when you go to a General Motors dealership, nowadays you bump into likenesses of NASCAR drivers in places you may never expect to: on TV, in toy stores, and even in supermarkets.

This chapter tells you how and why NASCAR competition means big money.

Sponsors Pay the Bills

NASCAR racing is more sponsor-oriented than any other sport in the world. The entire race is often sponsored by a big-time company — note the DieHard 500, NAPA AutoCare 500, Pepsi 400, and Coca-Cola 600, among others. Sometimes, those race titles go a little overboard: Just try sounding natural when saying "Yeah, I was really glad to win the UAW-GM Quality 500 today, but it wasn't as challenging as the Goody's Headache Powder 500 was last week. Now, that race was almost as hard as the SaveMart/Kragen 350." Let me tell you, it ain't easy.

NASCAR racing is filled with sponsors every place else, too. In fact, it's hard to get away from them. Cars are covered with decals of the companies that sponsor race teams. The drivers' uniforms are also covered with those company names — on the chest, on the back, going down both sleeves and going down the sides of both legs. (See the color photo section, near the center of this book.) Even the racing team has the sponsor plastered all over its uniforms.

When drivers are walking around in casual clothes, the sponsors still get their names in plain view, by having drivers wear hats, golf shirts, or button-down shirts with the sponsors' names on them. This serves as a constant reminder of the relationship between driver and sponsor — especially for the fans, who use the sponsor to identify and differentiate drivers and teams.

There are different levels of sponsorship, based on how much the company pays to the team. But no matter how much or how little the company spends, they all do it for the same reason: Sponsoring a race team gives companies a fantastic marketing tool on race day — a 200-mile-an-hour billboard. Many companies, including *Fortune* 500 companies, take advantage of that.

The primary sponsors are loaded

Primary sponsors are the bigwig companies that pay big bucks to put their name on the car's hood, which is the best place to advertise because fans can see it so well. The price tag for sponsoring a NASCAR Winston Cup Series team is $5 million per season on the average — but higher profile and more successful teams get much more, many times in excess of $10 million. Teams must secure a good primary sponsor because the costs of equipment, travel, and personnel are just too expensive for a team owner to absorb by himself. Without a constant flow of cash, a team can't hire the best employees or get the best equipment — and in racing today, those factors are keys to winning.

Valvoline, the motor oil company, has been my primary sponsor since 1992 — but I've had other primary sponsors in the past, including Folger's Coffee, Stroh's beer, Apache Stoves, and Amzoil. You can find all sorts of companies involved in racing today — companies you'd never expect to be interested in stock-car racing at all: McDonald's, Kellogg's, Tide, M&Ms, and The Home Depot. Even Betty Crocker sponsored a car for a while. The diversity of those sponsors shows how much the sport has moved away from the grease-and-oil days when oil and gasoline companies were the most common types of sponsors.

Not only do primary sponsors get more exposure on uniforms and cars than do associate sponsors (see the following section for more on associate sponsors), they also get more of a commitment from the driver in terms of sponsor appearances. When a driver makes an *appearance,* he shows up to sign posters, programs, and trading cards for fans or employees at supermarket grand openings, auto shows, conventions, car dealerships, fairgrounds, auto stores, or other venues. Sometimes, sponsors also ask drivers to give a speech or host a question-and-answer session for fans or employees. It's not obvious that being a race car driver requires public speaking skills, but with sponsors' increasing involvement in the sport, public speaking and public relations are big parts of a driver's life.

At the beginning of the season, a driver signs a contract with each of his sponsors and that contract lists how many appearances the driver is obliged to provide the sponsor. Primary sponsors get the most appearances because they pay the most money. (See Chapter 7 for more information on a driver's sponsor obligations.)

You'll have better luck meeting a driver at an appearance than at the race-track. Most of the time, only a handful of people with special passes gain access into the garage area where the drivers are. (Some tracks sell tickets that give you access to the garage, but not many.) But being in the garage doesn't necessarily mean you're going to meet drivers or get autographs. When drivers are at the track, they're focused on racing, not on meeting the public, so, when fans swarm around them for photos and autographs, the drivers may not be in the best mood.

To meet drivers under friendlier circumstances — when their minds are focused on *you* and not on their race cars — go to their personal appearances. Most of the time when races come to a town, drivers make local appearances at car dealerships or shopping malls, so keep an eye on the newspaper for those dates and places. You also can find out where they'll be during the week by checking with their fan clubs or going onto the Internet. Go to Chapter 15 to find a driver's fan club and Web site addresses. Going onto NASCAR's Web site at `www.nascar.com` also can send you in the right direction.

If you want an autograph, but don't mind not seeing your favorite driver in person, get the autograph through the mail. As a NASCAR fan, you can send anything you want to a driver and ask them to get it signed. While it may take a while, that driver will sign the trading card, diecast car, T-shirt, poster, magazine or whatever, and then send it back to you if you include postage. Plenty of people take advantage of that. At my shop in North Carolina, I have boxes and boxes of things people have sent me to sign, so whenever I'm there I try to sign as many things as possible and send them back to the fans. Sometimes I wonder why people trust me with the things they send — some things are really valuable collectors' items — but in racing, that's just the way things are. Fans trust their drivers and drivers value their fans.

Associate sponsors — the price is right

Companies that can't afford to spend millions of dollars still get a chance to sponsor a race team. Those companies, called *associate sponsors,* sponsor racing teams in a smaller way. They pay less money and, in turn, don't get as much exposure on the car or the uniform as the primary sponsors do. They still have the advertising and marketing capabilities, however, even though their advertising is on a smaller scale than that of the primary sponsors. The associates get to use the driver in TV commercials or print ads and also get the driver for a few appearances each season. So being an associate sponsor is never a bad thing because the company's logo is still on the car — and on every diecast collector's car, in every photo of the car, and also on TV when the car is shown during races.

The various levels of associate sponsorships and costs vary depending on the team and the size of the company's decal on the car. In the NASCAR Winston Cup Series, associate sponsorships cost from $750,000 to $4 million, with sponsorship of the higher-profile teams costing more. The highest level of associate sponsorship is *major associate*, which is the level just below a primary sponsor but above a regular associate. Cummins Engine Company is a major associate sponsor on my car, so I have more appearances for it and more commitments to it than I do my other associates. Sometimes, it's almost like having two primary sponsors, but one just happens to pay less and demand less than the other. (See the color photo near the center of this book for examples of sponsorship logos.)

Contingency programs: Stick with these guys to make some money

Much of a race car is covered with sponsor decals, including more than a dozen companies who are involved in *contingency programs*. Teams must put contingency program stickers on their cars if they want to be eligible for bonus awards. Winning those awards is contingent on the driver having the company's decal on the car and, in some instances, also using the company's product. For example, a driver wins $10,000 for leading the race at the mid-point — which is winning the Gatorade Front Runner Award if he has a Gatorade sticker on his car. A driver gets $5,000 for winning the MCI Fast Pace Award if he runs the fastest lap during an event and has an MCI sticker on his car. The catch is, the team must have those companies' decals on its car in order to be eligible for the money. It's a way for companies to advertise on most of the cars without dishing out money to just one team.

Crazy fans equal crazy sponsors

Sponsors know what they're doing. There's a reason why races are named the Jiffy Lube 300 and not "That 300-lap race at New Hampshire International Speedway." There's a reason why Charlotte Motor Speedway was renamed Lowe's [Home Improvement Warehouse] Motor Speedway. And there's a reason drivers thank their "Ford Quality Care Service/Ford Credit Ford Taurus" team whenever they have a great day at the racetrack. It's because many NASCAR fans live and die by every word spoken by their favorite driver, every sponsor's logo shown on their favorite driver's car, and every paint scheme change or uniform change. NASCAR fans are loyal — a recent study revealed 72 percent of them use NASCAR sponsors' products.

A *paint scheme* on a race car refers to the way a car is painted and decorated, and it usually stays the same way throughout a season. However, sometimes sponsors change that look for specific races, perhaps to market a specific brand of their product. For example, sometimes I drive a car painted in a Zerex paint scheme, which is the antifreeze-coolant made by Valvoline, my primary sponsor. When a special paint scheme is unveiled, fans tend to flock to stores to seek out souvenirs — many of which will become collectors' items.

From cars to T-shirts to motor oil — NASCAR fans have the goods on their drivers

You can see evidence of how loyal NASCAR fans are without even going to a race. Just drive down the highway and look at bumper stickers: some just display the car number of their favorite driver; others show the car number of their least-favorite driver with a big, thick line through it. The same goes for the car manufacturers involved in the sport — some fans don't necessarily prefer any one driver, but root exclusively for Ford drivers. Not surprisingly, those fans usually have a bunch of Fords parked in their driveways — and vow never to own a General Motors car in their lifetime. Car companies couldn't be happier about fans like that, particularly because those companies initially became involved in racing to market and sell more of their vehicles.

Keeping up appearances

A rookie driver who hasn't proven himself yet really doesn't have much control over which company will sponsor his team. In most cases, that driver is so eager for a sponsor that he'll take anyone — he's not in a position to be choosy. In my early years as a driver, I was thrilled to get a call from any company at all. Now, though, I can be choosy because of my success in the sport. I've been lucky to have Valvoline and Cummins Engine Company as sponsors because I believe in their products — products that I've used for years. They're everyday products with an all-American image, so I feel proud to represent them. It would be impossible for me to sound gung-ho in a commercial for a company with products that I'm reluctant to endorse, so I couldn't be happier about the way things worked out.

Going to a NASCAR race, you'll see a perfect example of how NASCAR fans show their support for their favorite drivers. You can see my fans from a mile away, wearing Mark Martin T-shirts, Mark Martin hats, Mark Martin jackets, and even Mark Martin sneakers. It would be a tough task to find a fan in the grandstands wearing a plain, old shirt with no logos on it — except for the guys who get sunburned because they don't wear any shirts at all!

When I was racing on the short tracks of Arkansas, I never thought I'd see people wearing T-shirts with my face on them or wearing hats with my name on them. But now it's really cool because it shows how many people support me at the racetrack and cheer for me when I drive by. Because I wear an ear piece while in the car (for the in-car radio) as well as a tight helmet, and have to contend with the roar of the engine, I can't hear fans cheering when I'm driving. But seeing fans wearing my name on their clothes lets me know that I have people behind me.

NASCAR fan loyalty goes way beyond filling wardrobes with logo-covered T-shirts. NASCAR fans are extremely faithful to the companies who sponsor their favorite driver. That's where a big chunk of the big business and big bucks come in. Not only do NASCAR fans support their driver by rooting for him, they also support him by buying his sponsors' goods. So, it's a good guess Petty fans fill their cars with quarts of STP oil, because STP has been a sponsor with Petty Enterprises for many years. My fans most likely use Valvoline oil (definitely not STP!) because Valvoline sponsors my team. NASCAR fans tend to use their drivers' brands, so sponsorships have become such a huge part of the sport. And that makes NASCAR appealing to companies who want an interesting and effective marketing tool.

Licenses Aren't Just for Driving Anymore

With fans buying up all that NASCAR merchandise, it's not surprising some people would do anything to sell stuff to fans and get in on some of the action — and to make some pretty good money. But making that money isn't simple. Just like you need a license to drive on the highway, you need a license to sell merchandise bearing the NASCAR name or drivers' names. Otherwise, you can be fined and/or arrested. Getting licensed is a serious deal. Unless you want the cops chasing after you, taking all of your merchandise, and giving you a big, fat ticket — get licensed if you're interested in selling NASCAR paraphernalia.

Licensing gives people the authority to sell particular goods with a particular name, logo, or likeness on it. Now there's a good reason why that's necessary, at least as far as I see things: It's embarrassing to have my name or picture on something ridiculously ugly, poorly made, or extremely inappropriate. As a driver, souvenirs are part of the image, so a driver doesn't want to be part of something that's too hokey or that's a cheap rip-off. Considering all of the souvenir items floating around out there, drivers have lots of opportunities to be part of cheesy, junky stuff — so somebody had better be watching out for their interests. There's also a selfish aspect to insisting everyone sells licensed merchandise. Drivers make royalties off the licensed goods vendors sell — either a percentage of the selling price or just a flat fee.

When buying NASCAR souvenirs, make sure to check out the label to see if the proper authority licenses them. If it has an official NASCAR logo on it or the official logo of a race team, which will say it's "officially licensed," then it's guaranteed to be quality stuff. That ensures you won't buy a shoddy souvenir that will fall apart the moment you put it on or bring it home. The imitation may be cheaper than a licensed item, but don't be fooled — the low price may mean low quality. Buying souvenirs from a driver's souvenir trailer, which is located outside the track during races, is a sure way to be safe because it sells licensed merchandise only.

You can find nearly every souvenir imaginable relating to NASCAR, including some everyday items — and some really strange things:

- ✔ **Clothing:** The most obvious souvenirs are T-shirts, jackets, hats, and button-down shirts. Some less obvious (for NASCAR fans who like a complete look) are socks with a driver's name and car number on them, or even children's underwear for kids who want to stay close and connected to their favorite driver.

- ✔ **Jewelry:** While a majority of NASCAR fans are men, women have become increasingly interested in the sport, so NASCAR jewelry for women has taken off in popularity. You can find almost any kind of NASCAR jewelry, including necklaces, bracelets, rings, or anklets. I'm not sure whether NASCAR navel rings have become popular yet, though.

- ✔ **Home decorating:** NASCAR fans don't have to go far to fix up their homes with a NASCAR motif. Some licensees sell just about anything for the home, and a lot of that stuff has my name on it, too. You can find Mark Martin wallpaper, Mark Martin quilts, Mark Martin sheets, Mark Martin chairs, Mark Martin dishes, and even Mark Martin carpeting. You can even purchase NASCAR crystal platters and silverware for entertaining purposes. I'm not telling you that buying all this stuff will make your house stylish, but it will definitely get a point across to your guests — that you're a NASCAR fan through and through.

- ✔ **Office supplies:** Looking for NASCAR scissors or a Mark Martin ruler? Don't fret, you can find them, along with stationery, pens, pencils, telephones, and nearly everything else you'll need to get your work done fast enough to take a couple days off to go to a NASCAR race.

- ✔ **Games:** The toy business is involved in stock-car racing, also. NASCAR video games are a big deal and a huge seller in stores. You can also find board games and card games relating to the sport — they're less hightech but just as much fun.

✔ **Diecast cars:** Perhaps the best-selling NASCAR souvenirs over the years have been diecast cars, made up with the current year's paint scheme on them and a driver's name above the door, just like on real stock cars. These babies aren't just your run-of-the-mill toy cars, though. They have working hoods, detailed cockpits, tiny engines and functioning wheels. Many fans see them as collector's items — and their price usually reflects that. Although they come in all sorts of sizes (1:64 scale to 1:24 scale), most of the time their price tags are hefty. Some cars, particularly older ones with a hard-to-find paint scheme, go for more than $200. For those fancy-pants collectors, some are made of 24-karat gold and platinum.

My fans had a perfect chance at buying the quintessential Mark Martin souvenir through the Neiman Marcus catalog in 1998-99. The store had one of my race cars for sale, all painted up with a working race engine under the hood. I guess it was for die-hard fans only because it cost $125,000 and wasn't even legal to drive on the street! In fact, the headlights were only decals, as in all NASCAR cars, so driving it home from the store at night would have been challenging. But I bet the trip would have been quicker than usual.

Smile, You're on NASCAR Camera!

There's one tell-tale sign that NASCAR is popular in the United States: its races are on TV. Every NASCAR Winston Cup Series and NASCAR Busch Series race is broadcast live on television. Qualifying rounds and even some practices are on television, too. That's amazing, considering the first NASCAR race was broadcast live, flag-to-flag, only 21 years ago. That race, the 1979 Daytona 500 on CBS, brought racing action into America's living rooms for an afternoon. Now, however, racing is more than just a once-in-a-while show on TV. You can find it every day, especially because racing season lasts from February through late November, which is the longest season of any professional sport.

Knock-down, drag-out NASCAR coverage

The first NASCAR race broadcast on live TV certainly made racing seem exciting to non-NASCAR fans who tuned in. It also made racing seem lawless. While Richard Petty won that 1979 Daytona 500, the most thrills came from drivers off the track. Bobby Allison and his brother Donnie Allison got into a fistfight with Cale Yarborough, with the TV cameras rolling as America got its first taste of NASCAR. Although this incident doesn't fit with the squeaky-clean image that many NASCAR drivers have, it shows how emotional the sport can get. It also reveals that, just like any other pro sport, competitors can't help but lose their tempers at times.

In the spotlight, under pressure

While sponsors drool when thinking about how much TV coverage of the sport has grown (more TV means more footage of cars on the track, all zooming around with big corporate logos stuck onto them), for drivers, that exposure heightens the pressure to lead races, particularly because the TV camera gets plenty of shots of the car out front.

TV coverage also puts a lot of pressure on drivers to speak well and behave well in front of the camera. Every time drivers climb out of cars, camera lenses are watching, and reporters with microphones are asking questions. Even after a

wreck, drivers have to explain why the car crashed, how it happened, and how they feel about destroying one of the coolest cars in the world. Even if it was his fault and just a bone-headed mistake on his part, the driver has to face up to it. And that's pretty tough to take. Pro football, baseball, and hockey players at least get to cool off for a while in the locker room before the cameras and microphones come running. But for NASCAR drivers, that immediate media blitz has become a way of life since TV came into the picture.

If you're curious about racing but not ready to devote yourself to it, you can catch a peek of the sport before you dive into it as a fan. Turning on your TV is the first step. Then it won't be long until you stumble upon a *racing show,* in which races, qualifying, and practices are dissected, and everyone from the driver to the car owner to the guy that puts gas in the car is interviewed. You can find out more about racing than you ever wanted to know if you watch those shows long enough. (Or sometimes just for an afternoon.)

You can find NASCAR race broadcasts on cable and also on the major broadcast networks. The networks are beginning to delve into the sport more and more, especially because TV ratings have grown nearly each year since NASCAR races began showing up on TV. NASCAR is even thinking about starting up an all-NASCAR cable channel with 24 hours of NASCAR news, so that insatiable NASCAR fans won't have to get off their sofas at all. I'm sure there'll be some takers.

TV has become such a big deal in racing these days that broadcasters are quite innovative in the way they bring the sport to viewers. Their most recent development has been mounting cameras inside and outside the race cars, which give viewers an up-close look of what's going on in the cockpit or just in front of the bumpers. From inside the car, viewers can see the driver turn the wheel and shift. From outside, viewers can see a car ahead of the driver or behind the driver — and also see if there is any contact between the two cars. When a driver crashes, the camera picks up plenty more action — like a wall coming straight at it at 200 mph or another car smacking into the rear bumper, and then flying off into another car to cause mayhem on the track. In really hard crashes, the camera can take only so much. Upon impact, the camera breaks and the transmission goes black. Not all cars have these cameras for every race, but the shots from those cameras give great insight into what is going on during a race — a real feel for what's going on — while regular cameras may come up short.

Shying away from cameras

When I began racing, I didn't want to talk that much — much less look into a camera for the entire world to see. All I wanted to do was drive race cars and win races, and I was pretty shy about everything else. I figured that if I wanted to be famous and on TV, I wouldn't be much of a racer.

As my career progressed, however, I figured out that being on TV was a great way to market myself, so I forced myself to get used to all that stuff early on. I was interviewed a lot when I ran on short tracks in the Midwestern U.S., mostly on local radio stations or on local television stations, so I had a lot of practice before graduating to the NASCAR Winston Cup Series. Now, I don't even think about being nervous because I'm on TV. I just think about winning races, as all top-level drivers do. Compared to that, the TV part is easy.

Chapter 3

Understanding Every NASCAR Series

*N*ASCAR racing is more than just one group of drivers traveling all over the United States to race. NASCAR has many different series featuring drivers from different places and with different levels of talent. From its smaller series to its biggest series, NASCAR racing has a series for every driver. And for every fan, too.

NASCAR Winston Cup Series: Where the Superstars Are

NASCAR's highest-profile circuit is the NASCAR Winston Cup Series, a racing league akin to the top leagues of other sports. The best hitters play in Major League Baseball, the best quarterbacks play in the National Football League, and the best stock-car drivers race in the NASCAR Winston Cup Series. It features the most recognized drivers in stock-car racing, including ones you've probably seen on TV in some way or another — whether driving in a race, selling souvenirs on a 24-hour shopping network, or smiling into the camera during a commercial. Some of the most popular NASCAR Winston Cup Series drivers today include the following:

✔ **Dale Earnhardt,** the seven-time NASCAR Winston Cup Series champion, was nicknamed "The Intimidator" because of his hard-nosed and hard-headed driving style. Take it from me, when an opponent looked in his rear-view mirror and saw Dale Earnhardt, it wasn't the most comforting feeling in the world. Drivers knew he wasn't the most gentle or courteous guy on the track, but that's what made him so successful and popular with fans. His father, Ralph Earnhardt, was also an accomplished stock car racer. Earnhardt's souvenir sales revealed his popularity, as he was consistently in the top ten for souvenir revenues among sports figures. Earnhardt developed a love for the sport that would ultimately fuel one of the most successful careers in the history of motor sports.

✔ **Bill Elliott,** from Dawsonville, Georgia, helped bring the sport into the mainstream by making it onto the cover of *Sports Illustrated* in 1985, after winning the $1 million in the Winston Million bonus program run by the NASCAR Winston Cup Series' sponsor, R.J. Reynolds Tobacco Co. Elliott, dubbed "Million-Dollar Bill," won the prize by winning three of NASCAR's four crown jewel races that year, including the Daytona 500. The other crown jewel events are the World 600 (now called the Coca-Cola 600), the Winston 500, and the Southern 500. The only one Elliott didn't win that year was the World 600 at Charlotte Motor Speedway. Not only did Elliott win a $1 million prize in 1985, he also won the championship. Now he is an annual winner of the NASCAR Winston Cup Series' Most Popular Driver Award, walking away with the honor more than a dozen times.

✔ **Jeff Gordon** began NASCAR Winston Cup Series racing in 1993 and quickly earned the nickname "Wonder Boy" because he was only 21 back then. He legitimized that nickname when he won his first NASCAR Winston Cup Series in 1995 at 24, becoming the youngest champion in NASCAR's modern era, which dates back to 1972. Gordon followed that title with back-to-back championships in 1997 and 1998, breaking records, winning races, and frustrating his older and more experienced competitors. Since arriving on the circuit, though, Gordon has grown out of his Wonder Boy nickname and into a more mature role. He's NASCAR's unofficial spokesman, especially to new fans who may not be familiar with the sport and who may not be from the southern United States. Gordon's no good ol' boy — he grew up in California before moving to Indiana when he was 13.

✔ **Dale Jarrett,** son of two-time NASCAR Winston Cup Series champion Ned Jarrett, grew up watching his dad win races. Now he's trying to live up to the family name, and he's doing a great job at it. Over the past few years, Jarrett has won more than 20 NASCAR Winston Cup Series races and has been a consistent contender for the championship. He finally won the title in 1999, driving the No. 88 Ford for Robert Yates Racing, to make him and his father only the second father-son duo to win championships in NASCAR Winston Cup Series history. He and his father joined Lee and Richard Petty as the only father-son champions.

✔ **Terry Labonte,** a two-time NASCAR Winston Cup Series champion from Texas, is called "Mr. Consistency" by his peers because he has been so consistently good for so long, but also because his seasons usually aren't filled with too many highs and lows. For example, in both years he won the championship (1984 and 1996) he won only two races, but was always racing near the front of the pack. People also call him "The Ice Man" because of his even temper both on and off the track. Labonte's younger brother, Bobby, also races in the series.

✔ **Rusty Wallace,** the 1989 NASCAR Winston Cup Series champion, grew up in St. Louis and learned how to drive on tracks in the Midwestern U.S. before moving up to the NASCAR Winston Cup Series. He's known as one of the most knowledgeable drivers when preparing a car to race — a reputation he earned by building and working on his own race cars before coming to NASCAR. He still works on his cars today, helping his crew get his car just right. Wallace's two brothers also are involved in racing. Rusty's brother Mike drives in the NASCAR Craftsman Truck Series, while his youngest brother, Kenny, is in the NASCAR Winston Cup Series.

✔ **Darrell Waltrip** earned the name "Jaws" back in the 1980s when he talked as much as he won races — and that was a lot. Waltrip, whose younger brother, Michael, races in the NASCAR Winston Cup Series, won 84 races in his career, as well as three NASCAR Winston Cup Series championships. Those wins tie him for third with Bobby Allison on NASCAR's all-time wins list. Just ask him how he made it to Victory Lane so many times, and you're bound to get a confident and quick-witted answer because Waltrip has always been quite an entertainer, particularly when he's winning. After he retires at the end of the 2000 season, Waltrip plans to head to the broadcasting booth — that way, he'll get paid to talk!

My goal always has been to make it to NASCAR Winston Cup Series racing, which I believed and still believe is the hardest and most recognized racing series in the world. If you race open-wheel cars (see Chapter 1), you dream about making it to Formula One someday. But if you race stock cars, you think about the NASCAR Winston Cup Series day and night: It gets the most live TV coverage, pays the most money, and earns the most fame for its drivers. It's also the ultimate challenge in stock-car racing, because the governing body makes sure races are close, and because each driver is so talented.

Not only does the NASCAR Winston Cup Series feature some of the best and most colorful drivers in motorsports, it also features some of the closest finishes. Many times, cars race bumper-to-bumper and side-by-side during an event — mostly because NASCAR monitors its rules so closely that no car or car manufacturer has an unfair edge over the competition. Even after a 500-mile race, it's not uncommon for drivers to cross the finish line within less than one second of each other. Even in qualifying, where drivers complete only one or two laps at full speed in order to earn a spot in the race, the fastest car and the slowest car are often separated by a fraction of a second.

NASCAR Winston Cup Series races are held at tracks all across the U.S. — from Daytona Beach, Florida to Sonoma, California and Loudon, New Hampshire. Races are held nearly every weekend of the year, too. The NASCAR Winston Cup Series had 34 races in 1999, making it one of the most — if not the most — grueling schedule in all of professional sports. But don't think that drivers only work 34 days per year. A race weekend entails at least two, and most often three, days of work (qualifying, practice, and a race) as well as one day of travel. See Chapter 7 for a day-by-day account of a driver's life.

Even so, drivers and crew members don't mind the rigorous schedule that much, particularly because they realize how fortunate they are to have made it to the top level of stock-car racing. While some drivers were able to get a job in the NASCAR Winston Cup Series early in their racing careers, most drivers spend years trying to get there. Those drivers dedicated their lives to their goal of making it to the NASCAR Winston Cup Series, spending a lot of time away from their families while competing in the various series that travel throughout the country.

NASCAR Busch Series — One Route to the NASCAR Winston Cup Series

A lot of drivers, including me, ended up in NASCAR Winston Cup Series via the NASCAR Busch Series — a place where drivers can train themselves by getting experience, making mistakes, and learning from those errors. NASCAR Busch Series races are usually held on Saturdays, while NASCAR Winston Cup Series races are most often on Sundays. But that's not the only difference.

While the cars look similar to fans or to outsiders, there are some major differences for drivers. NASCAR Busch Series racers drive stock cars and follow the same on-track rules (see Chapter 5) as in the NASCAR Winston Cup Series, but the cars have several of the following fundamental differences (see Figure 3-1):

✔ **Weight:** NASCAR Winston Cup Series cars weigh 3,400 pounds with all their fuel, oil, and water tanks filled. NASCAR Busch Series cars are 100 pounds lighter, at 3,300 pounds, but are more difficult to handle because a heavier car's extra weight makes it hug the track. The extra weight also makes the NASCAR Winston Cup Series cars more stable, which is important when driving 200 mph, trying to weave in and out of traffic, and pass other drivers along the way.

✔ **Size:** Although both cars are the same height (51 inches) and width (72½ inches), their *wheelbase* (the distance between the front and rear axles) is slightly different. On a NASCAR Winston Cup Series car, the wheelbase is 110 inches, while on a NASCAR Busch Series car it is 105 inches. The NASCAR Winston Cup Series cars still have an advantage here: Their longer wheelbase gives them more stability.

✔ **Horsepower:** The biggest difference between the two cars is how powerful their engines are. The NASCAR Winston Cup Series cars have significantly more oomph to them, producing about 750 horsepower. *Horsepower* is a unit of measurement representing how much power an engine generates. So, the more horsepower, the faster a car goes. NASCAR Busch Series engines only generate around 550 horsepower. So that should mean the NASCAR Winston Cup Series cars go faster, right? Technically, yes, but in practice, not really. Because the NASCAR Busch Series cars are 100 pounds lighter and have a shorter wheelbase, they reach speeds almost, but not quite, as high as the NASCAR Winston Cup Series cars do. Even though NASCAR Busch Series cars have a smaller engine, the engine doesn't have to lug around all the weight that a NASCAR Winston Cup Series engine does.

✔ **Compression ratio:** The difference in the compression ratio between the two types of cars is partly why the NASCAR Winston Cup Series cars are more powerful. *Compression ratio* is the volume inside a piston compared to the volume it compresses to when the piston is fully extended. (A *carburetor* is the part of the engine where air and fuel mix in an internal combustion engine. Nowadays, passenger cars don't have carburetors like they used to, but NASCAR cars still have them.) At that point, the mixture of fuel and air inside the piston is compressed into a small area, primed for the spark plug to fire. When the spark plug fires, the energy inside that small space is dispersed — boom! — and it pushes the piston back up and into its initial position. (For more details on the technical aspects of stock cars, check out Chapter 4.) The higher the ratio, the less space the mixture of fuel and air is shoved into, so the greater the potential for energy. More energy equals more horsepower. (So, higher ratio equals more power.) Because NASCAR Winston Cup Series engines have a compression ratio of 12 to1 and NASCAR Busch Series engines have a compression ratio of 9½ to1, NASCAR Winston Cup Series engines produce more horsepower.

The NASCAR Busch Series was a valuable training ground for me, and I haven't turned my back on those races now, even though I have been successful in the NASCAR Winston Cup Series for more than a decade. I still compete in a limited number of NASCAR Busch Series races every year, mostly because I love to race — and win. Because the cars are so different, though, I can't translate information from my NASCAR Busch Series car to my NASCAR Winston Cup Series car, such as information on how my crew can prepare the car so it will race well on a certain track. Also, winning on Saturday, when NASCAR Busch Series races normally are held, gives me more confidence for Sunday's NASCAR Winston Cup Series races. And I've won plenty of races on Saturdays. In fact, I've won more NASCAR Busch Series races than anyone in history — through the 1999 season, I've been to Victory Lane 40 times!

Figure 3-1:
NASCAR
Winston
Cup Series
cars may
look like
NASCAR
Busch
Series cars,
but they are
heavier and
have more
horsepower.

NASCAR Winston Cup Series car

NASCAR Busch Series, Grand National Division car

The tough part is competing in two races on the same weekend. During weeks like that, I hardly have any time to stop and take a breath. I get to the garage early to check out the Saturday car and talk to my Saturday crew chief, then hop over to my NASCAR Winston Cup Series car. Then I have to juggle NASCAR Busch Series practice with NASCAR Winston Cup Series practice, and then qualify for both races. Sometimes I'm so busy with that, and also signing autographs on my way from one garage to the other, that I forget to eat!

The NASCAR Busch Series — not bush league

Even though the NASCAR Busch Series, which evolved from the NASCAR Late Model Sportsman Series, is considered a stepping-stone for the NASCAR Winston Cup Series, many drivers bristle at that image. Some, like two-time NASCAR Busch Series champion Randy LaJoie, love racing in that series and have made a career out of it, saying it has the same intense competition as the NASCAR Winston Cup Series and doesn't have to be considered only a stepping stone. LaJoie especially likes the fact that, even though he doesn't get paid as much as NASCAR Winston Cup Series drivers do, he doesn't have to deal with nearly as much pressure.

The NASCAR Busch Series began in 1982 and has grown from races at small, unknown tracks to competitions at large, well-known facilities, and includes nearly as many races as the NASCAR Winston Cup Series does — 32 races in 1999. Many events are companion events to NASCAR Winston Cup Series races and are held on Saturday of a race weekend at a particular track. That gives NASCAR Winston Cup Series drivers a chance to drive, as I do, in both races in one weekend. And even though NASCAR Busch Series drivers themselves are quite popular with fans, having NASCAR Winston Cup Series drivers in the race lures even more people to the racetrack. But even without those well-known drivers competing, NASCAR Busch Series races have become popular events in their own right.

Pickup Trucks with Racing Stripes

In 1994, NASCAR decided to branch out and create another major racing series. But they didn't opt for just another stock-car series, which may have been too similar to the NASCAR Winston Cup Series or the NASCAR Busch Series. Instead, they chose something completely different. And quite creative. They started racing pickup trucks.

Racing trucks probably didn't improve NASCAR racing's image of being a redneck sport, but NASCAR didn't care — they sensed that the series would catch on because an overwhelming majority of truck owners are interested in some type of motorsports. The truck manufacturers were into the idea and plenty of talented drivers were looking for jobs, so why not?

In 1995, the NASCAR Craftsman Truck Series was created with Mike Skinner taking the first championship. And the series worked as a breeding ground, too — Skinner drives a NASCAR Winston Cup Series car now.

Some drivers say trucks are more similar to NASCAR Winston Cup Series cars than to NASCAR Busch Series cars because they have nearly the same horsepower: 750 for the car and 710 for the truck. NASCAR Busch Series cars, on the other hand, produce about 550.

Even though NASCAR Craftsman Truck Series trucks don't look or feel much like NASCAR Winston Cup Series cars, good drivers can handle both vehicles pretty well. (I've only raced in two truck races in my life, but was fortunate enough to win the second one.) To me, a vehicle is a vehicle and a race is a race, no matter what kind of vehicle I'm driving. If a driver is skillful enough to be able to control a vehicle, he can succeed in any series and in any vehicle.

The following are some differences between passenger trucks (such as a Ford F150, Chevrolet Silverado, or Dodge Ram) and their NASCAR Craftsman Truck Series counterparts (see Figure 3-2):

- **Horsepower:** A passenger truck has 160 horsepower. Compare that to the race truck, which has about 710.

- **Length:** Passenger trucks are an average 194.5 inches long, while a race truck is 222 inches (18 feet, 6 inches) long.

- **Width:** Passenger trucks are an average of 76.8 inches wide. A race truck is 78 to 80 inches.

- **Height:** Passenger trucks are an average of 70.4 inches high, while race trucks are 59 inches — shorter and much closer to the ground than their passenger truck counterparts.

- **Weight:** A passenger truck weighs an average of 3,829 pounds. A race truck is 3,400 pounds, just like a NASCAR Winston Cup Series car. But the race trucks don't have to be sturdy to haul things like fill dirt or your neighbor's couch. Their bodies are much lighter, making them as streamlined as possible.

- **Wheelbase:** A passenger truck's front and rear wheels are 117.5 inches apart. On a race truck, that measurement is 112 inches.

- **Engine:** A passenger truck's engine is a 4.3 liter, V6 with fuel injection. A race truck has an 8-cylinder engine with a carburetor.

- **Compression ratio:** A passenger truck's compression ratio is 9 to 1. A race truck's ratio is 9½ to 1. See the "NASCAR Busch Series — One Route to the NASCAR Winston Cup Series" section, earlier in this chapter, for more information on compression ratio.

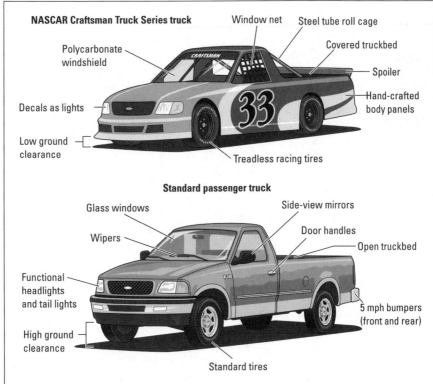

NASCAR Craftsman Truck Series truck

Window net
Steel tube roll cage
Covered truckbed
Polycarbonate windshield
Spoiler
Hand-crafted body panels
Decals as lights
Low ground clearance
Treadless racing tires

Standard passenger truck

Glass windows
Side-view mirrors
Wipers
Door handles
Open truckbed
Functional headlights and tail lights
High ground clearance
5 mph bumpers (front and rear)
Standard tires

Figure 3-2: Race trucks certainly aren't for bringing hay bales to the farm. They are finely-tuned racing machines, just like their NASCAR Winston Cup Series cousins.

NASCAR Touring Division: Where Stars Get Their Start

Before drivers get to the big-time, they first have to hone their skills. If you're interested in trying your hand at driving a race car, there are plenty of ways to start — and plenty of ways to become a serious race car driver. But before drivers get to the higher-profile series, they usually gain experience on one of NASCAR's touring divisions. These are called touring divisions because they tour, or travel, around to different racetracks in the same region during their seasons.

Going overseas

Even though NASCAR racing is based in the United States, it has held several exhibition races outside the country. Drivers most recently raced in Japan, once each year from 1996 to 1998 — twice on a road course in Suzuka and once on a newly-built oval track in Motegi. It was quite a culture shock for NASCAR drivers and their teams to travel about 8,000 miles from home and arrive in a place where they didn't understand the language, customs, or food and drink. You've got to remember: sushi, which is raw fish, and sake, which is a beverage made from fermented rice, aren't exactly part of the menu when racers travel to events in Talladega, Alabama, or Darlington, South Carolina. When I went to Japan in 1997, however, I didn't think about the food or surroundings as much as I thought about the race. I won the pole at the road course in Suzuka and finished second in the race, right behind Mike Skinner.

Most stock-car drivers start their careers on short tracks, which are oval tracks that are less than a mile in length. They begin competing at tracks near their homes, perhaps driving at the same track every week, perhaps eventually winning the track championship. After winning — and learning — on that level, drivers can move into a higher-profile series, where they can make a living as professionals. The following are brief descriptions of NASCAR's ten series other than the three most famous ones:

- **NASCAR Winston West Series:** These cars are nearly identical to NASCAR Winston Cup Series cars, but have less powerful engines. The series is the only series that competes outside the United States as part of its regular season: drivers travel to Japan, where they compete for points. Other than the jaunt to Japan, the series is held primarily in the western part of the U.S.

- **Busch North Series:** NASCAR Busch North Series cars are similar to Busch Series cars. They compete in the northern United States, in an area bordered by Portland, Maine; Buffalo, New York; Pittsburgh, Pennsylvania; and Philadelphia, Pennsylvania.

- **Slim Jim All Pro Series:** The All Pro Series cars are models of American-made passenger cars, such as the Buick LeSabre, Pontiac Grand Prix, and Ford Taurus, but they have a V8 engine. Races are held on short tracks throughout the eastern and Midwestern U.S., from Illinois to Florida.

- **Featherlite Modified Series:** This series is the NASCAR Touring Division's only open-wheel series, which features cars with engine modifications and without fenders — called *modified* stock cars.

- **Featherlite Southwest Series:** The Featherlite Southwest Series features cars similar to, but smaller than, NASCAR Winston Cup Series cars, and holds events in California, Nevada, Arizona, and Colorado.

- **Goody's Dash Series:** *Dash cars* are sub-compact stock cars, such as the Ford Probe, Chevrolet Cavalier, and Pontiac Sunfire. They are the smallest cars in NASCAR, known as *baby grands* because they're scaled-down NASCAR Winston Cup Series cars with V6 engines. The series races up and down the east coast of the U.S., from Virginia to Florida.

- **Busch All-Star Series:** The Busch All-Star Series is NASCAR's only dirt track series and it is based in the Midwestern U.S. It features cars with wide-tread tires that grip the dirt, but drivers slide through the turns anyway. The key is to control the car while it slides.

- **RE/MAX Challenge Series:** This series races on asphalt short tracks in the Midwestern U.S. and the Rocky Mountain states, with cars similar to the Slim Jim All Pro Series cars and the Raybestos Brakes Northwest Touring Series cars.

- **Raybestos Brakes Northwest Touring Series:** This series uses small versions of NASCAR Winston Cup Series cars and holds races in Washington, Oregon, Idaho, and Montana. The cars are similar in size to the RE/MAX Challenge Series cars and Slim Jim All Pro Series cars.

- **NASCAR Weekly Racing Series:** Before drivers compete in touring divisions, they usually start racing on local tracks, which each have track championships. NASCAR sanctions more than 100 of these tracks around the nation, so their track championships become part of the NASCAR Weekly Racing Series. In these events, held in ten different racing series regions, drivers compete for track championships and are also evaluated with a formula called the *Competition Performance Index* or *CPI*. The CPI is similar to the quarterback rating in pro football because it factors in the average finish, number of wins, driver attendance, and the average number of cars in the field. At the end of the year, the driver with the highest CPI in each region wins the regional championship, and the driver with the highest CPI out of all the regions wins the national championship.

So, You Want to Drive a Race Car?

Suppose you're sitting at home one day on the couch watching a NASCAR race, and you decide that NASCAR racing is for you. You want to be a rich and famous driver and you want to do it now. So, what's the first step?

Well, you can't just go out and buy a NASCAR Winston Cup Series car and race in the Daytona 500. In fact, you can't even buy a NASCAR Busch Series car or a NASCAR Craftsman Truck Series truck and head for the races, either. You must have some training, then a lot of practice before you're allowed to race at those levels. You also have to have a lot of cash — or the ability to get a lot of cash from sponsors, friends, or a rich uncle. Racing isn't cheap. A good car for racing at a local track can cost $40,000 and the engine can cost another $20,000. You also need more money after the initial purchase to maintain the car; buy tires, oil, gas; and fix the car when you crash it. And, believe me, you *will* crash it — because every driver, no matter how talented he may be, crashes every once in a while. Some more often than others.

Pre-stock car (not prehistoric) vehicles

If you don't have enough money to buy a full-fledged stock car, you can race more inexpensively with a go-kart. Go-karts are similar to the ones you see on tracks adjacent to miniature golf courses. They are tiny vehicles — tiny in relation to stock cars, that is — with engines attached to the back. But starting out in go-karts doesn't mean you're starting out in racing kindergarten. Certain go-karts can reach up to 100 mph and they even race on a course at Daytona International Speedway, using part of its high-banked track. Also, you have to sharpen the same driving skills to drive a go-kart that you would for a NASCAR Winston Cup Series car or a NASCAR Busch Series car. Ricky Rudd showed the virtues of go-karts when he went straight from them to the NASCAR Winston Cup Series. So go-karts are a viable option — and a great place to get started — if you're itching to race.

You can also find all sorts of other programs for kids who want to start young. Midget cars are one of them. Midgets are specialized open-wheel race cars that are small, fast, lightweight, and have no fenders — very similar to sprint cars. They graduate in size, going from quarter midgets to three-quarter midgets to midgets, the largest cars in the class. Quarter midgets are the cars kids squeeze into for some fun. Jeff Gordon started out in midget cars, so you must be able to learn a thing or two there, right?

My son, Matt, started racing quarter midgets this year and watching him race is one of the most exciting things in my life. It's fun to teach him all about the engine, the racing, and the competition — but it's up to him to figure out how to win. And he's already done that by winning the championships in his division, showing that he has some racing talent in his genes. Even though he's young and is involved in the sport mainly to have fun, he is developing valuable skills when driving and controlling a car. Who knows — those skills may help him win a NASCAR Winston Cup Series championship someday.

Never too young for racing

If you're a minor and aren't old enough for a regular driver's license, don't worry — you don't need a state driver's license to be eligible for a NASCAR license. If you are too young for a state license, though, you may have to go through a test session, so that officials can watch you race. If officials deem you competent, they allow you to race on their track. If not, you have to practice somewhere else (please, not the highway!) or wait until you're old enough to get a state driver's license. When you are, they'll be less suspicious of your driving ability.

You've got a car — now what?

If you've scrounged up enough money to buy a stock car and want to begin your training, what should you do next? Taking a trip to your local short track is a start. There, you can pick up an application for a NASCAR license. Your car owner and your pit crew (everyone directly involved in your race team at the track) needs to get a license, too. After you receive your NASCAR license (sent to you or to the track), you're ready to race.

To request an application for a NASCAR license, call NASCAR's Member Services Department at 904-253-0611, or write to NASCAR, Member Services Department, P.O. Box 2875, Daytona Beach, FL 32114-1234.

Memorize the rules, and then get a crew

With your NASCAR license, you also receive a rule book for the series in which you plan to compete. In that book, you can find a rule for every aspect of racing — especially for all the details and measurements of your car — so you should plan to tweak your car for at least a week or two before setting a date for your first race. In the meantime, gather up people for your pit crew, because you'll need those people — at least two of them — on race day. Your pit crew will be in charge of your car, tires, and fuel, and will talk to you on the radio during the race. So when choosing a pit crew, choose carefully. Your 70-pound kid brother may not be the best choice.

Moving up and out

As you become successful on your local short track, you can move up to a touring series, which travels from track to track — and sometimes all over the nation. To be eligible for a touring series like one of the NASCAR Touring Divisions, you must first get a license for that particular series, just as you do when you first started racing at your local track.

The better the series, the harder it is to get there

When you want to try your hand at the NASCAR Craftsman Truck Series, the Busch Series, or the NASCAR Winston Cup Series, NASCAR officials get more involved in the licensing process. They do this mostly because they don't want some unskilled guy off the street getting in a truck or a car and taking out the whole field because he doesn't know how to drive. Before you get on the track in NASCAR's top series, you must fill out a résumé and an application, then send it to NASCAR for official review. Officials license you to race in those series when they determine that you're good enough, judging by your résumé and records in other series. Your car owner, race team, and everyone who participates in your team also has to obtain a license — the only difference is that they don't have to submit a résumé. After you're approved, you must pay an annual fee for your license.

Working on a Crew

It's much easier to become a member of a race team than it is to become the driver, mainly because each car has only one driver, but dozens of crew members. So more slots are available for mechanics, pit crew members, and garage sweepers than for drivers. If you're wondering why I mentioned garage sweepers in the same sentence as crew members — then you might want to read more closely here.

You can't really become a NASCAR mechanic if you can't fix a car. So, some people learn all about cars after getting their initial jobs at race shops. They show interest and learn from experts, all without getting caught under people's feet. I've got to warn you, though, it may take you a substantially long time to get promoted from sweeper to mechanic or from sweeper to fabricator (the ones who build the outside or body of the car) if you're learning along the way. If you already have a working knowledge of cars, you'll be promoted much faster.

Fabricators are the people who put sheet metal on the car's frame and mold it to the shape of the car. They're the ones who create the body or outside shell of the car. (And the ones who grumble the most when you wreck a car — because they're the ones who have to fix all the dents and rebuild the body, if necessary.)

Pit crews aren't the pits

If you don't want to work on the car all week at the shop, but just want to help out during pit stops on race day, there are opportunities for you in NASCAR racing. (See Chapter 10 for more details on making pit stops.) You may have a tough time getting a job on a pit crew if you don't know somebody on the team, though, so be prepared to schmooze or make friends fast. Also, pit stops have become such a big factor in racing that you have to try out for the pit crew before you get the job. You'd better lift some weights and practice changing tires before you show up at a race team's door.

The easiest way to get on a crew is to be willing to do anything, including sweeping floors, to get your foot in the door. If you're an efficient, enthusiastic floor sweeper, people will notice you and you'll get promoted before you know it. It's true what they say: floor sweeper today, crew chief tomorrow. Well, maybe it takes longer than that, but that strategy has definitely worked in the past. Some people I know, including my former crew chiefs Robin Pemberton and Steve Hmiel, wanted to be on a race team when they were young, so they were brave enough to make a bold move. They just packed up, left their hometowns and headed for Charlotte, North Carolina, where most of the NASCAR Winston Cup Series race shops are, hoping to get a job (any job!) with a team. Obviously, it worked out for Robin and Steve, but others have gone that route successfully, too.

Another way to sharpen your car skills is to go to a vocational school and take classes on how to fix engines or work on bodies. Some schools offer a specific curriculum that focuses on teaching students how to build and repair NASCAR-type cars. In the future, NASCAR plans to have its own technical schools it will use to prepare crew members for jobs in the sport. It recently announced a partnership with Universal Technical Institute, a vocational school with locations across the country, to build a NASCAR Technical Institute in Charlotte, North Carolina. After the Charlotte location is up and running, NASCAR plans to branch out to other cities.

Part II
What Makes It Stock Car Racing?

The 5th Wave   By Rich Tennant

"No, really—thank the engineers at Nerf, but I don't think it'll get past the inspectors."

In this part . . .

*N*ASCAR stock cars have no doors, no speedometer, no side-view mirrors, and no stereo with a sub-woofer. If these facts bewilder you, dive into this part. Tucked into nearly every paragraph of this section, you can find information about NASCAR race cars and how they differ from passenger cars. In the end, you'll realize why it's impractical and impossible for you to enter your four-door Ford Taurus in the Daytona 500, even though there will be a herd of Ford Tauruses entered in the event.

Even if you're fluent in Spanish or the pig Latin you learned in seventh grade, understanding the language of NASCAR may still difficult. Sway bar? Carburetor restrictor plate? Engine dynamometer? These phrases are commonly used in NASCAR racing, but not at your local moose lodge, bingo parlor, gym, hair salon, or high school. Heck, you can't even find them in your run-of-the-mill dictionary. But never fear, I define those words and plenty more racing terms in this part.

In addition to helping you understand the basic components of a stock car, this part fills you in on the rules and inspections of NASCAR racing, in all their ever-changing glory. You'll meet all the people who have to follow those rules, including the important members of race teams. You also find out that I do other things besides drive a race car on Sundays — really, I do!

Chapter 4

What Makes Them Stock Cars?

*N*ASCAR racing has changed since its early days when race cars were passenger cars with numbers painted or taped on the sides of them — the cars raced were often the cars driven to the track. Races featured cars that fans could go out and buy the same day they saw them race. Manufacturers wanted their cars to win so that they could benefit from the unique type of advertising — the saying went, "Win on Sunday, sell on Monday."

Today, however, the cars are anything but "stock." Teams have engineered ways to make the cars' bodies more aerodynamic, devised methods of producing more horsepower while keeping the engine sturdy, and installed safety features to protect the drivers. After all of these innovations, describing the differences between a passenger car and a stock-car race car is like describing the differences between putt-putt golf and the PGA tour.

In this chapter, we discuss the major differences between passenger cars and NASCAR stock cars, giving you an overview of what you see on the track every weekend.

What Cars Will I See Racing?

Three car models have made up the entries in the NASCAR Winston Cup Series for many years:

Manufacturer loyalty

While some fans cheer for a particular driver or team, others have an allegiance to a specific car manufacturer. For example, if your grandfather drove a Chevy his whole life and your dad drove a Chevy his whole life, you may be persuaded to root for Chevys on race day. It's that kind of loyalty that car manufacturers love — and it's that kind of loyalty that keeps them in racing.

- ✔ Chevrolet Monte Carlo (manufactured by General Motors)
- ✔ Ford Taurus
- ✔ Pontiac Grand Prix (manufactured by General Motors)

In addition to those three, Chrysler enters the series in 2001 with Dodge Intrepids.

Each car model has a staff of engineers working in its racing division — located in or near Detroit — in order to make that car more competitive on the track. They work on developing better aerodynamics, engines, and engine parts, and also work with their respective race teams to try to get an advantage over the other car makes. But, as I talk about in Chapter 5, NASCAR officials try to keep that from happening, wanting every car to have an equal chance of winning, so that fans aren't bored by the same car and the same driver winning each race.

With the many differences between a race car and a passenger car, it's not easy to tell one car from another if you're not familiar with racing. So manufacturers make teams slap the name of the car on every vehicle. For example, the Chevrolet Monte Carlos have a big decal with the words "Monte Carlo" on the nose of the car, Ford Tauruses have a big "Taurus" in the same spot, and the Pontiac Grand Prixs have a "Grand Prix" decal where everybody can see it near the front bumper. When in doubt, check the front of the car to know which model is which.

What Is "Stock" about a Stock Car?

Not much of a NASCAR stock car is similar to a passenger car. Stock cars are built for speed, not to take the kids to soccer practice, so they don't have cup holders or vanity mirrors, and none of them have an automatic transmission. Performance, not comfort or convenience, is what counts — which explains why stock cars last an average of three years, unlike passenger cars, which are manufactured for longevity.

The following are some things that you may be used to seeing on a passenger car, but won't find on a NASCAR stock car:

- **Doors:** That's why drivers climb through the window opening to get in.

- **Windows:** There's just an opening with no glass on the driver's side. On the passenger's side, there's a plastic window that doesn't roll down, but only when cars race on tracks 1½ miles or longer. On tracks shorter than that, there's nothing covering the window.

- **A normal windshield:** In race cars, the windshield is in three sections instead of just one and it's made of Lexan, which is hard, shatterproof plastic, not glass, as you'll find in passenger cars.

- **Back seats or passenger seats:** There's just one seat — the driver's seat.

- **Side-view mirrors**

- **Brake lights or headlights:** The lights you see on the race car aren't real — they're just stickers.

- **Speedometer**

- **Gas gauge**

- **Storage space in the trunk**

- **Stereo system or speakers**

- **An air conditioning or heating system**

- **Automatic transmission**

- **Anti-lock brakes**

- **Cruise control**

- **An ignition where you insert a key:** Drivers just flip a switch to get the car going.

- **Air bags**

- **Locks**

- **Glove compartment**

- **A horn**

Show cars

If you want to see a race car up close, you don't necessarily have to go to the racetrack. From time to time, you can see one at your local mall or grocery store. Teams have *show cars* that travel around the country just so that fans can get a taste of NASCAR without having to pay for race tickets. While the cars are just for show, they are real race cars that were taken out of commission for being too old, suffering irreparable damage, or because they just weren't suited to the driver.

The car has everything that a real race car has, including a working engine so the show-car driver can demonstrate to fans how loud a NASCAR car gets. The *show-car driver,* whose job is to drive the show car all over the country, brings the car to stores, fairs, and driver appearances. It doesn't cost anything to check it out, so if you're curious about race cars, these appearances are perfect opportunities to see one in person and get a good look at it.

The body

The body of a NASCAR stock car is only partly stock. The hood, the *rear deck lid* (or *trunk lid,* as it's normally called), the roof, the front grille, and the bumper panels come from the factory. Those parts are similar to the ones on passenger cars because they're obtained from the manufacturer, although those parts can be modified by the manufacturer from their passenger car counterparts (see Figure 4-1). Those are the only parts of a NASCAR car's body that aren't hand-crafted. Car builders make the rest of stock-car bodies from scratch. The few factory-made parts on NASCAR cars, however, make them recognizable as one of their cousins that you see driving down the highway. It also helps that teams place decals of headlights on the cars to make them look similar to passenger cars.

Aerodynamic features

NASCAR stock cars each have a rear *spoiler,* which is a metal blade that runs the width of the car atop the back of its trunk (see Figure 4-2). The spoiler helps regulate air as it flows over the car, and helps provide stability to the back end of the vehicle. (Turn to Chapter 13 to read more on aerodynamics.) The spoiler collects air as it flows over the vehicle, and that air forces the back end into the ground, making it more stable. You may see passenger cars with spoilers on them, but most of the time they are for looks, not for aerodynamic purposes. They need to be big enough and mounted at the right angle to help control airflow.

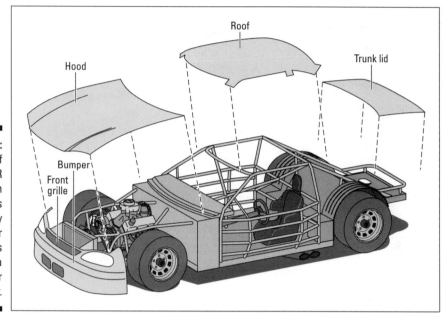

Figure 4-1:
Few parts of a NASCAR Winston Cup Series car's body are similar to the ones on a passenger car.

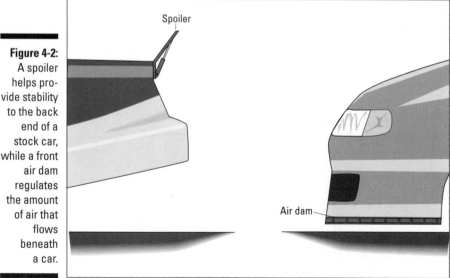

Figure 4-2:
A spoiler helps provide stability to the back end of a stock car, while a front air dam regulates the amount of air that flows beneath a car.

GARAGE TALK

Some fancier sports cars or snazzier passenger cars may have an *air dam* that's attached to the front bumper and goes nearly to the ground (refer to Figure 4-2). Every NASCAR race car has one, though, because it plays an important role in aerodynamics — which is how a car cuts through the air. An air dam blocks air as it hits the front of a car, keeping too much of it from flowing under the vehicle and reducing speed. The closer an air dam is to the ground, the easier a car can cut through the air. Just as a spoiler does in the rear of a car, the air dam keeps the front stable.

The engine

A NASCAR Winston Cup Series car uses an 8-cylinder engine, just as the most powerful, sportiest passenger cars do. And, like its body, most of the car's engine parts aren't the same ones used in the engines of passenger cars — see Figure 4-3.

There are similarities between a NASCAR race car and passenger car:

- ✔ The number of cylinders
- ✔ The angle of the cylinders
- ✔ The location of the camshaft
- ✔ The location of the spark plugs
- ✔ The number of valves per cylinder
- ✔ The number of intake ports
- ✔ The number of exhaust ports

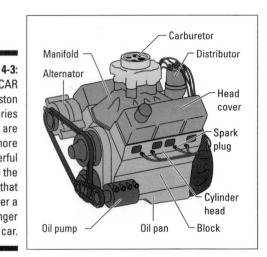

Figure 4-3: NASCAR Winston Cup Series engines are much more powerful than the engines that power a passenger car.

Carburetor
Manifold
Distributor
Alternator
Head cover
Spark plug
Cylinder head
Oil pump
Oil pan
Block

The manufacturers provide teams with engine blocks that have an engine displacement between 350 and 358 cubic inches — cubic inches are one way to measure the size of the engine. A run-of-the-mill passenger car engine has an average of 150 to 200 cubic inches. In racing, the bigger the engine, the more horsepower it will produce.

The manufacturers also outfit the teams with certain performance parts built to withstand 500-mile races, high speeds, and other stresses of racing. After teams get these parts, they start tweaking them to their liking — and that's why not every engine produces the same amount of horsepower. Most produce about 750, much more than a production car, which averages about 200. Their *rpm*, or revolutions per minute, can approach 8,900, which would blow your passenger car's engine to smithereens because its engine shouldn't rev over 5,000 rpm for long. (Rpm describe how many times the crankshaft turns. The crankshaft is the part of an engine that cranks the pistons up and down in a circular motion.) With all that wear on a NASCAR Winston Cup Series engine, teams must replace many of its parts after every race, including the pistons, valves, and springs — basically anything that may have been worn even slightly. That way, the team prevents the engine from breaking or blowing during the following event — although it's not a guarantee. It takes about two days of work to freshen up a used engine, even if nothing needs to be repaired, because team members must replace many parts and meticulously comb over the engine for potential wear or defects.

Carburetors

Unlike passenger cars that were switched to fuel-injected engines because they produce better fuel mileage and fewer emissions that can be harmful to the environment, NASCAR stock cars still use carburetors. The difference is that a *carburetor* mixes air and fuel that pass into the engine's cylinders for combustion, while in a *fuel-injected engine,* an electric pulse triggers the release of a specific amount of fuel, which is then sprayed into each cylinder for combustion. To put it simply, NASCAR teams can get more horsepower from an engine with a carburetor (shown in Figure 4-4) than with fuel injection. On the downside, their engines only get about four miles per gallon.

While teams can fiddle with the engines to enhance their performance, they can't do just anything that pops into their heads. NASCAR sets certain parameters for the equipment and makes sure teams follow the rules by policing engines during inspections (see Chapter 5). NASCAR officials must approve all parts before teams use them, which is done to ensure no one has an unfair advantage. NASCAR's goal is to make races as close and exciting as possible, so no one with an engine made of spaceship parts gets to use it.

Figure 4-4:
Race cars have carburetors, not fuel injection as passenger cars do, although the drive trains on the two cars are similar.

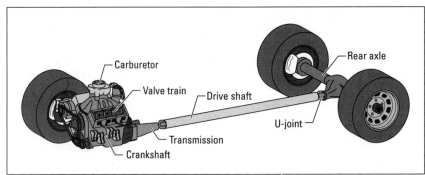

Built for strength and speed

In racing, people make their living building high-performance engines that produce a lot of horsepower, but can also withstand the grueling conditions of a long race. If that engine builder is a good one, he's bound to make a nice salary because good engines are vital to winning races.

An engine builder in NASCAR racing reinforces parts of the engine, such as the sections around the crankshaft (refer to Figure 4-4) by adding material to the bearing, which is a metal part that protects the crankshaft and the connecting rods from overheating and friction — and that's one of the things that helps prevent the engine from breaking down during a race. Only steel crankshafts are allowed, while most have been lightened and balanced for increased horsepower. Teams use other reinforced parts in a race engine — in fact, most parts are reinforced — including extra-strength valves, camshafts, connecting rods, and valve springs.

It takes an engine builder about seven working days to obtain parts, tweak those parts, and put together an entire engine. The cost of that completed engine is about $70,000 to $80,000. Some teams build their own engines, while others buy them from outside companies. Sometimes, teams even lease engines if they're trying to qualify for an important race or racing in a marquee event. The price of a leased engine isn't pocket change, though. It can range anywhere from $10,000 to $40,000 or even more — and you have to give the engine back when you're done.

Engine builders and engine tuners, who work on the engine after it's built to make it produce more horsepower, have turned high-tech along with every-thing else in NASCAR racing. They use special machines, called *engine dynamometers* (see Figure 4-5), that test an engine's performance, measuring the amount of horsepower that an engine produces. During these tests, team members can run an engine for several hours, mimicking a 500-mile race, just to see how the engine will hold up or wear during a real race and how much horsepower it produces. If the team finds problems, the engine builder or tuner can make repairs before the car hits the track. The information from the dynos is relayed to computers so that team members can analyze the data.

Figure 4-5:
Teams run their engines on an engine dynamome-ter, which tests an engine's performance while computers collect the data.

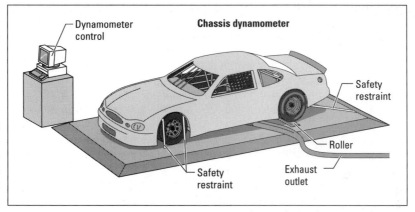

Teams also use machines called *chassis dynamometers* that measure the amount of power translated from the wheels to the ground. The entire race car gets hooked up to the large gizmo — different from an engine dynamome-ter, which only tests the engine when it's not in the race car.

Teams don't build just one engine for a race, and then hope it holds out for the duration of race weekend. They bring several engines to an event. Well-funded teams can have three engines just for qualifying — a primary, a backup, and a backup to the backup. They also may bring as many as three race engines. The qualifying engine is built for maximum power, not for maxi-mum durability, and while it lasts for several laps, pushing it longer than that is risky. After qualifying, teams use a hydraulic lift to remove the engine from the car, and then replace it with a more durable race engine.

Suspension

Perfecting the *suspension* — or the parts that affect the handling of a race car — is one of the most complex aspects of racing. If you struggled through physics in high school, you may have a tough time understanding it. The gist of making the suspension just right is figuring out how much force to put on each corner of the car. That determines how the car rides and how easily the driver is able to control the car.

The suspension in passenger cars is quite simple: Replace four springs and four shock absorbers, and the car should ride smoothly and comfortably. In racing cars, however, a team can make hundreds of changes to the suspension to improve the car's performance. The key is getting the right combination. (NASCAR cars have independent suspension on the front only, meaning the front wheels act and react separately from one another, while the back ones react the same to every bump, turn, or dip — see Figure 4-6 for a complete look.) The parts of the suspension are some of the most important parts of a car's *setup*, which is how the car is prepared to drive on the track with optimum handling and speed.

- ✔ **Air pressure:** Changing the air pressure in the tires is the change most teams use as their first option to improve a car during a race. That's because they can change the air pressure in the new tires they will put on the car *before* their pit stop, so they don't lose any time on pit road. If the car needs more drastic changes because it still isn't riding to a driver's liking, teams make other adjustments. They can put different amounts of air pressure in each of the tires, change one tire, or change a combination of tires. The amount of air pressure put in or taken out depends on where the driver has problems on the track and whether he feels the car isn't performing up to potential.

- ✔ **Camber:** Before the race, teams monitor their tire wear and tire temperatures to see how the tire is performing on the track. If the tires are wearing out too much on one side, or are too hot on one side, teams will change the *camber of the tires* — changing the angle of the tire so it can touch less or more of the racing surface. Camber is measured in degrees from vertical.

- ✔ **Shock absorbers:** *Shock absorbers* are cylinders attached to the car's wheel that make the car ride smoother over bumps. They take care of the tire and control how fast the wheel moves. The key is to figure out the optimum combination of a smooth ride and fast wheel speed. To do that, teams have hired specialists and engineers to build and test shocks, and devise ways for the shocks to make the car faster.

Teams even hook up the shock to a *shock dynamometer* (see Figure 4-6), which pumps the shock up and down as if it were in a real car. The computer prints out results of the test, which show how much force is used when the shock compresses and extends. That's how a team chooses shocks for qualifying or for a race.

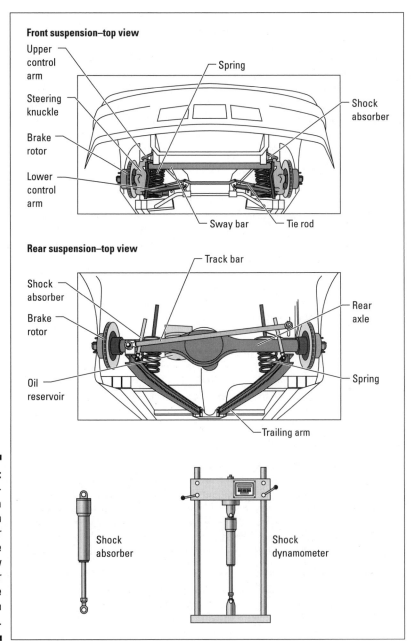

Figure 4-6:
The suspension plays a key role in how the car will handle and how fast a driver can drive during a race.

At superspeedways, shock technology has gone a bit too far recently, with the shocks depressing once the car gets on the track, but never traveling back up. This makes the car squat to the ground and improves the aerodynamics, letting the car cut through the air easier and faster. The problem is that the ride is too bumpy and nearly uncontrollable for drivers — particularly at superspeedways — so NASCAR decided to utilize a uniform shock for those racetracks. That means that teams pick up four shocks with equal specifications on qualifying day and race day at the superspeedways — Daytona International Speedway or Talladega Superspeedway — put the shocks on the car and drive off.

✔ **Springs:** Teams have a closetful of springs. The tension on each spring, which is the *spring rate*, determines how smooth the ride will be and how much weight is put on each tire. Some springs compress more easily than others. The key is to get the right spring with the right spring rate in the proper corner of the car. What makes it even more difficult is that you can put different springs in all four wheels. Teams can't change springs during a race, but they can take a *rubber* out of the spring or put a rubber in — the piece of rubber (cleverly called a "rubber") that's placed between the coils of the spring increases the tension. That makes the car looser or tighter, depending on which spring (and which wheel) the rubber goes into.

Loose is when a driver goes through a turn and the rear of his car gets all wiggly and starts to fishtail, making the driver feel as if he's losing control of the car and about to spin out. That's when the rear tires aren't sticking well to the track and providing enough traction. This is also called *oversteer*. *Tight* is the opposite: When a driver goes through the corners, the front of the car doesn't turn well because the front tires are losing traction before the rear tires are. When a car is tight, it also means it's *pushing* — and if a driver isn't careful, he'll end up zooming right into the wall.

✔ **Track bar or Panhard bar:** The *track bar* is a part of the rear suspension that's attached to the frame on one side and to the rear axle on the other. It keeps the tires centered within the car. Without the track bar, the frame of the car would sway from side to side, making the car unstable and difficult to drive. Teams can raise or lower the track bar by inserting a wrench into a hole located above the right rear tire, and this adjustment makes the car easier to control at high speeds.

✔ **Sway bar:** Most race cars have two sway bars — one in the front and one in the rear. The front sway bar, which is always used while the rear sway bar isn't used at some tracks, is attached to the frame and the lower control arms of the suspension. During practice, teams change *sway bars,* which alter the amount a car rolls to one side or the other through the turns. With different sway bars, they can change how much weight is transferring to the springs on each corner of the car. Teams can't make adjustments to the sway bar during a race, so they're stuck with what they put in before the event. At times, though, teams can disconnect the rear sway bar — which is connected to the frame and the rear-end housing — and remove it all together.

✔ **Wedge:** *Putting a wedge in* means putting more weight onto a wheel by compressing the spring. Teams can put wedge into the rear tires only during a race by inserting a wrench into a hole above the tires. *Putting a half round of wedge in* means they are turning the wrench in a half circle — and placing that much more pressure on the spring. *Taking two rounds of wedge out* means turning the wrench twice counterclockwise and loosening the spring. A round of wedge is also called *a round of bite*.

Other differences

Here are some other features that make a NASCAR stock car different than a passenger car:

✔ The steering wheel is detachable, making it easier for the driver to enter and exit the car (see Figure 4-7).

Figure 4-7:
Drivers can remove their steering wheels, so it's easier for them to enter and exit their car, as well as fit into their seat.

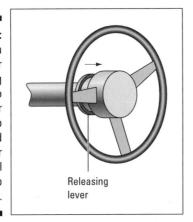

Releasing
lever

✔ The car has roof flaps which are rectangular pieces of metal that fly up when the car travels backwards to keep the car from becoming airborne. See Chapter 11 for more on roof flaps.

✔ The gas tank — also called a fuel cell — is basically located below the trunk, which is farther to the rear than in passenger cars (see Figure 4-8). It is made of steel with an internal rubber bladder that's much stronger and more durable than a passenger car's gas tank.

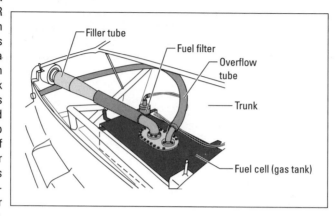

Figure 4-8:
NASCAR Winston Cup Series cars have a 22-gallon gas tank that's located farther to the rear of the car than its passenger-car counterpart.

- Filler tube
- Fuel filter
- Overflow tube
- Trunk
- Fuel cell (gas tank)

✔ The trunk and the hood are fastened down with steel pins, which allows for quick and easy access. Also, steel safety cables keep the hood and trunk lid from flying off in an accident.

✔ An internal roll cage, made of tubular steel (refer to Figure 4-1), is an added safety feature that protects drivers during crashes.

✔ The exhaust doesn't exit from pipes at the rear of the car. It exits on the left side of the car near the rear tires (see Figure 4-9), which makes it pretty hot and loud for the drivers.

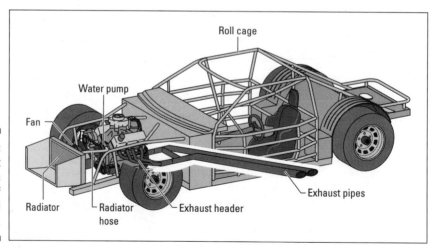

Figure 4-9:
The exhaust system is made up of several parts.

- Roll cage
- Water pump
- Fan
- Radiator
- Radiator hose
- Exhaust header
- Exhaust pipes

What's Inside?

If you peer inside a NASCAR Winston Cup Series car, you won't find luxurious, finely-upholstered leather seats, a radio, a clock, or a sun roof. It's as austere as possible, made for utility and function, not style or convenience — see Figure 4-10.

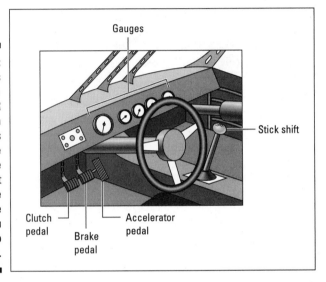

Gauges

Stick shift

Clutch pedal

Brake pedal

Accelerator pedal

Figure 4-10: The controls inside a NASCAR Winston Cup Series car are a little different than the ones on the car you drive to work.

The gauges on the dashboard are a perfect example of that. You won't find a speedometer to see how fast you're going or an odometer to see how far you've traveled. All cars, however, have a *tachometer* that measures the number of revolutions per minute — or *rpm* — of the engine. It indicates how hard the engine is working.

The gauges in a NASCAR Winston Cup Series car vary from car to car, depending on what the driver is used to, but some of the gauges — in addition to the tachometer — include the following:

✔ Oil temperature

✔ Water temperature

✔ Oil pressure

✔ Volt gauge to monitor the battery and electrical system

✔ Fuel pressure gauge

Next to those gauges, you'll find a few switches, which always include an ignition switch. That's why drivers don't need a key to start their cars. They just flip the switch and the engine roars. There also is a second ignition switch that controls a second ignition box. Sometimes in a race, you'll see a car suddenly drop way back, and then start moving toward the front again. That's an indication that the car may have stalled because of ignition failure, so the driver just hits the back-up ignition to remedy the problem.

Next to the ignition switches, you'll see switches that turn on a driver fan, which sends air into the driver's helmet and suit. Also, you may find a brake fan that blows air on the front brakes to keep them cool and keep them working. (Cars used at short tracks have rear brakes only, so the extra fans are in the rear in those cars.) There also may be a rear end fan which keeps the grease cool so the rear-end gear doesn't burn up.

If you look at the pedals on the floor of the driver's seat, you notice a brake pedal, a gas pedal, and a clutch pedal. In a passenger car, everyday drivers use their right foot to control the gas and brake pedals, and their left foot to control the clutch. In racing, on the other hand, it doesn't necessarily work that way. Most drivers use their right to hit the gas, and their left to hit the brake and the clutch. Some say this two-foot method, which is the method I use, is a faster and more efficient way to get on and off the gas and brake.

Take a Seat

A stock car has only one seat and that's for the driver. And it certainly doesn't look very comfortable to sit in — see Figure 4-11. The seats are made of aluminum, covered with padding, and custom-fitted to a driver's body. Even through a driver might spend three hours in that seat during a race, it can't be too comfortable, because that would mean it isn't safe enough. The seats must be snug so there's no room to move around, and that keeps a driver safer in case of an accident. To protect a driver's ribs, two extensions jut from each side, so that drivers have to wiggle into their seats instead of just sliding in. To protect a driver's legs, the seat also has extensions on both sides. To protect the driver's head and neck, some seats have extra protection around the head area. And no, the seat doesn't recline so the driver can relax when a caution flag slows traffic.

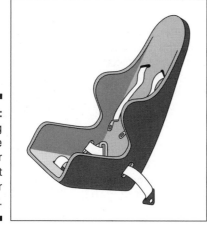

Figure 4-11: Racing seats are made for safety, not so much for comfort.

Tires

NASCAR uses high-performance Goodyear tires that don't look much like the ones you use on your family car. And they certainly cost much more than what you'd pay for the ones on your family car. (What do teams pay for these upscale beauties? Roughly $350 to $400. NASCAR tires are wider than passenger-car tires (see Figure 4-12) — the part that actually touches the ground is about 11 inches wide. They also don't have any tread — except for the ones used on road courses during wet weather. They don't have tread because the cars need as much traction as they can get — and that means the more rubber that touches the racing surface, the better.

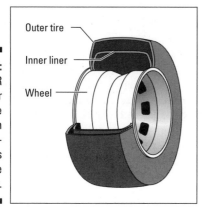

Outer tire

Inner liner

Wheel

Figure 4-12: NASCAR race car tires are wider than passenger-car tires and have no treads.

Goodyear employees come to every race and prepare the tires for the teams, including balancing and mounting each tire onto its wheel. Each team has its own set of wheels at each race, color-coordinated with the car's paint scheme, which a separate company transports to and from each racetrack. Having a separate company deal with the wheels makes it easier for teams because it frees up room on their haulers (see Chapter 6) for other equipment. It also makes it easier because the Goodyear *tirebusters,* who mount and balance the tires, can start working even before the teams unload their equipment.

Each team gets a maximum of three sets of tires (12 tires total) for practice and first-day qualifying. If a team tries to qualify on the second day (see Chapter 8), it gets one more set of tires. When race day rolls around, though, teams use as many tires as Goodyear allows, and that varies from track to track.

Technology

NASCAR cars are supposed to be simple, not high-tech. They aren't outfitted with on-board sensors the way Formula One cars are (see Chapter 1 for more on other types of race cars). Stock cars are made to appeal to fans who can relate to them instead of being perplexed by the technology. NASCAR officials make sure cars stay that way by checking the car before every race for computerized items, including the following outlawed instruments:

- On-board computers
- Recording devices
- Electronic memory chips
- Traction control devices
- Digital gauges

In certain cases, though, cars are outfitted with sensors — called *telemetry* — at the request of the network that's broadcasting the race. The sensors are placed throughout the car to monitor the rpm (revolutions per minute), mph (miles per hour the car is travelling), when and how often the brake and gas pedals are pressed, and which gear the driver selected (with the stick shift). The sensors read that information and transmit it to a remote computer. Some networks broadcast that information during the race to show the speed of a certain car or other information.

GARAGE TALK

Every team has one electronic transmitter on its car during a race and that's a *transponder*. The transponder, shown in Figure 4-13, is a transmitter that teams affix to the bottom of their car — on the right side of the box tht protects the fuel cell — that's used to monitor lap times around a track. Every time the transponder hits a certain point on the track, it records the lap time on a remote computer. Teams huddle around a computer during qualifying to see lap times pop up and who is qualifying where. Also, during a race, those times register on a computer in the pits, so that teams can figure out how fast their car is going relative to the other cars on the track.

Figure 4-13: The transponder is attached to the bottom of the car and helps time how long it takes the car to complete a lap on a racetrack.

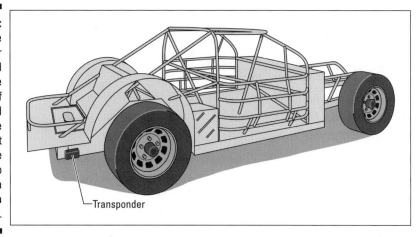

Transponder

Chapter 5

The Rules of the Road

In This Chapter

▶ Understanding the rules and regulations of NASCAR

▶ Watching cars go through inspection

▶ Knowing how teams get around the rules

▶ Deciphering the flags

*W*hen sitting in the grandstands at a NASCAR race for the first time, you may have trouble making sense of what the heck is going on. With your binoculars, you can probably see a lot of activity in the garage area, and with your own eyes, you can see what's happening out on the track — but you may not have any idea what to make of it. Don't fret. This chapter gives you the lowdown so that you won't feel so lost.

To Live and Die by the Rule Book

At the beginning of each year, NASCAR officials hand out rule books to every driver, crew member, car owner, and anyone else with a NASCAR license, making sure everyone in the garage receives a copy for his or her reading pleasure. They don't give tests on the material, but they do have a clever, effective way to find out if the racing teams know the rules: NASCAR officials inspect everyone's car several times during each race weekend, checking to see that teams follow the regulations. Inspecting the cars isn't an easy task, considering there are so many regulations to abide by — and so many that teams try to get around.

The rule book is crammed with pages and pages of specifications, mandates and "suggestions" (which are really rules in disguise). These rules give the racing team details of how to do almost everything it needs to do in order to compete, including how to build a car to NASCAR's liking, what safety measures to implement on the car, and how to fill out paperwork such as entry blanks for races. The team can even find a detailed blueprint of a car from which teams can build their first NASCAR car.

Some of the other rules deal with the following issues:

- ✔ **Engine:** A team can't have just any engine in their car. It has to be a certain size and must be set up in a certain way, so cancel your call to those NASA engineers for their advice.

- ✔ **Body:** Even though most NASCAR car bodies are hand-crafted in a race shop, NASCAR still enforces rules on the basic shape of each vehicle. That means a team can't have a Ford Taurus body that looks like one of those rocket-type cars on *The Jetsons*.

- ✔ **Tires:** NASCAR always tries to cut down on costs for car owners, so it has specific rules about how many sets of tires a team can use for qualifying and practice.

- ✔ **Gas tank:** Many times, races may come down to which team gets better fuel mileage (meaning which team can make it farther on a single tank of gas), so NASCAR makes sure to check that the *fuel cell* — the fancy word for gas tank — isn't bigger than it is supposed to be.

- ✔ **Testing policies:** NASCAR Winston Cup Series teams get only seven tests — or extended, two-day practice sessions — per year at tracks where they compete in NASCAR races. NASCAR makes sure teams don't abuse those allotted tests by sneaking into tracks for extra sessions, which would give those teams more information than — and an unfair advantage over — other teams. Unfair advantages may mean blowout races, which may turn fans away from the sport.

  Rookie drivers are allowed 12 test sessions per year to allow them to become familiar with tracks that they've never driven on before.

- ✔ **Pit stops:** When a car comes in for tires or fuel during the race, the team's pit crew jumps over the wall to service the vehicle. But that group can't just do whatever it wants. NASCAR specifies how many people can go "over the wall" to work on a car during a race and has certain rules for how the team should conduct the stop. For more on pit stops and the rules that govern them, see Chapter 8.

While NASCAR has many, many guidelines for building and preparing a race car for competition, it doesn't have specific rules that govern how drivers race against each other. NASCAR does reserve the right to penalize drivers for *rough driving*, though, which is an infraction not precisely defined in the rule book. It's an action such as bumping into the back of another car to pass it or causing another car to crash when an accident could have been avoided. But the bottom line is, the rule is vague.

Drivers also have unspoken rules among themselves called *gentlemen's agreements*. They are unwritten rules for how aggressive you should be on the track. Not everybody, however, follows those rules. It depends on the driver. Some are known to race like bullies, knocking cars out of the way to pass them. Others are known to race *clean*, which means they are courteous and pass other cars without making contact.

NASCAR's rule book is packed with so many regulations regarding the race-car that you'd be hard pressed to come up with something that it doesn't have a regulation for (except for driving etiquette, which is governed by non-written rules). Still, teams haven't stopped trying to skirt the rules. Every crew member of every team has a NASCAR rule book for the series they're involved in, and many of them spend a lot of time figuring ways to get around the rules. So, when you see a crew member walking around with a rule book in hand, it's not because he is studying what *to* do — he's most likely figuring out what *not to do*. Most teams practice some form of getting around the rules, but we get more into that in the "Being Creative with the Rules" section, later in this chapter.

Don't look for the NASCAR rule book at your local souvenir store because NASCAR issues it only to people with a NASCAR license. (Turn to Chapter 3 to learn more about obtaining a NASCAR license.) NASCAR keeps the rule book under lock and key, safeguarding their rules and the blueprints on how to build a race-ready stock car. NASCAR only wants legitimate teams and dedicated, professional competitors to compete.

NASCAR teams and drivers really don't have to sit down with the rule book and study it from cover to cover. They have a pretty good idea of what's inside already, just from starting out on local tracks and making their way through the ranks. If any specific rule changes are made for on-track activity — such as making a pit stop in a very small *pit box* (the area a driver must pull into so a crew can service the car) or starting the race on a restart at a particular point on the track — NASCAR officials review those changes during a drivers' meeting. That meeting is normally held two hours before the event, and it's the one time during a race weekend when all the drivers and crew chiefs are in the same place at the same time.

There are even rules for the drivers' meetings. Drivers and their crew chiefs must attend the meeting — and be on time — or get penalized for it. If a driver or his crew chief misses the meeting, the driver automatically starts the race from the last-place spot, no matter where he qualified. This could be embarrassing for a driver who, let's say, qualified third but overslept, missed the meeting, and had to start the race in last place. His team gets upset over that because all of the work it put in to qualify up front goes to waste. The sponsors aren't too happy about the driver falling back to last place in the field, either. Companies don't pay hundreds of thousands of dollars — sometimes millions of dollars — to see their cars start in last place.

Even though drivers know the rules, they occasionally may ask questions at the drivers' meeting in order to clarify something for the race. For example, if a driver isn't sure where to start accelerating when the green flag falls (signaling the start or restart of the race), he asks a NASCAR official to go over that point. Or sometimes a driver uses the drivers' meeting as a chance to speak up about something that has been bothering him. If practice before the race was particularly out of control, a driver may warn his fellow competitors that the race isn't necessarily won by who goes the fastest — it's won by who goes the fastest without getting into or causing an accident. NASCAR officials warn the competitors, too. Often at the drivers' meeting, NASCAR officials tell the drivers, "You can't win the race unless you finish the race." That means, "Be careful or you're likely to get into an accident."

Many times, the drivers' meeting is held in an empty bay in the garage area, where chairs are set up for the drivers and crew chiefs. Sometimes, when there is enough room, fans are allowed to watch the meetings — but only from outside of roped-off areas. If you have a garage pass, get to the area early because many fans show up to see the proceedings. This is a great time to take a peek at your favorite drivers and snap their pictures while they sit still at the meeting, relaxing and interacting with other drivers. Don't make noise, though, because NASCAR officials can throw you out of the meeting area. You also shouldn't storm the drivers and crew chiefs for autographs as they leave the meeting. That's one way to upset them, particularly because they don't have that much time to prepare for the race. They're trying to focus on the competition, not on the T-shirt that you'd like them to autograph.

Teams Expect to Be Inspected

Long before drivers go to drivers' meetings or teams put the final touches on their race cars, their cars must be approved to race by NASCAR officials. Throughout race weekend, NASCAR inspects cars to see if teams abide by the rules. If they do follow the rules, officials give teams permission for their cars to go on the track. If they don't, teams must work on the cars until officials deem them ready to race. Formally, those processes are called *inspections*.

A race weekend in the NASCAR Winston Cup Series, the NASCAR Busch Series, and the NASCAR Craftsman Truck Series usually begins on Fridays — and inspections begin not long after the garage opens that morning. Teams arrive at the garage early in the morning, and then start preparing their cars for NASCAR inspectors to examine. If the car doesn't pass inspection the first time through, team members know right away that the weekend won't be an easy one.

As soon as teams show up at the track, the inspectors head to the garages and begin the inspection process.

Surviving the initial inspection

The initial inspection begins the morning the track opens, when each car is put on four stands without tires. Inspectors do a quick check of the following:

- **Body:** Even though stock-car racing involves only Fords, Chevrolets, and Pontiacs, there's a lot of room for tweaking. So officials must make sure that each of the cars conforms to a certain shape. No missiles or bullet trains allowed.

- **Safety belts and nets:** An inspector takes a quick look around the inside to make sure everything is in order, especially the seatbelts and the window net, which are safety features on the cars. The seatbelts strap the driver in with five adjoining belts, while the *window net* is a piece of mesh fastened to the inside of the window. The net keeps the driver's head or arms from coming out of the window during an accident. To make sure these items work, the inspector examines them to see if they are made of the correct material and also to ensure that their locking mechanisms are functioning.

- **Roll bars:** *Roll bars* are the part of the car's frame that protects the driver because they're made of strong tubing with a minimum thickness — like a tubular cage. If a driver rolls his car over, the roll bars ideally protect him from getting crushed. An inspector leans into the car window to check the thickness of these bars with a special instrument that measures the diameter and thickness of the steel tubing.

- **Fuel cell:** Whenever fuel or the fuel cell (the fancy phrase for "gas tank") is involved, NASCAR officials get nervous because of the potential fire hazard. In the initial inspection, officials check the fuel tank to make sure it holds the correct amount of fuel (22 gallons) and that it has a foam rubber interior to prevent it from breaking open and spilling gasoline. The inspector also takes a look at the *check-valve,* which is a valve that prevents fuel spills if the car turns over.

- **Engine volume and compression ratio:** Even though the engine is checked more thoroughly in subsequent inspections, officials like to give it a once-over at this stage. They check to see if the engine is the right size and if the compression ratio is correct — and that both follow NASCAR rules. Bigger engines (with more volume) produce more horsepower. Higher compression ratios produce more power, too. (For more information on compression ratios, flip to Chapter 3.)

- **Metal check:** To ensure teams aren't cheating by substituting a lighter material, such as titanium, for steel (to make their car lighter and faster), inspectors go over the main parts of the car with a magnet. If the magnet doesn't stick, then they've caught a team trying to break the rules.

If officials catch teams cheating or see something they don't like in this initial inspection, they can ask teams to fix or replace the part or parts in question. If NASCAR gives them an initial okay, the team's next step is to head for a more-thorough inspection, where officials examine the car more closely. If a team doesn't fix or replace a questioned part, officials don't let its car on the track.

Heading to the inspection line

Even though a team may have gotten through the initial inspection, they're not done being inspected for the day. Even before they can think about practicing, teams must take their car through a technical inspection line where several officials — not just one, as before — look at their car. Cars must go through *tech,* which is NASCAR lingo for technical inspection, at the following times:

✔ Before the first practice of the race weekend

✔ Before qualifying

✔ After qualifying if they win the pole or are the fastest car in the second-round qualifying

✔ Just before the race, which is why you may see a line of cars snaking through the garage the morning of race day, with a bunch of crew members shepherding their cars through the line

The day isn't even over after the race ends. Certain cars must be inspected one more time before teams pack up and go home. Check out the "Even when a car wins, it's not over" section later in this chapter for more on post-race inspections.

In the inspection line, officials conduct a more thorough check of the cars. If a car doesn't pass, even if it's just one part of the multi-step inspection, the team must roll the car back to the garage and fix the item in question. Then, the team must roll the car through the inspection line again, whether it cuts into practice time or not. When the team gets to the front of the line, officials don't only check the item that didn't pass the initial inspection — they inspect every part of the car all over again. That's just to make sure the team didn't fiddle with anything when they went back to the garage area. If the car passes the inspection, officials put a sticker on the car's windshield indicating it can go out on the track.

In the NASCAR Winston Cup Series, inspection officials review the following:

✔ **Weight:** Crew members push their car through the inspection line with the car's engine off. In order to be weighed, the car must go through inspection *wet,* which means filled with fuel, oil, and water. Without the driver, NASCAR Winston Cup Series cars must weigh at least 3,400 pounds, with at least 1,600 pounds of that weight on the right side.

With the driver, the car must weigh at least 3,600 pounds. While cars are weighed each time they go through technical inspection, drivers are weighed only twice a year — once at the start of the season and again halfway through. At those weigh-ins, some drivers get sneaky because drivers who weigh less than 200 pounds must add weight to their cars in ten-pound increments (up to a maximum of 50 pounds). Nobody wants to add weight to their cars, so some drivers take it upon themselves to miraculously get heavier just before the weigh-in. They drink tons of water or stuff themselves with food to add a couple extra pounds. Also, if they can get away with it, they get weighed with a fair amount of clothes on. For me, though, it's almost no use to try and fool anybody. I'm 5'5", 135 pounds and couldn't look much heavier.

✔ **Compression ratio and engine displacement:** Inspectors use instruments to ensure the compression ratio is 12:1. (See Chapter 3 for more on compression ratios.) With higher ratios, engines produce more power. They also do a check for the overall engine displacement, which reveals the volume of the engine. NASCAR Winston Cup Series engines must be a maximum of 358 cubic inches. Any bigger, and those engines would generate more horsepower. Inspectors also check one of the engine's eight cylinders — a different cylinder every time — each week to keep teams on their toes and make sure no one is cheating.

✔ **Safety:** As with the initial check, NASCAR officials examine the inside of the car, looking for sharp edges on which a driver could injure himself. They also check the safety belts and window nets for wear and tear.

✔ **Heights:** As the car rolls on the scales, it also rolls under an arch of metal with a pin attached to its center. That pin reaches down to the car's roof, measuring the roof height of the vehicle.

✔ **Ground clearance:** Teams always want their cars to be as low to the ground as possible (without scraping the ground, of course) so that their cars can cut through the air as easily as possible. But NASCAR wants to make sure those cars aren't too low. Officials use an instrument to measure the ground clearance at various points on the vehicle, ensuring teams aren't trying to get their cars to squat lower than the rules allow in order to get an unfair advantage.

▶ **Rear spoiler:** The *rear spoiler* is a piece of metal that runs the width of the car and is attached to the car's trunk. It plays a big role in determining how air flows over the car to affect speed and handling (see Chapter 13). Officials check the height of the spoiler, from the top of the spoiler to where it meets the top of the trunk, and also check the angle of the spoiler to ensure it meets NASCAR standards.

▶ **Body:** In each of NASCAR's series, each brand of car or truck has a set of *templates* — individual pieces of metal that conform to the body of a car — in order to ensure the car fits NASCAR specifications (see Figure 5-1). Each piece conforms to the car in different places, making it a metal blueprint for the shape of a car's exterior. In NASCAR Winston Cup Series, my Ford Taurus has at least 18 of those templates. They check the shape of nearly every inch of my car's body — including the nose, the length of the body, the trunk, and the width of the body — in several places.

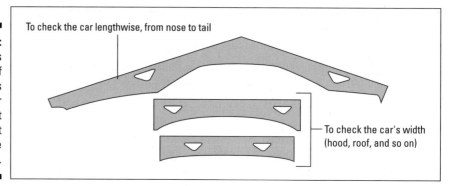

Figure 5-1: Templates are sets of blueprints each car must fit before it goes on the track.

To check the car lengthwise, from nose to tail

To check the car's width (hood, roof, and so on)

When drivers are fast, officials say "not so fast"

Think a team is off the hook just because their car passed through tech before it went on the track for practice? Not yet. NASCAR officials want to make sure teams aren't cheating, so they make cars go through tech inspection several other times during a race weekend. Cars go through tech just before qualifying (see Chapter 8). Afterward, they can't go back to the garage and must take their place in line on pit road to wait for qualifying to begin.

The top five qualifiers go through inspection again, where officials check height, weight, and the car's body. Even then, the car of the pole winner, who had the fastest qualifying lap, isn't finished with inspection. During that weekend, the pole-winning team members must *tear down,* meaning take apart, the car's engine while officials watch over their shoulders. When they have the engine in pieces, officials check everything over yet again to make sure that the engine is the right size and that all the parts conform to NASCAR rules.

Cars that didn't make the race during first-day qualifying also must go through tech before they get one last chance to make the race during second-round qualifying (usually held on Saturday mornings). The fastest car of the second round goes through tech after its fast lap. Then, that team tears down its engine so NASCAR officials can check to see if it's legal.

Even though NASCAR officials do a great job inspecting cars, they have some help making sure everyone follows the rules. The teams standing in line waiting for inspection take on that job, especially because they have nothing else to do while waiting in line — but mostly because NASCAR racing has become so competitive. The team in line behind a car being inspected watches officials do their jobs. Right along with the officials, that team makes sure the car fits all the templates and is the right height and weight. If something looks funny, that team will protest, but NASCAR doesn't mind. Other teams are NASCAR's second defense against cheating, and those teams help keep racing fair.

Special tests for special tracks

NASCAR officials use an especially thorough process to inspect cars at Daytona International Speedway and Talladega Superspeedway. Those tracks are NASCAR's two superspeedways, which are NASCAR's fastest tracks. (Flip to Chapter 13 to get a more detailed look at those two tracks.) Officials conduct special tests at those tracks to ensure driver and fan safety because of the high speeds — more than 190 mph — that cars run there.

At Daytona and Talladega, where carburetor restrictor plates are required to reduce horsepower and slow down cars — an official handles the restrictor plates at all times. (See Chapter 13 for more on restrictor plates.) Teams receive their restrictor plates when they go through inspection, but they can't just grab one and slap it on their car's carburetor. It's a carefully regulated process. A team member reaches over a barrier to choose a plate randomly, then an official lifts the plate over his head for everyone to see. After that, the official places the restrictor plate on a pole that measures the diameter of the hole, ensuring it is the same size as every one else's restrictor plate. Finally, he places the plate on the car's engine — see Figure 5-2. Then the engine is sealed, as it always is, with an official NASCAR seal to make sure none of the teams tamper with the engine after it passes inspection.

NASCAR officials take the inspection process at superspeedways further than they do on other tracks. They often X-ray parts of a car's engine after the races, nearly eliminating the chance of a team getting away with even the minutest infraction. If there are holes in the carburetor, even ones the naked eye can't see, more air leaks into the engine — and the car goes faster, defeating the purpose of the restrictor plates. NASCAR ensures that no holes exist.

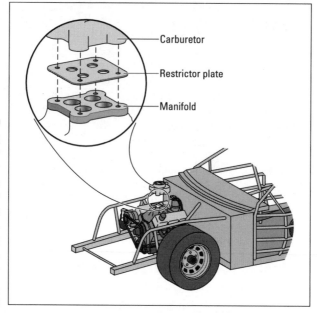

Figure 5-2:
Carburetor restrictor plates restrict air flowing into a car's carburetor, and thus reduce horsepower and speed.

Carburetor

Restrictor plate

Manifold

Even when a car wins, it's not over

Even after crossing the finish line first and driving into Victory Lane, the inspection process isn't over. In fact, the hardest part is yet to come. After a driver wins a race, officials follow his car into Victory Lane and watch over it — just to make sure his team doesn't tamper with it while he poses for pictures or sprays champagne over the crowd. (But that would be a great distraction, don't you think?) After the driver is done whooping it up, the team rolls the car over to the gas pumps where the other cars that finished in the top five already filled up their gas tanks. Then the top five cars go through inspection again, during which NASCAR officials weigh them — which is why they need to fill their gas tanks — and place templates on the bodies for the last time.

The battery of inspections continues because the top two or three cars — depending on how many NASCAR officials choose — head for an empty garage to be inspected again. Another car, chosen randomly during the race, also gets the privilege of joining them. (The first driver who falls out of the race because of an accident or mechanical failure picks a number out of a hat — whichever car finishes in that place becomes the random car to be torn down.) Having a random car torn down is the way NASCAR officials can police cars that consistently finish out of the top five. Every other car heads home right after the race without getting the once-over.

MARK SAYS

Just when you think you've got 'em beat

I don't mind post-race inspections much, probably because if my car has to go through them, it usually that means I've done well in a race or won the whole thing. But in 1990, I didn't like my inspection at Richmond one bit. I had won the second race of the season that year, taking the lead with 16 laps to go to finish three seconds ahead of Dale Earnhardt.

In the inspection, NASCAR officials found something in my engine that they thought was illegal. There was a carburetor spacer on the engine's manifold that was one-half-inch thicker than the two inches allowed, something NASCAR thought was a pretty big deal even though all we had to do was weld the spacer together to make it legal. I thought it was just a technicality, but it turned out to be a huge deal when officials decided to take 46 points away from me and fine

my team $40,000. Those 46 points represented the difference between first and tenth place, which is where the last car on the lead lap finished. (Turn to Chapter 8 for more information on NASCAR's scoring system.) My team appealed the penalty to the National Stock Car Racing Commission — a group of individuals appointed by NASCAR, including several track presidents and NASCAR executives. But the fine and the penalty stood.

The whole incident was heartbreaking for me, especially when I ended up losing the NASCAR Winston Cup Series championship to Earnhardt that year — by only 26 points. That slip-up cost me the title, so it's no wonder I don't usually stick around post-race inspections. They make me nervous.

GARAGE TALK

When cars are *torn down,* teams take apart the cars' engines, but tear downs also can include whatever NASCAR officials want. Usually, the winning team goes through a *thorough tear-down,* meaning it will take apart the engine, the suspension, the power train, and whatever else officials want to check out.

Unlike other inspections during the weekend, post-race inspections can take several hours because the teams must tear down their cars nearly to the bare bones. After they do that, officials check different parts of the car, doing it as thoroughly or as cursorily as they deem necessary. Not only do officials check for obviously illegal parts, but they also look for parts not approved by NASCAR (which may have been modified in hidden places) and illegal additives used in the fuel. Those things may appear legal at first glance.

NASCAR officials check for the following during a post-race inspection:

- ✔ Engine: size, compression, and so on
- ✔ Ignition
- ✔ Rear-end gear
- ✔ Fuel tank

> ✔ Body
>
> ✔ Power train
>
> ✔ Fuel (fuel additives)

While teams are happy to win a race, they aren't so thrilled about their post-celebration work at tear-downs. At that point, they've had a long day, often beginning before dawn, and want to go home, without spending another hour or two in the garage taking their car apart. When NASCAR officials finally give a team the okay, they place all the car's engine parts into a box to be shipped back in the team truck. The team must put the engine back together at another time, which isn't a big deal because teams use different cars at different tracks anyway. Each team has a fleet of about 12 cars at their shop, each built specifically for a different type of racetrack — some for superspeedways, some for high-banked tracks, some for flat tracks — all covered in Chapter 13. (Flip to Chapter 4 to find out more about engines and what teams do to prepare them for a race.)

Being Creative with the Rules

NASCAR racing has become so competitive over the years — with so much money at stake — that teams try to do everything possible to get an edge over the competition. That includes cheating. But in NASCAR, cheating isn't always called cheating — it's called *getting around the rules, interpreting the rules, reading between the lines, using the gray area,* or *being creative.*

I'll use the templates as an example. Back when templates first came out, there were only two or three of them. So even though teams had to build their car to fit those two or three templates, they did whatever they wanted on every other part of their cars. Now, even though more than a dozen templates exist for each car, teams try to do the same thing. That's why NASCAR officials keep adding more and more templates — because teams keep trying to get around the rules.

Here is a list of some of the ways teams try to skirt the rules:

> ✔ **Body:** Teams can get an aerodynamic advantage by putting all sorts of nearly indistinguishable bumps and ruts into a car's body. They may put a bump on the door to disturb the air flowing down the side of the car, which may create turbulence for other cars when the cars race in a pack.
>
> ✔ **Tires:** NASCAR officials don't check teams' tires, so some teams try to use that to their advantage. Teams have soaked or chemically treated the tires to make them softer and better to grip the track — which does make the car faster, but only for short runs because the soaked or altered tires aren't very durable.

✔ **Engine:** Teams try to lower the *motor mounts,* where the motor sits in relation to the body of the car, so that the car will have a lower center of gravity and handle better.

✔ **Roof flaps or other parts:** To lighten the car, teams constantly try to figure out how to make parts out of lighter material — which is illegal in certain cases where parts must be made out of NASCAR-mandated materials, such as steel. Still, teams are constantly substituting those materials for lighter ones when they install roof flaps, drive shafts, wheel hubs, suspension components, or even nuts or bolts on the engine. They can also drill holes in these parts, another way to make the car lighter. Teams transfer the weight they save to a spot lower on the car to improve handling.

While figuring out ways to cheat can be quite a creative process, if a team is caught cheating, NASCAR is pretty tough on it. If officials discover something illegal on your car before the race, they make the crew fix or replace the part, and later slap the team with a big fine or put the crew chief on probation. *Being on probation* means that if a team member is caught doing anything illegal, he can be temporarily or permanently kicked out of the garage. If NASCAR officials discover an illegal part on a car after qualifying or after the race, then they can fine the driver *and* make him requalify or take points away from him.

The king of cheaters takes over

Teams don't cheat as much as they used to because the NASCAR rule book has gotten thicker and thicker over the years. But in the NASCAR Winston Cup Series, there is another reason. Gary Nelson, the NASCAR Winston Cup Series Director, is in charge. Nelson became series director in 1992 after 14 years of working as a NASCAR Winston Cup Series crew chief. In those 14 years, Nelson was the biggest rule bender around. Because of his background, he can catch cheaters in a second. As Ricky Rudd put it, "When NASCAR hired Gary Nelson, I guess they figured, "Hire a crook to stop a crook."

During Nelson's stint as a crew chief, one of his most ingenious ideas was when he was Darrell Waltrip's crew chief at DiGard Racing. To get around the rules, Nelson filled the frame rails of Waltrip's car with lead buckshot and rigged it so that Waltrip could pull a lever and let the buckshot dribble out of a hole and onto the racetrack during the race. Without the extra weight of the buckshot, the car would be lighter than any other car in the field — and would rocket to the front. Back then, cars weren't weighed after an event, so Nelson got away with his little trick for a while until another team figured out his scheme.

With a crew chief's mentality, Nelson knows where teams try to get an advantage and, because of that insight, cheating has become less and less common in NASCAR Winston Cup Series racing. But because of the fierce competition, it'll never disappear completely.

Watching the Flagman

After all of those inspections, cars are ready to get out on the track. From that point on, keep your eye on the *flagman,* who is perched above the racetrack at the start/finish line in a crow's nest of sorts. You can't miss him — he's the guy waving all those flags.

What do all those flags mean? Here's the lowdown:

- ✔ **Green:** To keep things simple, green means go. The flagman waves the green flag to signal the start of the race. During a few pace laps, which are run at a slower pace so that cars can warm up their engines and tires, a pace car with lights on its roof leads the field. Just before the race starts, though, the pace car peels off onto pit road as the flagman waves the green flag. Then, they're off!

- ✔ **Yellow:** The yellow flag, or *caution flag,* comes out when drivers need to slow down because the track is unsafe. This happens in the event of an accident, rain, or when debris or oil is on the track. When the yellow flag is waved, drivers speed back to the start/finish line to begin the first lap of caution. Sometimes drivers who have fallen a lap behind the leader will track to get back on the lead lap when the yellow flag comes out. They can do this by passing the leaders on the way to the start/finish line.

Most of the time, though, drivers don't try to pass other cars on the way back to the start/finish line as part of a gentlemen's agreement. There is an exception, though. When the yellow comes out near the end of the race, drivers race back to the start/finish line because the race may end under caution. Caution laps are counted as part of the total laps in a race, so if the caution comes out with two laps to go (and it takes at least that many laps for officials to clean up the accident on the track), then drivers race their way to the finish in order to win.

Some fans don't appreciate paying to attend a NASCAR race, only to see it end under a caution flag — which is completely understandable. For me, though, ending under a caution flag is just fine. It seems to me that every time a race is restarted with a few laps to go, something bad happens. At the Pepsi 400 at Daytona International Speedway in 1997, cars lined up for a restart with only one lap to go, giving fans the action they came for. I was in the lead then, but not for long. It was mayhem as soon as the green flag fell, with cars trying wildly to get to the front. The fans got their action all right, there was a big crash where a bunch of the top cars were collected, including me. So not only did that knock me a bit silly, it also reinforced my feelings that a race should end on a caution flag, and shouldn't be set up for a last-lap shootout. If I were assured that no accidents would happen on that final lap and that every driver would use his head, I wouldn't mind it. After all, the fans are the reason that NASCAR is so popular, and I'm all for giving them a good race. But given what can happen with 43 cars bunched together racing all-out for two crazy laps, I think it's safer and smarter just to end the race after a late yellow-flag period and conclude the event under caution.

Drivers don't always feel the same way when a caution comes out. Sometimes, they are happy about it because they need a pit stop for gas or fresh tires, or because the car in the lead is a mile ahead of everyone and cars are bunched back up for a restart after a caution, bringing everyone closer to the leader. Sometimes, though, a driver hates to see a caution flag — especially when he's leading by a mile or when his car drives better after long runs at full speed.

✔ **Red:** When a red flag waves, cars must stop wherever they are on the track. The pace car then comes out and slowly leads them to a safe place designated by NASCAR. If drivers are on a part of the track where they can't see the red flag, their crew chief gets on the two-way, in-car radio and tells them to stop. A red flag comes out when a dangerous situation exists on the track — like a lot of oil or fluid covering the surface or a damaged wall or fence — and it would be unsafe or impossible for cars to continue to circle the track under caution. Also, if it is raining so much that drivers can't see the track (or if the track is too wet and slippery), the red flag stops the race until the conditions improve. Depending on how long a race is under the red flag, drivers may sit in their cars, get out and talk with one another, or — during a long rain delay — head for their trailers parked in the infield.

✔ **Black:** A black flag signals to the driver that he must get off the track and go to his pits. This happens when something is wrong with his car, such as oil leaking or smoke billowing from the exhaust, which may create a dangerous situation for other cars on the track. The black flag can also come out when a driver breaks the rules, like when he jumps the start.

When a driver is black-flagged, he knows it. Not only does the flagman wave that ominous, dark flag at him, but his car number also is displayed at the start/finish line so drivers know exactly who's in trouble. A driver can't really ignore getting black flagged, either, and just stay out on the track to race, because at some point, officials get peeved and the flagman breaks out a black flag with a white "X" on it, indicating the driver won't be scored any longer. In that case, a driver should give up and head to the pits.

✔ **Blue with diagonal yellow stripe:** When a driver sees this flag, it signifies that faster, lead-lap cars are about to pass him and he must yield to those cars. A flagman usually waves this flag at a driver who is one lap down and is significantly slower than the cars racing for the win.

✔ **White:** This flag signals that the driver in the lead is on his final lap.

✔ **Checkered:** When a flagman waves the checkered flag, it means that the winner has just crossed the finish line.

Chapter 6

The Race Team

Y ou may not think of stock-car racing as a team sport — racing certainly seems like an individual sport, considering all the attention a driver gets. While a driver is arguably the most important part of a race team, he isn't the only reason a team wins or loses. Dozens of people work on a race team and contribute to the performance of a car every weekend. From the owner to the crew chief, the engine builder, and the guy who orders parts, everyone on a team has to work well — and work well together — in order for the team to succeed.

Consider the driver racing's version of a quarterback. And a good quarter-back can't accomplish much if his team lets him get sacked.

The Owner Is the Boss

In NASCAR Winston Cup Series racing, just as in any sport, the players — in this case, the drivers — get most of the credit. But drivers wouldn't have jobs if somebody didn't employ them. The person that employs NASCAR drivers is the team owner.

The *owner* has the final say in hiring everyone who works on the team, from the driver to the crew chief to everyone who prepares the cars for racing. The owner spends money on cars and parts, which are quite pricey, consider-ing a set of racing tires alone can cost more than $1,500. The owner shells out cash for the payroll — which isn't cheap, considering how competitive the sport is and how valuable talented employees are. With all those bills to pay and paychecks to sign, an owner has to be a shrewd and savvy businessperson, because that money has to come from somewhere — ideally not his own pockets. So in order to make sure he has enough money to pay everybody, the owner has to do one thing first: Secure a sponsor.

The owner approaches large corporations and asks for anywhere from $4 to $10 million to sponsor a race team for the season. The owner has to convince the companies that paying that kind of money will lead to exposure, and ultimately, better sales for their product. So the owner needs to understand the business world beyond the business of running a race team. But he also needs to know racing. An owner has to be able to recognize driving talent on the racetrack, and much like a team owner or a coach in other sports, he needs to be able to create an environment in which that talent can flourish.

While most NASCAR owners are men, just as most drivers and team members are, a few women own teams — including the mother of Jack Roush, my team owner. Georgetta Roush owns one of Roush Racing's five teams, but she isn't involved in the day-to-day operations of the team, as is the case for many female team owners.

Many multicar teams, which I talk more about in the "Multicar teams — the more the merrier" section later in this chapter, have several different owners on paper. This is done because only two teams per owner are eligible for NASCAR's bonus programs. Those programs can generate a good deal of money, depending on a team's performance, so every team owner wants to be involved — even it means fudging a bit when it come to team ownership.

Some NASCAR Winston Cup Series team owners have become as famous and as popular as their drivers. For instance, some fans have a stronger allegiance to a team owner than they do to a driver. So, they'll cheer for any car that, for example, Robert Yates owns — no matter who's behind the wheel.

In NASCAR racing, each car has its own *car number*, just as each pro basketball player has a number on his or her jersey. It's an easy way to identify a car on the track, especially when you can't see the driver's face as he zooms by. Car numbers are vital to know if you want to be a knowledgeable race fan and fit in with the race crowd. A lot of times people refer to a car number only, and not the team name or driver, when they're talking about a car. They'd say, for example, "The 2 was the strongest car out there, don't you think?" What they just said was they thought Rusty Wallace's Ford Taurus was great that day. (See Appendix C for a list of drivers and their car numbers.)

A few of the better, more successful racers have become linked to their car numbers for an eternity, such as Dale Earnhardt and his No. 3 Chevy or Richard Petty and his No. 43 car. Even Jeff Gordon, who hasn't been in NASCAR Winston Cup Series racing for that long, will always be known as the driver of the No. 24 Chevy — particularly because he announced in 1999 he will drive the car until he retires.

Good team owners don't come around often

My car owner, Jack Roush, is, in my opinion, the best team owner in racing and I also consider him my surrogate father since my father, Julian, died in a plane crash in August 1998. Jack has looked out for me since we teamed up in 1988 on his new NASCAR Winston Cup Series race team, and we've been together ever since, through the good times (winning races and nearly winning NASCAR Winston Cup Series championships) and the bad times (going winless throughout the entire 1996 season). It's not an exaggeration to say that I wouldn't have been as successful a driver as I am now if it weren't for Jack Roush. (Check out the color insert, near the center of this book, for a photo of Jack.)

The best relationships between owners and drivers are the ones with give and take, and lots of trust. You can see that trust in the top driver-owner relationships, including the relationship between Jack Roush and me, Dale Earnhardt and Richard Childress (who were together nearly 20 years), and Rusty Wallace and Roger Penske (who have worked together for almost ten years). Without mutual trust, they wouldn't have had as much success as they had during that time.

Jack and I get along well right now because we're both proud of the team we've built and the success we've had in recent years. Also, Jack and I have similar approaches to dealing with the team and the race car. He's one of the most hands-on owners in NASCAR Winston Cup Series racing, overseeing everything for each of his race teams, from the engine program to the body shop to the processes at the racetrack. And I'm one of the more hands-on drivers in the series, working with the crew chief, car chief, and engine specialist to understand exactly how the car is working and precisely what can be done to make it go faster. Some owners and drivers, on the other hand, sit back and let the team figure things out, which definitely isn't our style. Over the years, I've come to understand that Jack and I are similar in the way we do things — and we both care about making our team as good as possible so that Roush Racing can win its first championship.

The following are a few of the more famous — perhaps even legendary — NASCAR Winston Cup Series team owners today:

- ✔ **Richard Childress:** Childress was the longtime car owner of one of the most well-known drivers on the circuit — seven-time NASCAR Winston Cup Series champion Dale Earnhardt. Together, the Childress-Earnhardt No. 3 Chevy team won six titles. Childress was a race car driver before deciding to go the ownership route, which turned out quite well for him. He didn't win any NASCAR Winston Cup Series races as a driver, but has won more than 65 races as a car owner.

- ✔ **Rick Hendrick:** Hendrick became a NASCAR Winston Cup Series team owner in 1984 with Geoffrey Bodine as driver, and then became one of the first multicar teams (see the "Multicar teams — the more the merrier" section) on the circuit. But in the 1990s, Hendrick won four consecutive championships — one with Terry Labonte and three with Jeff Gordon from 1995 to 1998.

✔ **Roger Penske:** Penske's love for racing began as an open-wheel car driver when he was young. He then branched out into ownership. He owns Rusty Wallace's team, but also owns a team in the Championship Auto Racing Teams series, which is one of the nation's two major series featuring open-wheel cars. (Turn to Chapter 1 for more on open-wheel cars.) But Penske didn't stop there. He also developed several major-league racetracks in the U.S., including Michigan Speedway.

✔ **Richard Petty:** Petty is known as the King of stock-car racing because of his seven NASCAR Winston Cup Series championships and NASCAR-record 200 wins, but he also has been a successful car owner. There's a good reason for that — Petty owned his own car for most of his career so he knows what he's doing. Back when he first began driving in 1958, many drivers owned their own teams because it was so much less expensive than it is today. But Petty stayed an owner, even when costs skyrocketed through the years. It helped that STP oil company was his longtime sponsor and helped out financially — it also helped that he won so many championships and races. Today, Petty owns cars driven by his son, Kyle, and by John Andretti, nephew of the legendary open-wheel driver Mario Andretti. Andretti drives the No. 43 car, which was Petty's number until he retired in 1992.

✔ **The Wood Brothers:** Glen and Eddie Wood's father began racing in 1953 — just a few years after NASCAR began in 1949. The two sons continue to keep up the tradition as one of the longest-running team owners in the business. Elliott Sadler, who is from Virginia just as the Woods are, drives the Wood Brothers' No. 21 Ford.

✔ **Robert Yates:** Team owner Robert Yates, perhaps the best engine builder in NASCAR, finally won a championship in 1999, after years of coming close. Dale Jarrett, one of his two drivers, dominated most of the season in the No. 88 Ford to win the title. Some of the greatest drivers drove for Yates after he became a team owner in 1989, including the late Davey Allison who drove the No. 28 Ford. Jarrett and Ricky Rudd, who will drive the No. 28 Ford, will be teammates in 2000.

The sponsor doesn't give commands

Even though *sponsors* — the companies that pay for the right to have their names on cars — pay most of the bills, they don't get to hang out at the race shop as much as they want or give advice to drivers on how to make their cars run faster. While some sponsors show up at the track or the race shop more often than others, their role on the race team is usually limited to paying the bills or marketing the race team.

Some sponsors don't like this limited role very much. Considering how much cash their companies are laying out, some sponsors feel they should have a say in how a race team functions, meaning which driver to hire, and which changes should be made to the race car. When a sponsor starts making those sorts of decisions, however, it's almost never good for the race team — unless that sponsor has been a successful NASCAR Winston Cup Series team owner, driver, or crew chief! Running a race team is usually best left up to the people involved in racing: those who know the business and are responsible for a team's performance on the track. Everyone else should just enjoy the results.

Multicar teams — the more the merrier

In the old days, guys used to haul one car down to the track, gather up whoever was around to change tires or fill up the tank during pit stops, and go racing. Even when the sport got more technical and more advanced in the '70s and '80s, one owner usually employed one driver and one race team.

That's not the case any more. Owners have begun to realize that they can share expenses and information with multicar teams. One of the most crucial components in being successful in racing is information: What a crew learns about the car and the tracks; what a team can find out about what makes the car go fast and what doesn't. With more money coming into the sport during the 1990s, owners quickly realized that one way to get more information was to use more than one team. When an owner has only one driver and team, he only has one source of information. But when he adds another team, he doubles his chances for getting more — and better — information.

NASCAR limits teams to seven test sessions a year, so an owner who has two teams can double his test sessions to 14 — and then exchange the information between the two teams. At the racetrack, two-car teams can do a bit of experimenting. One car can run one set of specifications — spring ratios and tire pressures and other things — while the other team tries something slightly different. Then as practice goes on, the crews determine which car handles better and which one runs faster. After practice is over, they exchange the data and determine which setup is best.

Because the demand for information has grown so much in recent years, it has become harder and harder for single-car teams to survive. One team owner with one car simply can't learn enough about new tracks and new technologies to really contend for a championship. So as stock-car racing moves into the 21st century, expect nearly all owners to field more than one car in each race.

When teaming up pays off

When I started racing for Jack Roush in 1988, I was his only driver and we were the only NASCAR Winston Cup Series team he had to worry about. But Jack was one of the first owners to realize the benefits of owning two teams. So in 1992, I had my first teammate — Wally Dallenbach Jr. And on paper, it paid off. I won twice that year, was second five more times and had 17 top-ten finishes all together. In 1996, Jack added a third team when he brought on Jeff Burton, with whom I've worked closely ever since. Jeff has been my best teammate because he knows so much about race cars, just like I do. I've often said that if you laid out all the parts of a NASCAR Winston Cup Series car in front of the drivers in the garage, Jeff would be able to build the best car from scratch because he knows so much. We also think a lot alike, so it's easy for us to communicate about what's going on with our cars and what we should tell our crew chiefs.

Our crews work well together, too, telling each other what we've learned and making suggestions for how we can each go faster. Now, Jack owns five NASCAR Winston Cup Series teams, and I've even got my hand in the ownership of one of them. I think getting the teams to work together helps all of us have more success.

On the track, the teammate relationship exists — but to a much lesser extent. If I'm leading a race and Jeff or another teammate isn't running so well and is a lap down, I may let him get back on the lead lap by allowing him to pass me. Or if one of my teammates has a faster car than I do and I know it, I may not try to fight him off — I'll probably just allow him to pass. But believe me, if I were battling for the win with one of my teammates, I'd race him just as hard as I would anyone else. Even though we're teammates, we still want to kick the pants off each another.

Team Managers Organize the Operation

When I started racing, I thought of a team manager as the kid in high school who got water and cleaned towels for the football team. But in racing, the *team manager* serves as the owner's representative in the shop: someone who oversees everything, including ordering equipment, hiring personnel, and organizing test sessions. There are just too many details for the owner and crew chief to deal with, so the team manager position was created as a mix of both those positions. Not every race team has a team manager. But anytime a team can have another experienced person around, it's bound to help. Just don't confuse him with the guy who's supposed to get water for the driver.

The team manager is usually someone with a lot of experience working on race cars, often someone who had been a long-time crew chief, but wanted to step back and take a more administrative role. The team manager isn't concerned with how the car is running at a specific time, but, instead, interviews candidates for specific jobs, and frequently makes the hiring decisions — with the owner's approval, of course.

After the team is assembled, the team manager's job is to get the people to work together, to make sure each individual person is doing his individual job. He works closely with the crew chief in overseeing everyone, and — if the owner owns more than one race team — he makes sure the teams are working together, sharing ideas and information that may benefit both on race day.

Our team manager is Buddy Parrott — a manager who has lots of experience in racing. Buddy was a crew chief for almost 20 years in the NASCAR Winston Cup Series before he came to Roush Racing. He works for my team and Jeff Burton's team, overseeing nearly everything and everyone that goes on in our joint race shop in Mooresville, North Carolina. With all of his experience, Buddy has helped improve the communication between our teams — which I think is responsible for our two teams racing so well over the past few years.

The Crew Chief — a Race Team's Head Honcho

No driver can "will" a lousy car into Victory Lane. It just can't happen. Racing isn't like other sports, where the equipment is the same across the board. Michael Jordan didn't suddenly have to shoot a deflated basketball while the other team got to use the regular kind. Mark McGwire doesn't have to swing a hollow bat while everyone else gets a solid one. But some days, drivers are presented with race cars that just aren't fast enough to win.

That's where the crew chief comes in. A *crew chief* oversees everyone in the shop to make sure they're building cars that will go fast on the racetrack. He works from his own experience, knowing how cars have reacted in the past on certain tracks under certain conditions. The crew chief tells each of the workers under him the specifications for doing their jobs, both at the shop and at the racetrack. He determines how the bodies are built, how the springs and shocks are adjusted, what level of air pressure to run the tires at — everything. It's a big job. Because of that, he usually works longer hours than anyone on the team, looking at numbers and considering possibilities. A great crew chief needs to know everything about a race car, and everything about his driver and the track he's going to run next.

Although drivers get a lot of attention, crew chiefs have started to become stars in their own right, too. The top crew chiefs have their own trading cards, and they're often asked to sign nearly as many autographs as the drivers — all for doing a job that used to be considered anonymous and not very glamorous. They deserve all of the attention they get, though, because they have as much to do with success as anyone involved. Here are some of the better-known crew chiefs:

MARK SAYS

A good crew chief is hard to find

When I raced in the American Speed Association (ASA) Series, a non-NASCAR stock-car series based in the Midwest, I worked with Jimmy Fennig and we hit it off right away. He was as intensely dedicated to racing as I was, so it was a perfect match. Jimmy and I won the 1986 ASA championship in just our second year together. In those two years, we recorded nine races and 13 poles, which is amazing considering we hadn't worked with each other for that long. We couldn't stay together forever, though. While he was the crew chief in 1986 when I ran my first five NASCAR Winston Cup Series races, I wasn't ready to drive full time in that series — and he was, so he had to move on without me.

Jimmy, who is from Milwaukee, Wisconsin, worked with NASCAR Winston Cup Series champion Bobby Allison and almost a dozen other drivers until we decided to work together again in 1996 — and that's the best move we've ever made, considering what great chemistry there is between us, even after all those years. In 1998, we won seven races, the most I've ever won in a season, and finished second in the championship. Without Jimmy, I couldn't have done that.

- ✔ **Ray Evernham:** Some people say Jeff Gordon wouldn't have won any of his three championships without Evernham setting up his cars and talking him through a race. While that may or may not be true, there's no doubt that Evernham and Gordon had one of the best combinations in racing when they were together until late 1999. They had that special chemistry that a team needs to win races. Evernham left the team to start his own NASCAR Winston Cup Series program in 2001, however, saying that he needed a bigger challenge.

- ✔ **Larry McReynolds:** Even though McReynolds isn't Dale Earnhardt's crew chief any more, he is one of the best crew chiefs — and one of the best teachers — in the garage. He's known for his expertise at helping develop drivers, and for his patience as drivers are gaining experience.

- ✔ **Todd Parrott:** Racing runs in the Parrott family. Todd won the 1999 NASCAR Winston Cup Series championship (with Dale Jarrett as the driver) with his younger brother, Brad, by his side as a crew member. Todd's father, Buddy, is the general manager of Roush Racing and one of the most respected people (a former crew chief) in the garage. Buddy began his career in 1970 and worked with some of the best drivers in racing, including Darrell Waltrip, Rusty Wallace, Richard Petty, Buddy Baker, and all of today's Roush Racing drivers.

- ✔ **Robin Pemberton:** Pemberton was my crew chief from 1988 to 1991, and is Rusty Wallace's crew chief nowadays. His brother, Ryan, also is a crew chief on the circuit, so technical skills run in the Pemberton family.

Robin left my team to be Kyle Petty's crew chief, but not because we had a falling out. He just needed to move on with his career and pursue other challenges, just as other people do when they change jobs to try something new.

If You Need Something Done, Go to the Car Chief

Racing has gotten so big over the past few years that owners have had to add another job to their teams — the car chief. The *car chief* is the person who works closely with the crew chief in figuring out setups for the car, but is the actual guy who makes sure it gets done. That allows the crew chief more time to work on a computer or look through notes to figure out better setups. When the crew chief does decide on a setup, he discusses it with the car chief — and then the car chief goes to the garage and implements the changes. The car chief gathers other crew members together, tells them what to do, and then rolls up his sleeves and helps get the job done.

Believe It or Not, the Driver Does More than Drive the Car

The driver often ends up getting all of the credit — and a lot of the blame — for how a race team performs. But when you look at the whole picture of a team, the driver is really just a small part. That's particularly true before the race starts.

During the week leading up to a race, the driver may or may not come to the race shop where the cars are being prepared. The crew chief has conversations with the driver about how the car should be set up, but for the most part, the team does all the work at the shop.

After everyone arrives at the track for a race, teams try to improve their cars during *practice sessions* (when drivers complete laps around the track, and then come into the garage to tell their crew chiefs what the car is doing). Drivers describe whether the car is reacting correctly to the track and where it needs to go faster — on the corners or in the straightaways. The crew chief then determines which adjustments to make.

After the race starts, the driver's role may seem rather obvious — get to the finish line before everyone else. But it's a little more complicated than that. I talk more about the driver's role, and what he has to do during an entire week, in Chapter 7.

GARAGE TALK

Meeting the team scorer

On race day, each team has its own *scorer* who counts how many laps a car has made around the track. He or she scores by hand (using a good, old-fashioned pen and a piece of paper), but also by computer. Each time the car completes a lap, the scorer presses a button on a computer to record that lap. But those scorers aren't the official scorers of the race.

Instead, NASCAR Timing & Scoring (presented by MCI) has a technical way of keeping track of cars on the track. Each car has a *transponder* (which is a small box) attached to its underside. That transponder transmits a signal to NASCAR computers every time it completes a lap. That's how NASCAR knows exactly who led the most laps, just in case people start to question it.

GARAGE TALK

Practice for a NASCAR Winston Cup Series race is some of the most important time of the whole weekend. While the cars may appear to be simply driving around in circles, in reality, everyone is involved — the driver, the crew chief, the team manager, and the crew. The team is finding out everything they need to know about how the car will perform under race conditions.

Practice in stock-car racing is a little different than in other sports, in which practice takes place behind closed doors. You don't see the Packers practicing in front of the Broncos before the Super Bowl. But in racing, everybody gets to see how fast everyone else is running. (How a driver runs in practice usually determines how fast he'll run during a race.)

And the Rest of the Team . . .

Besides the owner, the crew chief, the car chief, and the driver, other team members work the garage, too. Those team members, who are dressed in matching uniforms, do much more than just strut around looking important. Even though they aren't the primary decision makers on a team, they're important components to building a winning program. Keep in mind that not every team member goes to a race, only a set group goes. The others stay at the race shop and work on cars for future races. Here are some that go to the track:

GARAGE TALK

✔ Engine specialist: The *engine specialist,* or *engine tuner,* is in charge of taking care of the engines after they get to the racetrack. They're the guys you see running around with a tray of spark plugs and a magnifying glass. The engine tuner *reads* a spark plug by examining the insides of it and checking for signs of heat — color variations or spots. After reading spark plugs, the engine tuner determines what he needs do in order to get the optimum power output from the engine.

✔ **Tire specialist:** The tire specialist isn't tough to spot — he's the guy who spends the entire day hanging around the team's tires, changing the air pressure, checking the heat buildup, or measuring the wear of a tire after it has taken a few laps on the track. The tire specialist uses an instrument to figure out how the tire has worn in certain places — the inside, middle, and outside of the tread. He also measures the temperature of the tire in these locations to determine the heat buildup. The way a tire wears or how hot it is in certain places reveals how the car is driving on the track. If one tire is too hot in one spot or worn out in one specific place, crew members change the car's setup so that tires travel on the racing surface more evenly and smoothly — and many times, that means the car goes faster. The measurements a tire specialist makes are miniscule, so the job may seem insignificant, but it's critical.

✔ **Engineers:** NASCAR racing prides itself on not using any on-board computers to maximize the car's output the way that other racing series do. Still, that doesn't mean NASCAR is dead-set on staying behind the times. Over the past few years, stock-car racing has seen an influx of engineers who've used their master's degrees and doctorates to improve how a car runs. Many teams use engineers to calculate the exact setup for a car on a certain track, including precisely how each shock should be built, which springs should be used, and what tire pressures will be best. At first, many old-timers in the sport — and some of the young people, too — resented the engineers for bringing too much technology to NASCAR racing, which had traditionally been a grass-roots, low-budget sport. They felt that stock-car racing should stay as basic as possible, and remain accessible to people without fancy-schmancy college degrees. While engineers have yet to become an integral part of a race team, people are getting more and more used to them being around. And, as racing becomes more competitive, I guarantee that in a few years, everyone will have an engineer working for them in some way.

✔ **General mechanics:** While many team members have specialized titles with specialized jobs, some are all-around workers who can do just about anything. The people who are general mechanics can help the car chief set up the car, build shocks back in the trailer, or rework the body of a car after a driver crashes it into the wall. Every team has to have a few general mechanics to get by — and I feel kind of funny saying that because in the past, everyone was a general mechanic. But now, it seems everything is changing and becoming more specialized. Ask the shock builder how to change an engine and he may laugh at you and run away (hopefully not with your shocks in his hands). So every team has to have some people with versatility.

✔ **Pit crew:** A maximum of seven people are allowed to go over the pit wall and service a car during a pit stop. While some crew members — mechanics, crew chiefs, car chiefs, and tire specialists — still do double-duty by working at the shop and on the car and pitting the car as well, some teams fly specialized pit crew members to the track on race morning. To find out more about pit crews and pit stops, turn to Chapter 10.

✔ **Truck driver:** Being a team's truck driver may not seem like an important job, but it is. If the driver doesn't do his job right, the team may show up at the racetrack and not have any equipment. The driver must be on time and be careful driving the rig with millions of dollars of equipment in it, including the following items:

- The primary car

- The backup car

Every team brings more than one car to the racetrack, just in case the driver crashes one of them irreparably. The best car for that track is the *primary car*, which is the car a driver starts out driving during a race weekend. If something happens to that car, however, a team must unload the backup car from the truck. This is never a good sign for a team because the *backup car* isn't their first choice for their driver to use at that racetrack. It's usually another car out of the team's fleet of about a dozen at the race shop, a car used on tracks similar to the one they're at, but not exactly like it. If the driver crashes that car, too, he may be in trouble at another racetrack — the track where the backup car was supposed to be the primary car.

- Extra parts for the suspension, the engines, and every other piece of the car

- Shock dynamometers to figure out how a shock reacts on the track (see Chapter 4 for further explanation)

- Extra sheet metal, noses, and rear sections — called *rear clips* — for the car, in case of an accident

- Cabinets and drawers filled with snacks for the team to munch on during long days at the track

The *team hauler* is the place where the team hangs out when it's not in the garage area. It's a place to relax and grab some lunch — as well as a place to hold ultra-serious meetings on how to make the race car better. Most haulers have a lounge in front, equipped with a TV, stereo, desk, table, and a couple of comfortable couches. The team hauler is where a crew chief goes to crunch numbers for setups, where a driver goes to take naps, where a team owner goes to fire or hire a driver at the track. Basically, it's the only private place in the garage area where team members can sleep, hold important meetings, or work in peace.

The People Behind the Scenes

The work doesn't end when the race ends. Dozens of team members wait back at the shop for the car to return from the race so they can fix it up and prepare it for the next race it will run, whether that's the following week or a month or two. Dozens of team members also build engines, build car bodies, and test parts. While these team members work behind the scenes, they shouldn't be overlooked:

✔ **Fabricators:** *Fabricators* have a special talent. They take flat sheet metal and mold it into sleek, aerodynamic race cars. They size the metal, cut the metal, then make it fit the car's frame precisely — called *hanging a body* in racing terms. If the body isn't hung properly, the aerodynamics of the car won't be as good as they should be. And that'll slow the car down.

✔ **Engine builders and engine assemblers:** An engine doesn't just show up at a race shop ready to be put into a car. Some team members are in charge of building the engine nearly from scratch. Engine builders figure out how to make the engine as light, but durable, as possible. Then engine assemblers put the engines together. The engine tuner, discussed in the "And the rest of the team . . ." section earlier in this chapter, takes over from there.

✔ **Parts specialists:** At the race shop, teams have a specialist for everything, for example, a suspension specialist who's responsible for taking apart the suspension from a race car that just raced, and then testing to see which parts need to be replaced. Having tons of specialists running around isn't a bad thing, considering how much pressure there is to win races. Teams can't afford to lose races because some small, insignificant part falls apart after too much use. That's why everybody on the team is so meticulous when building and improving the car.

The team's schedule

A race weekend in the NASCAR Winston Cup Series isn't easy or relaxing for a race team because it consists of several long, grueling days. The weekends usually begin on Thursday for the drivers and teams, when they get on a plane to travel to the racetrack. In the late afternoon or early evening, teams and drivers arrive in the town the race will be held, go to dinner, and then get a good night's sleep for Friday's activities, which usually consist of qualifying and two practice sessions. The team needs plenty of sleep because the garage usually opens even before dawn and closes past dinnertime. Teams practice and qualify their cars on Friday, then practice and requalify on Saturday if their car was too slow to make the field for the race based on their first-round qualifying speed. (See Chapter 8 for more on qualifying.) Sunday is race day, of course.

Race weekends in the NASCAR Busch Series and the NASCAR Craftsman Truck Series aren't quite as exhausting because, most of the time, they aren't as long. Many events in those two series last just two days, with qualifying on the first day and the race on the second day.

Chapter 7

Who's in the Driver's Seat?

Despite what you may think, NASCAR drivers do much more than just hop in their cars, drive around in circles, win races and make money! Much more goes into racing than that, so much so that test sessions, races, sponsor luncheons, and commercial shoots take up nearly every second of a driver's day.

With so many non-racing activities filling a driver's schedule, racers today must be versatile — they must be great drivers, competent public speakers, astute businessmen, and half-decent actors (though not necessarily Oscar winners).

The Role of the Driver on the Racing Team

Even though drivers are super-versatile, it doesn't mean they play any less important role on a race team. They're still the ones who get into cars and take chances, risking their lives for three or so hours every Sunday — and nothing will ever change that. They're also the ones who have the best feel for their cars, so they can tell their crews how to make them race faster and handle better on the track. My crew is one of the best I've ever had, but they're not mind-readers, so it's up to me to tell them what I need them to do to make the car better.

A driver isn't just a figurehead who gets all the credit and all the headlines in the newspapers. He has to work to make his money, just like everybody else.

During practice, a driver doesn't shut up

It's not to a driver's advantage to be shy when practice begins. It's his job to jabber as much as he wants to his team, face-to-face or over the in-car radio. The more talk, the better, because the more input the team gets about the car, the better work they can perform.

Here's a scenario of what the driver may say to his team throughout a typical race weekend:

✔ The driver shows up for practice, dressed in his driving uniform and ready to go. He slides into his car and takes a few laps, but notices the car is *loose* as he enters the turns, meaning the rear of the car is starting to fishtail because the rear tires are losing traction. He contacts his crew via the two-way, in-car radio, tells them what's going on, and then heads into the garage.

✔ After the car rolls into the garage, the crew chief (or another important team member like the car chief or the engine specialist) runs to the driver's window to talk more about what the car was doing. They may, for example, decide to change the air pressure in one of the tires to see if that will do the trick. Of course they're trying to do everything in a rush because they only have a limited time for practice — and it never seems like enough when your car isn't running well and your team is scrambling to find out what's wrong and still have time to make changes.

✔ The driver takes to the track with his new setup, but quickly finds that the car isn't driving smoothly and that he's having trouble turning the car — which is the opposite problem than he had before. He radios his crew and darts back into the garage, hoping his team has enough time to remedy the problem.

✔ This time, the crew changes two shock absorbers and adjusts the springs in the car to further change how the car rides. These changes make the car drive differently.

The driver zooms onto the track and back into the garage throughout the practice session, so that the team can get the car running exactly as the driver needs in order to qualify for the race (see Chapter 8). Each time, the team tweaks something else on the car based on what the driver tells it.

Although driver input is critical in preparing the car for qualifying, the initial practice sometimes — although very rarely — goes somewhat differently than the scenario I just described. This is when the team unloads the car off the truck, and the car runs perfectly. The driver has no complaints about the car during the first practice, raving to his team the whole time about how great a job they did. When this happens, a driver usually says his car was great *right off the truck*.

When the race starts, there's no zoning out

When the green flag drops, the driver can't just start daydreaming about what he's going to eat for dinner or when he's going to do his laundry. Not only does he have to concentrate on the racetrack, he has to make some pretty important decisions. He has to figure out when to make a pass, when to be patient, when to be aggressive, and when to *save his tires* (meaning that he takes it easy through the turns and doesn't run the car too hard). So, even during a 600-mile race like the Coca-Cola 600 at Lowe's Motor Speedway, the longest NASCAR Winston Cup Series race of the year, drivers must stay focused at all times.

Staying focused for three or four hours, the length of a typical 400- or 500-mile race, isn't easy. That's why drivers must be mentally disciplined — generally, the more focused the driver is, the better he is. Focused drivers are constantly thinking about their cars and how to make them better. The driver is in constant contact with his crew chief throughout a race, exchanging information on the car and what the team needs to do during a pit stop to help improve the car's performance.

Some drivers talk more over the radio than others do during practice and races. I prefer to say one or two things to my crew chief from time to time instead of talking over the radio throughout the race. That gives me the opportunity to concentrate on taking the fastest route around the track. To do that, some drivers try to *hit certain points* on the track — a route they've mapped out in their heads that they think will get them around the track in the fastest time. If it works, they try to repeat the previous lap by hitting the points again — either by picking out a spot on the wall in one corner or choosing a line on the inside of the track in another corner — anything that helps them repeat the same lap every time. By hitting these points, drivers try to run the fastest lap possible on the track. It's not that drivers veer all over the place if they don't hit their points, but they may not be running the fastest lap they could if they took different routes around the racetrack.

No time to pal around

It's no secret that a lot of people consider me the most focused driver around. And I take that as a compliment, although sometimes people can take my ultra-focused attitude the wrong way, especially at the track. When I head for my car just before practice or walk to pit road to start the race, it's not easy for me to smile the whole way or stop and sign autographs every two seconds, because I'm already thinking about the race and what I have to accomplish. So, it's not time for me to pal around with other drivers or joke with fans. Just like any other athlete, it's my time to get in a zone.

Need space and distractions? Don't try racing!

If you're the claustrophobic type, stock-car racing isn't for you. Drivers have to squeeze into their tight-fitting seats and stay strapped in for several hours during a race. You can't stretch, and you don't get much air flow. You contemplate the road ahead, how your car is running, and ways to win a race — and that's pretty much it.

If you have a short attention span, driving a race car isn't for you, either. You won't find a radio or a CD player in a race car. You can't hear much besides the drone of the engine and you don't really see much — just the same scenery over and over again. Drivers are used to that, though. After years of training, they can focus on the road for hours without even flinching.

No time for timeouts

NASCAR racing, unlike baseball, football, or basketball, doesn't incorporate timeouts into the competition. That's one of the things that makes stock-car racing so challenging. Drivers can't get out of their cars or take a bathroom break while driving 200 miles an hour (drivers do get a bottle of water at each pit stop, however). After they're in their cars, they're in there for the long run. That's why you may see drivers running to portable toilets before the race. After that, they just have to hold it until the race is over — three or four hours later. Often times, though, drivers sweat so much during a race, they don't need to go to the bathroom because they're so dehydrated.

Why Drivers Are Athletes

Some people think that drivers aren't athletes because a lot of them aren't in top physical shape with tons of muscles and lungs the size of North Dakota. And other people think drivers aren't athletes because stock-car racing doesn't involve a ball, a bat, a hoop or some other traditional piece of sports equipment. But if those people were to get into a race car, on a typical summer day, weaving through traffic going 200 miles an hour, I'm sure they'd change their minds.

While many drivers aren't perfect, or even nearly perfect, physical specimens, they do have many physical qualities that lend to their success. How else can they stay in a sauna-hot car for more than three hours at a time, concentrating on the road and the car without getting distracted? Not just anybody can do that, so there has to be some athleticism involved.

They have to react quickly

Imagine flying down the highway, going about 100 miles an hour when the car just ahead of you spins out and starts rocketing right toward you. You'd probably end up with at least a couple injuries and one majorly damaged car. But most NASCAR drivers have the ability to avoid getting into that wreck. It's called *fast reaction time*.

Drivers have incredibly quick reaction time. It's the same ability pro baseball players have to be able to smack balls out of the park, even when those balls come hurling at them at more than 95 miles an hour. Not just anybody can get into a race car and drive inches away from the guy ahead of him. Not just anybody can avoid an accident that happens in a split-second, just feet ahead of them. But drivers can, that's why they're able to avoid wrecks every weekend and sometimes make it home without a dent on their race cars.

No clumsiness allowed

Driving a race car isn't anything like driving your dad's El Camino to the foodmart on the corner. Drivers need much more coordination to operate their manual transmission, high-performance race cars. They must shift gears quickly, turn the wheel smoothly, step on the brake, and jam on the accelerator — all while driving at breakneck speeds. Sometimes, drivers even control the brake and clutch pedals with their left foot and depress the gas pedal with their right foot, which is different than what you learned in your high school driver's education class. Your teacher told you to use your right foot to control the gas *and* the brake. Of course in racing, people break those rules all the time. In most cases, using the two-foot technique — which means you're a *left-footed braker* — is quicker than using the same foot on both the gas and brake pedals. In all cases, driving a race car is more difficult and takes a lot more coordination than you may think. Professional race car drivers can't be a klutzes — otherwise, they may find themselves careening headfirst into the car in front of them when they accidentally press the gas instead of the brake.

Endurance is key

Even if you're the best driver in the world, if you don't have endurance, you won't make it as a stock-car driver. Drivers may not look as in shape as long distance running stars or cyclists in the Tour de France, but drivers' bodies can endure a lot — heat, mental strain, pressure to avoid an accident, and then the accidents themselves. Drivers are also able to handle the intense pressure of competition, racing 42 other drivers who are among the best in the world. Without endurance, we'd never make it through a race. Then again, we wouldn't be drivers in the first place.

Getting into peak condition

Some drivers would rather eat a live rattlesnake than work out on a consistent basis, but I think staying in shape is critical to being a successful race car driver. And, as the sport becomes more and more competitive, drivers will have to be in better physical condition to get an edge over everybody else — especially the newcomers who may have youth on their side.

As a racer, being in good physical shape helps in several ways:

✔ When drivers get into accidents, they won't injure themselves as much if they're in shape — muscles protect their bones and internal organs. If a driver is flabby, he has nothing protecting his insides. A driver who's in good shape also rebounds from an injury faster than other drivers.

✔ If a driver is cardiovascularly fit or in shape aerobically, he has an easier time sitting in a steaming-hot car for an afternoon while sweating off pound after pound. When in a hot car, a driver's pulse naturally rises, so if a driver's heart isn't in shape, it'll be tougher for him to make it through a race than it is for someone whose heart is used to being taxed.

✔ With a strong upper body, it's easier for a driver to wrestle the car around a racetrack if it's not handling well. A driver can't just leisurely put one hand on the wheel and expect to steer effectively. If his upper body is weak, he'll have a hard time steering.

MARK SAYS

Driving with injuries

NASCAR doesn't have an injured reserve list like other major sports do. Instead, drivers tend to get right back into their cars after getting into accidents, even major accidents. They can't afford to take time off because a driver doesn't get any points toward the championship if he doesn't start a race. That's why you see drivers with broken arms and broken legs getting into their race car to at least start a race and gain some points (see Chapter 8 for more on the points system).

I got into a bad wreck the day before the Pepsi 400 at Daytona International Speedway in 1999 — I was really hurting after hitting the wall in practice and had plenty of injuries to show for it, including a broken left wrist, a broken rib, and a broken right knee cap. Even so, I had two guys from my team pick me up and slide me into the car so I could race (see the color photo section, near the center of this book). I finished 17th.

MARK SAYS

Staying in great shape is one of my obsessions, including when I'm away from home at the racetrack. From Monday through Friday, even the Monday after a 500-mile race, I wake up at 5:45 in the morning and get to the gym by 6:00. When I'm at home, I don't have far to go because I have a gym set up in my airplane hangar, which is connected to my house. When I'm at a race, I work out in a gym set up under a tent in the motorhome lot. Wherever I end up working out, my main objective is to lift weights and keep my muscles strong for racing, something I've been doing since the late 1980s.

Drivers Are Hot Stuff

Even on cool days, it gets extremely hot for drivers inside a stock car. That's not only because the engine runs incredibly hot — even though that plays a big part in it. It's because there's no air conditioning. And, on days when the external temperature is in the 90s — like it is plenty of times at places like Daytona Beach, Florida; Talladega, Alabama; or Darlington, South Carolina — the temperature inside the car can soar above 120 degrees.

Without air conditioning, drivers get pretty uncomfortable inside their race cars during the three or four hours that typical races last. While drivers need to wear a suit to protect them from possible fires, a helmet in case of an accident, and gloves to protect them from heat and blisters while grabbing the steering wheel and throwing the stick shift into gear, all of that equipment makes the conditions even hotter. It's not uncommon for a driver to lose anywhere from three to ten pounds after sweating during a single race.

The fact that the car's main exhaust system travels through a pipe directly under the driver's seat (see Figure 7-1) only adds to the heat. Occasionally, the seat gets so unbelievably hot that I feel it on my back and legs for days afterward.

Figure 7-1:
Soon after the race starts, the inside of a race car gets unbearably hot, consistently reaching temperatures above 120 degrees.

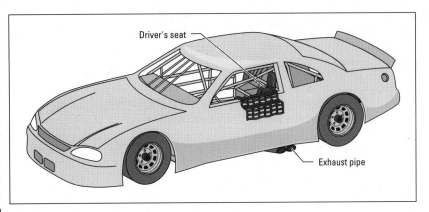

Driver's seat

Exhaust pipe

The floor of the car can get even hotter. That's why drivers wear special driving shoes with insulation in them, with silvery, aluminum-foil looking stuff around the heels and on the soles. They'd make Michael Jackson proud. But sometimes, drivers need additional help to protect their feet, so they strap extra pieces of insulation — called *heat shields* — onto their heels when the floor is extra hot. Some of the older drivers have figured out alternatives to protecting their feet, claiming the bottom part of a Styrofoam cup works better than anything else does to keep their feet cool. And Dave Marcis, one of the oldest of the old-timers, still claims his trusty old wing-tipped shoes do the job.

While drivers can't turn on the air conditioner or roll down the window for a shot of cold air or breeze, they're not left to suffer without fresh air flow: Most teams have rigged up a cooling system inside the car that injects air into the driver's helmet and up through holes in the seat (see Figure 7-2). It's a system of tubing that flows from a box with a fan (and sometimes dry ice) in it — without it, drivers would have trouble staying conscious on hot days.

Figure 7-2:
Without a cooling system, drivers may not be able to survive a three- or four-hour race in temperatures above 100 degrees.

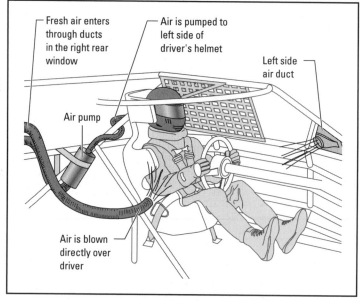

Fresh air enters through ducts in the right rear window

Air is pumped to left side of driver's helmet

Left side air duct

Air pump

Air is blown directly over driver

Ricky Rudd, a veteran racer who began his NASCAR Winston Cup Series career in 1974, found out the hard way how important an in-car ventilation system is on a hot day. His "air conditioner" malfunctioned during the fall race at Martinsville Speedway in 1998. It was more than 90 degrees outside that day, and approached 150 degrees in the car, when Rudd figured out that no cool air was blowing into his helmet or up through his seat. Even so, he held on to win the race and had to be helped out of his car in Victory Lane. He fell to the ground, with blisters and burns on his back and his backside, and paramedics gave him oxygen so that he wouldn't pass out. Even though he felt awful and could barely talk, Rudd still gave post-race interviews while lying on his back. Later, he was given intravenous fluids because he was so dehydrated.

Racing All Over the Nation

When drivers aren't racing, they're probably not lounging at home watching a TV shopping network or pulling weeds in the yard. Their schedules are so packed, they barely have enough time to sneeze after they get home from a race before they have to take off for another event. In 1999, the NASCAR Winston Cup Series had 34 races.

On top of that, two exhibition races every year don't count toward the NASCAR Winston Cup Series points championship: the Bud Shootout at Daytona International Speedway in February — a race that includes the previous season's pole winners and one wildcard driver — and The Winston held in May at Lowe's Motor Speedway in Concord, North Carolina, a race featuring past winners on the circuit and also one wildcard entry (see Chapter 13).

So, 36 weekends of the year are accounted for, which means that drivers still have plenty of time for themselves during the other 16 weekends, right? Wrong. With test sessions, sponsor commitments, commercial shoots, and series banquets, those additional weekends are spoken for.

The days early in a week, before the driver goes to a race, are filled with things to do, too. At most, he has one day at home to handle his personal business, then he's off to a test or to an autograph session someplace like Kalamazoo, Mich., or other places far from home.

Here's a snapshot of a typical week for a driver:

✔ **Monday:** If he's lucky, a driver gets to sleep in on Monday after what's usually a long day at the races on Sunday. Most of the time, it's the only day a driver can spend with his family at home or deal with personal business. More often than not, though, he has to go to a sponsor appearance and sign autographs — many times hundreds and even thousands of miles away.

✔ **Tuesday:** Teams conduct two-day testing sessions at racetracks and those sessions are often on Tuesdays. The tests take place at a track where the teams will race in a few weeks, not where they'll race that upcoming weekend. For example, drivers and teams test at Daytona

International Speedway for several days in January, but the Daytona 500 isn't until mid-February. It's just like preparing for an exam. Teams experiment with their cars, trying different setups in order to find just the right one for the upcoming qualifying session and race. They talk about the fastest way to get around the track, and they discuss what they'll do when they return for the real thing.

During a test, the driver has to be at the track early in the morning, prepared to slip into the driver's seat and start the session. Even though he's not racing against 42 other drivers during the test session, testing a race car still isn't easy. A session usually lasts from dawn until dark, and teams use every minute of that time because they get only seven testing sessions per year. And that makes every second of every session precious. (Rookie drivers get 12 tests, though, because they need to get used to driving on NASCAR Winston Cup Series tracks.)

✔ **Wednesday:** Frequently, Wednesday is the second day of a two-day test session. But if a driver isn't testing that day, he's at an appearance for one of his sponsors. Ideally, those appearances are held near a racetrack (at a car dealership or an auto parts store) where the series is racing that weekend.

The NASCAR Winston Cup Series has a special kind of appearance called a *Winner's Circle appearance*. NASCAR has a Winner's Circle program, which consists of drivers who've won races the season before. Those drivers get compensated for being in the program, but in turn they must make several appearances each year — each appearance hosted by a racetrack on the series. A representative from the racetrack sets up all sorts of media appearances for the driver for one day: Drivers go to radio stations, TV stations, and newspapers, giving interviews and hyping the upcoming race.

✔ **Thursday:** Thursday is a travel day for drivers because most racetracks open for practice on Friday. Drivers fly to the town where a race is held, and then head for the racetrack where their motorhomes are already prepared for their arrival. A motorhome driver, who works for the race car driver, drives the vehicle from track to track. After he gets to a certain track for a race weekend, that person stocks the motorhome with food, toiletries, and other essentials, and then checks into a hotel when the driver and the driver's family arrive.

Occasionally, drivers are already at the tracks on Thursday for pre-race events.

✔ **Friday:** On Friday, NASCAR Winston Cup Series drivers qualify their cars for the Sunday race (see Chapter 8). They also participate in several practice sessions during the day. After the garage closes, drivers often meet with fans and sponsors at an appearance, making the drivers' days quite long.

✔ **Saturday:** Drivers don't get Saturday off. They've got to go to the track and practice, making final changes on the car's engine or its setup for race day. Saturday is also the day for second-round qualifying, when the drivers who weren't among the 25 fastest during the first day of qualifying try again to make the field (see Chapter 8).

Happy Hour is the final hour of practice for the race, held the afternoon before race day. During this time, drivers and teams make last-minute — and sometimes harried — changes on their cars. Because of the urgency, Happy Hour is a crazed, rushed 60 minutes of cars whizzing in and out of the garage after running laps on the track. Not all teams leave the track happy after Happy Hour, however — especially the ones whose cars ran slowly or whose drivers got into a late-practice accident.

✔ **Sunday:** Most races are held on Sunday afternoons (although a few are on Saturdays and a few are at night). On race days, drivers have much more than just a race to drive in:

• **Meet the sponsors:** On race days, drivers wake up, get dressed in nice pants and a shirt with their sponsor's logo on it, and then head for the garage. Most of the time, they have a pre-scheduled meeting — called *hospitality* — with a group of employees of one of their sponsors. Drivers give a small talk and answer questions. It's a little strange for the driver to give a pep talk to *fans* only a few hours before the race, but that's all a part of racing and having a sponsor paying the bills. You don't see football players talking to people in the suites a couple of hours before game time, but that's the difference between racing and football.

Sometimes, thousands of employees from a sponsor's company show up at hospitality, where the sponsor sets up a tent and serves breakfast or lunch. So as a driver, I have to be ready to address all those people, even though I may be nervous about the race or thinking about my race car. As soon as a driver gets done with his talk, he signs autographs for a while before heading back to the garage for the drivers' meeting.

• **Drivers' meeting:** The most important thing on Sunday mornings for a driver is to make it to the drivers' meeting, held two hours before each race. (I discuss the meeting in detail in Chapter 5.) If a driver or his crew chief misses the meeting, the driver must start the race in last position, no matter where he qualified.

• **Church service:** Right after the drivers' meeting, many drivers, teams, and their families stay for a brief church service that's held each race morning.

• **Drivers' introductions:** About a half hour before the race, drivers assemble for drivers' introductions at a stage near the start/finish line. At this time, awards may be given out for teams who did well the week before or for the team that won the pole for that day's race. Each driver's name is then announced as he walks across the stage, waving to fans. Drivers sometimes ride in the back of a car or truck, taking a lap around the track to wave at all the fans.

- **The race:** This is the main event — it's what drivers do all the other stuff for.

- **Post-race:** When a driver wins, he spends nearly an hour in Victory Lane celebrating and taking pictures. Then he has to talk to the print media for another hour in the press box, and give TV interviews later. Drivers who come in second or third also give interviews with the press, explaining how their cars performed and what they saw during the race. Even drivers who didn't finish well usually stick around to make a few quick comments to the media. If a driver crashed, he can expect to be bombarded with reporters' questions.

  Throughout a race weekend, drivers must deal with reporters. Some are TV reporters wielding cameras and microphones. Some are newspaper reporters with pens, pads and tape recorders in hand. Some are radio reporters with headsets and microphones. Whoever they are, the driver has to talk to them at some point during the weekend — or at several points: Before practice, after practice, during practice, before qualifying, after qualifying, just after crashing during qualifying, after winning the pole, after losing the race, or after winning the race.

- **Getting home:** Because the racing season is long and the schedule is packed, almost every team and every driver has their own plane. So, right after the race, the driver (if he's not in Victory Lane) heads for a local airport and is in the air within the hour. The biggest problem is the traffic on the runway because nearly everyone in racing has a plane, and everyone is on their way home at the same time.

(Motor)home away from home

Drivers and their families spend at least three days and nights at the races. Three nights multiplied by 34 (the number of official NASCAR Winston Cup Series races per season) is 102 nights away from home! In the past dozen years or so, drivers, owners and some crew chiefs got tired of spending all those nights in a hotel room, so they began bringing motorhomes to the races.

The kind of motorhomes you find in the driver and owner motorhome area (called the *motorhome lot*) at the races isn't at all like a pop-up camper. Many times, they're quite luxurious with more amenities than the typical home. Most of them have TVs (connected to satellite dishes), a separate bedroom, a living room with leather couches, good-sized showers, glass cabinets, full-sized refrigerators, kitchen tables, and stereo systems. This way, drivers and their families are quite comfortable even though they're away from home so much.

Drivers don't get those kind of motorhomes to show off. They just want to make things as cozy as possible. The motorhomes also make it possible for the drivers to bring their wives and children to the races — and have them at the racetrack at all times. In the past, drivers were stuck at the track between practice and qualifying with nowhere to go or hang out, while their families were biding time in the hotel room or staying at home because they didn't think going to races was worth the trouble. So now, drivers have a private place to go to be with their families at any point of the day — a place where they don't have to deal with traffic, crowds, or rowdy fans. A place they can call home.

The motorhome lot is a small, mobile village with all the same people traveling from race to race. It's also kept safe by security guards who protect the entrance ways and monitor the grounds.

Motor Racing Outreach

While drivers couldn't be happier they have a place to spend time with their families, their days can get boring at times. Because of the popularity of the sport, drivers can't really take their wives out to a quiet dinner in town the night before a race — or any time during race weekend. While some restaurants cater to drivers and their crews, drivers usually can't go casually strolling through town looking for new restaurants, gyms to work out in, or places to go to church because they'd be swarmed by fans.

NASCAR Winston Cup Series racing has become a bona-fide traveling community, which is why the series has an organization, Motor Racing Outreach (MRO), that has a day care center for drivers' children, provides religious services, and organizes events for drivers and their families at the track. I don't know what drivers would do without it.

The following are the services MRO provides:

- ✔ Church services are held every race morning, just after the drivers' meeting. Drivers don't have time to go to a regular church on race day, especially with all the traffic headed toward the track, so the MRO inter-denominational Christian church services give them a chance to keep their faith alive. MRO also organizes prayer groups throughout the weekend, held in the motorhome lot.

- ✔ When the drivers are in the garage area, their wives don't necessarily have to stay put in the motorhome area and watch the kids. MRO has a motorhome, bought with donated funds from drivers and corporations, where children read and learn — all under the care of MRO volunteers.

✔ For those racing team members and families who want to stay in shape, there is a little workout center in the motorhome lot that travels to every race. It's set up next to the MRO motorhome and has a few tread-mills, bikes, and free weights.

Part III

What Happens On (And Off) the Track

The 5th Wave   By Rich Tennant

You seemed slow on the straightaway and hesitant in the turns. I think you should... hey-how long has your wife been in the back seat?

In this part . . .

NASCAR races aren't the simplest events to follow. They're not like football games where two teams play for 60 minutes and are done with it. NASCAR events last several days, beginning with qualifying for the race (usually on Friday) and ending with a long, drawn-out ceremony in Victory Lane (usually on Sunday).

This part decodes every move that teams and drivers make on the track and at in the garage during a race weekend, including race strategies and pit stops. I also explain why a driver can smack his car into a concrete wall, flip over several times, or barrel into another car at the track without getting even a scratch.

If you want to know what's going on during every moment of race weekend — or even just on race day — you'll have fun reading this part. Like a good mystery novel, you won't be able to put it down until you read every chapter and have all your questions answered.

Chapter 8

First, They Gotta Qualify

*B*efore drivers hear the famous "Gentlemen, start your engines!" command, they must first qualify for the race. That means they're not going anywhere unless they prove they're worthy to start the race — and to do that, they have to prove that their cars are fast enough. Regardless of how fast a car is, qualifying is nerve-wracking business.

Qualifying for a NASCAR race requires drivers to go as fast as they can around a speedway without crashing or losing control of their cars. They're trying to find the quickest way around the track, and it's not always easy. While each driver has a specific route — or line — mapped out in his head, it's like riding a runaway roller coaster that may derail at any second. Qualifying is different than racing because drivers "take it to the edge" as they like to say, circling a track as fast as they can go for just one or two laps. In a race, on the other hand, drivers must be patient and careful over 400 or 500 miles in order to make it to the finish line and win. If a driver is patient and careful during qualifying, he will most likely be watching the race from his living room sofa instead of competing in it.

Knowing the Track

NASCAR races are held mostly on oval-shaped tracks with four turns. People started labeling the turns so that drivers and crew chiefs could talk about the race track — and have some landmarks to help them figure out where the car is doing what. Now they can say, "The car scraped the wall in turn 2" and everyone can immediately picture what happened.

An *oval track* is two long strips of racetrack connected by sweeping turns at both ends. Drivers compete on the track by circling it counter-clockwise — see Figure 8-1. The strip of racetrack where the start/finish line is located is called the *frontstretch, front straight*, or *front straightaway*. It's where you see cars racing each other to the finish in the last seconds of a race. The strip of racetrack on the opposite side of the track is called the *backstretch, back straight,* or *back straightaway.* While NASCAR racing competes at all sorts of tracks — short tracks, intermediate tracks, superspeedways, and road courses (see Chapter 13) — most of them are ovals (except for the road courses and a handful of strangely configured tracks). The turns connect the two straightaways in the following way:

- ✔ Turn 1 is located at the end of the front straightaway and is the first turn the racers will make during a race. Drivers go from the frontstretch into turn 1.

- ✔ Turn 2 is at the beginning of the backstretch.

- ✔ Turn 3 is at the end of the backstretch.

- ✔ Turn 4 is at the beginning of the frontstretch.

NASCAR has a bunch of different tracks besides ovals. (For more information on NASCAR Winston Cup Series' different tracks, turn to Chapter 13.)

- ✔ Tri-ovals like Daytona International Speedway, which are modified ovals with a tiny extra turn.

- ✔ Quad ovals like Atlanta Motor Speedway, which are modified ovals with two extra, slight turns.

- ✔ A triangle, which is Pocono Raceway and completely out there in its own category.

- ✔ Road courses, which can be any shape and have a number of sharp, difficult turns.

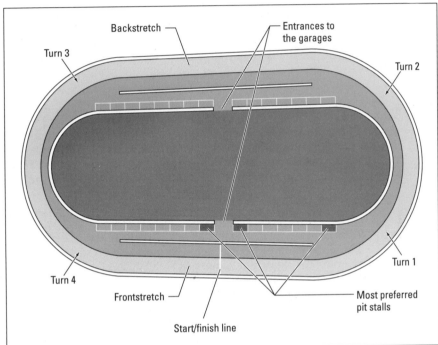

Backstretch

Entrances to
the garages

Turn 3

Turn 2

Turn 1

Turn 4

Frontstretch

Most preferred
pit stalls

Start/finish line

Figure 8-1:
The
standard
oval track.

How Many Drivers Make It?

No matter what the track shape is, drivers still have to *qualify* on it, which means they must complete one or two full-speed laps around it. This weeds out slower or unprepared teams that won't be able to get up to speed on race day.

In NASCAR Winston Cup Series racing, qualifying is normally held on the Friday before Sunday's race. Each week, 43 cars start every event, while in the NASCAR Busch Series and the NASCAR Craftsman Truck Series, the number of cars depends on the size of the track and how many cars it can accommodate safely. The smaller the track, the fewer the starting spots.

Even though 43 starters in NASCAR Winston Cup Series may seem like a lot, every week drivers leave the track wishing there were even more starting spots available for the race. Those drivers were unable to qualify, which guarantees them an entry in the race, because their cars didn't go fast enough during a timed lap. That's especially depressing for drivers and teams who travel across the nation for a race, and then don't even compete in it. It's like driving to California from the east coast for a concert, only to find that the concert is sold out.

Qualifying Order

Drivers just don't drive randomly onto the track to complete their qualifying laps. The whole process is precisely orchestrated — and it has to be. The qualifying times of all the drivers attempting to qualify for the race are frequently separated by less than one second. So if even one element is amiss, a driver's qualifying time could easily put him at the back of the pack.

To start the process, usually held on Fridays, representatives from each NASCAR Winston Cup Series team gather to determine the qualifying order. According to car owners' points (which I discuss in the "Provisional Entries" section later in this chapter), each representative picks a ball with a number on it out of a small rotating sphere — just like the ones used in your local bingo parlor. But instead of yelling, "BINGO!", the representative runs to his driver and crew to announce when the driver will go out to qualify. Why does everyone care so much when their driver qualifies? It's not because they want to get done early so they can catch the evening news.

Sometimes, qualifying order can be crucial because weather plays a key role in how fast the cars run on the track. In hot weather, the track is slippery, so the car doesn't stick very well, particularly going through turns. That means the driver must slow down to keep from losing control. In normal weather, the track is cooler and the tires adhere to the track better, so the drivers can go fast through the turns without worrying about crashing. (In cool weather, though, the tires may be cold, which results in little traction and often in a crash. That's why you see drivers swerving back and forth on the racetrack before a race. They're warming up their tires.)

The days before qualifying

In the old days, no one limited the number of cars that started a race. For example, 75 cars started the first Southern 500 back in 1950. They crammed onto the one-mile track, running perilously close to one another. Today, though, NASCAR is much more safety-oriented and it limits the number of cars that compete in a race.

In hot weather, the driver who picks the No. 1 qualifying spot and qualifies at the usual mid-afternoon start, may run at the hottest — and slowest — time of the day, while the driver who picks the last qualifying spot may be in luck, especially if the sun goes down by the time he races, and the track is faster. At times, though, choosing the first qualifying position isn't bad. For example, if a cloud just happens to float over the track at the right time, cooling the track's surface, a driver may get a fast lap. But if that cloud floats quickly away, the next driver may be out of luck. That's how delicate a situation it is — cloud cover can make the difference between winning the pole or starting 20th.

Starting up front is groovy

A lot of work goes into making a car qualify well because starting up front could be the difference between winning and losing the actual race. Some tracks are *one-groove racetracks*, which means there's only one comfortable way to get around a track fast without putting a driver at risk of crashing. A *groove* is a part of the track where cars' tires get the best grip, and if the car drifts out of that groove, it will become unstable and difficult to control. Some tracks have more than one groove — a *high groove* and a *low groove*, meaning cars can run side-by-side or two-wide around the track. Some tracks have *no grooves* because cars race easily on any part of the track. But on one-groove racetracks such as New Hampshire International Speedway, it is very difficult to pass another car, because when a driver pulls out of the groove to attempt a pass, his car doesn't handle well. And a car that doesn't handle well doesn't go very fast.

Qualifying well is important at one-groove racetracks because passing is so difficult. So, if a driver starts fifth, he has a chance of making it to the front. If he start 25th, though, he has less chance of advancing unless the cars ahead of him have problems.

Smaller isn't always better

Qualifying well is also important when racing on a smaller track, such as the .526-mile Martinsville Speedway. Most short tracks physically just don't have enough room for cars to race two-wide, so passing is difficult. Starting up front makes the day much less stressful. (For more on short tracks, see Chapter 13.)

Winning the pole

Drivers and crews scramble during the practice before qualifying in order to get the car just right for the run, a run they hope will be fast enough for them to win the pole. The *pole winner* (or *pole sitter*) is the driver who runs the fastest lap during qualifying. That driver is one of two drivers who starts the race on the front row. The pole winner starts on the inside of the front row, or the part closer to the infield, while the second-fastest qualifier starts on the *outside pole,* which is on the outside of the front row — the part of the track closer to the grandstands. NASCAR races start with only two cars in each row. So in NASCAR Winston Cup Series races, which have 43 cars, there are 21 rows of two cars, and one row, way at the back, with just a single car.

Winning the pole is a big deal because the driver who starts in that position is closest to winning — even before the race starts. For at a few moments, that driver has the best view of the racetrack. He also wins at least $5,000 for winning the pole, even if he gets passed right after the green flag drops.

Getting Ready for the Run

Winning the pole isn't as important as winning the race, but in NASCAR racing, every aspect of racing is competitive. So the drivers, crews, and team owners put a lot of effort into running the fastest lap on qualifying day. Not only does the driver get the extra money, but he also gets the prestige of being the best and going the fastest — which gives him confidence on race day.

Preparing the car for a qualifying run is hard work. First, the driver takes the car on the track during practice to see how fast it is and how it handles. After every practice session, NASCAR puts out a time sheet that ranks the cars from fastest to slowest. Then, the scrambling starts. If a driver's car isn't at the top or near the top of the list, he has to change something so his car can go faster. Some of the things drivers and crews change or fine-tune during practice include the following:

✔ **Balance:** The most important thing to perfect during practice for qualifying is the car's balance. A driver doesn't want one end of the car sticking to the track more than the other end, because an unbalanced car is a slow car and is hard to handle. When a car *sticks to the track* it means it has good traction, and a driver wants that traction to be as even as possible in the car's four tires. During practice, the driver gets a feel for how the car is driving and whether — and to where — the weight must be moved to make the car ride better. The weights that the teams redistribute are chunks of lead kept in the tubing of the car frame.

✔ **The engine:** In order to have a fast qualifying lap, a car's engine must run perfectly. So while taking practice laps, a driver looks at his *tachometer* (the gauge that measures how many revolutions an engine is making per minute), in order to see how hard the engine is working. If the engine is working too hard or not hard enough, a team changes the car's gears to maximize the engine's output. Teams also must consider the weather when deciding what gears to put in their cars. Usually, when it's really hot, a lower gear ratio is required, and vice versa.

Drivers listen to the engine to find out how it's working. They know exactly how it should sound when it's working right. If it sounds funny — too high-pitched or not smooth — they take the car right into the garage and have the crew look at it.

✔ **The shock and spring combination:** In qualifying, particularly at superspeedways where aerodynamics play such a crucial role, it's imperative to get the car as close to the ground as possible in order to cut through the air as fast as possible. Whenever air gets beneath a car, it slows it down. So teams try to figure out the right shock absorber and spring combination to get the car as close to the ground as possible without *bottoming out* (getting too close to the ground). (For more on aerodynamics, turn to Chapter 13. To find out about different components of the suspension, flip to Chapter 4.)

Practicing for the real thing

When a team wants to see exactly how they'll do in qualifying, they prepare the car for an all-out run. Part of that preparation is *taping the car off.* That means the team places heavy-duty tape over the car's grille. Teams place tape over the grille, which is the screen at the front of the car leading to the radiator, in order to keep air from going through the grille and slowing the car down. A car runs its fastest when air is flowing over it, instead of through it or under it. That way, the car is sleeker and faster as it moves through the air. (For more on aerodynamics, see Chapter 13.)

Teams can't tape off their car during the race, though. It will overheat because no air is flowing into the radiator to cool the engine. Several laps won't hurt, but a taped-off car wouldn't last very long in a 500-mile race. The engine would just go kaput after a certain point, when it became too hot.

Qualifying engines

Cars hit their top speeds during qualifying thanks to the engines they use, which aren't the same ones used in the race. They are engines specially built for qualifying and going as fast as possible — not for surviving the grueling, punishing conditions of a 500-mile race. Qualifying engines have lighter — and inherently weaker — parts so the savings in weight can be redistributed lower in the car. These engines aren't made to endure much more than several laps at top speed before they fail. After qualifying is over, the team hoists the qualifying engine out of the car and replaces it with a race engine, one that will last (hopefully) 500 miles.

You never hear teams discussing their laps using miles per hour. There's no, "What a great lap. We went 197.56 miles per hour!" In racing lingo, teams always refer to their lap times by how long it took their car to complete a lap. They may say, for example, "We ran a 79," which refers to the hundredths of a second of their timed lap, which may have been a 23.79-second lap. Racing is measured in split seconds, which is why teams are so precise when talking about laps.

First-round qualifying

After the crew puts the qualifying engine in the car, tapes off the grille, and performs last-minute changes, the driver is ready to hit the track. Even then, the process is still stressful — because only the 25 fastest drivers qualify for the race during the first of two rounds of qualifying. It's a reward for being fast the first day, while the rest of the drivers have to wait a day to try to qualify for the race in the second round.

Why do 25 drivers make the race on the first day of qualifying? That's like asking why there are nine innings in baseball and why a pro basketball player fouls out after six fouls. About four years ago, only 20 drivers made the race during the first round of qualifying, but NASCAR increased that number to 25 because so many more teams were trying to make races.

During the first round of qualifying, even veteran drivers get nervous and wound up inside. Drivers get jittery because they know if they mess up even a little, it could ruin the whole weekend for the team and the fans. So, qualifying well on the first day is a big deal. Drivers want to get it over with, and after they do, they can be much more relaxed until race day.

Qualifying butterflies

As the years have gone by, I've gotten more and more nervous on qualifying day — literally to the point where I'm on the verge of getting sick to my stomach. I guess that's because making a race has become more difficult as the sport grows. Every time I go out to qualify, I have to drive close to the edge in order to make the race. It's a tremendously intense experience whenever I go out there because the expectations, especially my own, are so high.

A scary lap

Drivers take one or two qualifying laps, depending on which track they're on. They each get one lap of warm-up on the track before they take the green flag at the start/finish line. At that point, the car, with a transmitter attached to its fuel cell runs over a sensor in the track to start the timed lap. During the lap, drivers push the car as much as they dare, hoping the tires have enough traction and stick to the track — and hoping the car doesn't spin out and crash. It's quite a relief when it's all over and the car zooms over that sensor again to end the lap.

After qualifying ends, cars are ranked by the speed recorded by NASCAR officials, who score all of the races and time all of the qualifying laps with sophisticated, high-tech equipment. Those officials reveal who had the fastest lap — that driver will start the race on the inside of the front row, or the *pole position*. The second-fastest qualifier gets to start the race on the outside of the front row, which is the *outside pole*. It's an honor to win the pole, because you go to Victory Lane, take photos, and accept awards — and your competition respects you a little more for it. They know how hard it is to be the best qualifier, considering the fastest car (1st) and the slowest car (43rd) are often separated by less than one second.

Sometimes really odd things happen during qualifying, like two cars recording the exact same time, but NASCAR has a back-up plan for that. If two or more cars record the exact same time for a lap, the team higher in car owner points gets the better starting position. (I discuss car owner points in the "Provisional Entries" section of this chapter.)

After the first day of qualifying is over, the top 25 qualifiers don't have to worry about qualifying anymore (at least for that race), because their spots in the race are locked in. The rest of the field, however, has some thinking to do.

Second-round qualifying

The second day of qualifying is more stressful than the first one, for the teams that haven't made the race. The teams still in limbo, wondering whether they're racing or going home, have to decide whether to requalify or just stand on their time. *Standing on your time* means a team isn't going to make their driver qualify again. The team is banking on the driver's time from the first-round of qualifying, and is hoping the time will be fast enough for them to make the race. If a team wants to stand on its time, it must tell NASCAR its decision within five minutes after the final practice and just before second-round qualifying. If a team doesn't tell NASCAR that it plans to stand on its time, it's obligated to requalify because the time from the first round is thrown out.

Daytona is different

Instead of holding two rounds of qualifying, NASCAR does things differently for the Daytona 500, NASCAR's Super Bowl held at the beginning of each season. For that premier race, drivers have several rounds of qualifying — but not all of them are held the usual way.

On the first day of qualifying, drivers do complete two laps around the speedway, but only the fastest two drivers lock in their starting spots for the race. The fastest two cars sit on the front row, while all the others must run in one of two qualifying races held the Thursday before the Daytona 500. First-round qualifying determines the starting lineup for those qualifying races, which are called the Gatorade Twin 125s (because they are each 125 miles long). Drivers have two more chances to improve their starting spots in the 125s, though, in second- and third-round qualifying. After those qualify-ing sessions are over, the field for the 125 is set. The cars that finished in an odd-numbered position, including the pole winner, race in the first qualifying race. The cars that finished in an even-numbered position, including the outside pole winner, compete in the second qualifying race.

The top 14 finishers in the first qualifying race line up behind the pole sitter in the Daytona 500. The top 14 finishers in the second race line up behind the outside pole sitter. Using that formula, 30 of 43 starting spots are filled. The next six positions (31 through 36) are given to cars not already in the race that were the fastest after the three qualifying rounds held earlier in the week. The remaining seven positions are given to teams that are entitled to provisional entries, which I talk about in the "Provisional Entries" section.

Several factors go into making the decision of whether or not to stand on one's time. Perhaps the most critical is looking at where the team qualified the day before. If the team almost made the first-round cutoff, they most likely will stand on their time. But if a team was average or really slow, it may want to qualify again — depending on the weather conditions. If the weather is hot throughout the day of second-day qualifying, even hotter than the afternoon before when the first-round was held, odds are teams that requalify will go slower than they did the day before because the track is so slick. If the weather is cool, and cooler than it was the day before, expect to see nearly everyone requalify because the track conditions are so conducive to fast laps.

Whatever teams decided to do, they have to consider that only the fastest 36 teams are guaranteed a spot in the race. The rest of the race entries are pro-visional entries, which I discuss in the "Provisional Entries" section later in this chapter.

Provisional Entries

There's hope for drivers who are having a bad weekend and who couldn't record a decent qualifying lap if you paid them a million bucks. NASCAR has a built-in safety valve for those drivers. And they're called *provisional entries* (often just called *provisionals*) — guaranteed spots in a race for cars that weren't one of the 36 fastest during qualifying. NASCAR hands out seven provisionals each race, with those drivers starting 37th through 43rd.

The provisional system is rather complicated, but the purpose is simple: It guarantees that star drivers get into the race. So even if Jeff Gordon or Dale Jarrett has a poor qualifying run, fans still get to see them race because they use provisional entries to make the field.

✔ A provisional is an entry allowed into a race that a car owner may receive when his team fails to qualify for a race on the basis of its timed qualifying lap. Provisionals are based on owner points, not driver points.

- *Driver points:* Drivers receive points for each race in which they compete, based on their finishing position in a particular race.

- *Car owner points:* Owners receive points for each race, based on the finishing positions of their cars in a particular race, no matter who's driving.

✔ Each car owner receives four provisionals at the start of each season. One additional provisional is provided to each car owner after he attempts to qualify for eight races, for a maximum season allotment of eight provisionals.

✔ Until the completion of four races for the current season, provisionals are assigned to six positions (37 through 42) based on the *prior* season's car owner points, not driver points. After the fourth race of the season until the end of the season, provisions for positions 37 through 42 are assigned based on the *current* season's car owner point standings.

✔ Provisionals are assigned starting with the car owner who ranks highest in car owner points but did not qualify for positions 1 through 36 during qualifying. The car owner who ranks next highest receives the next provisional, and so on, until all starting positions are filled.

If ten teams need to use provisionals, only the top six teams in car owner points get to race. The other four teams, unfortunately, have to pack up and go home.

✔ If a car owner is in the top 25 in car owner points and has to use a provisional, NASCAR doesn't take away one of his available provisionals because provisionals are intended for successful owners and drivers who happen to have a bad qualifying day.

If a car owner is not in the top 25 in car owner points and has to use a provisional, NASCAR swipes one of the freebies given to him. This provides motivation for an owner to stay in the top 25: The most provisionals that a car owner can receive is eight, but if he's in the top 25, using a provisional doesn't count against him.

✔ If all six provisionals are assigned for spots 37 through 42, and a provisional is needed by a car owner whose driver is a NASCAR Winston Cup Series champion, participated as a driver the previous season, and entered the race for his car owner before the entry deadline, a 43rd provisional — called the *champion's provisional* — is assigned to that car owner.

If more than one champion doesn't make the race, NASCAR gives the 43rd spot to the most recent champion. If no champion takes the last position, the next eligible team (according to car owner points) fills it.

Rain, Rain Go Away

If qualifying is rained out for a NASCAR Winston Cup Series race, the way NASCAR determines the starting lineup is a bit out of the ordinary. All but one provisional gets tossed aside. The rest goes like this:

✔ The first 35 starting spots are filled according to car owner points. The top 35 in points get the top 35 spots in the race. (If it's one of the first four races of the season, the points revert to the previous season's final points standings.)

✔ Next to make the race are the previous race winners (at the track where the race is being held) who aren't in the top 35 in points.

✔ One past champion's provisional goes to the most recent past champion who isn't already in the field based on the above criteria.

✔ The rest of the starting spots, if any are left, go to the teams that are organized and efficient with their paperwork. NASCAR fills the rest of the field by checking the postmarks on entry blanks for the race. The team that sent the entry blank in first gets the first available spot in the race, and so on down the line.

How the champion's provisionals got started

Champions haven't always had special provisionals set aside for them. NASCAR instituted the champion's provisional in 1989 when the King of the sport, Richard Petty, failed to make a NASCAR Winston Cup Series race at Richmond International Raceway. It was a shocking day for fans, drivers, and crew members to see NASCAR's winningest driver fail to make the cut. So, NASCAR officials got together and devised a system that would prevent something like that from happening again. They started using champion's provisionals the next year, so that drivers who reached the pinnacle of the sport could benefit, even when they had poor qualifying days. Right away, it was dubbed the "Petty Rule" because Petty's Richmond problem started it all. The mellow, easy-going Petty didn't mind, though. He started calling it the "Petty Rule," too.

Champion's provisionals worked flawlessly for several years until Darrell Waltrip went home from the UAW-GM Quality 500 in 1997 when Terry Labonte used the provisional because he was higher in points than Waltrip was. Then, in 1998, Waltrip ended up using 20 champion's provisionals in the 33 races. It was supposed to be a fall-back for a past champion, something used rarely and in an emergency. So, NASCAR changed the rule once again at the beginning of 1999. The updated rule said each champion would be limited to eight provisionals a year just like everybody else (only if he wasn't in the top 25 in points).

Chapter 9

Race-Day Strategies

- -

In This Chapter

▶ Passing other cars

▶ Listening to spotters

▶ Driving aggressively or hanging back

▶ Conserving tires and brakes

▶ Gambling during a pit stop

▶ Calculating fuel mileage

▶ Drafting at superspeedways

- -

*I*n stock-car racing, there's no such thing as drawing up a game plan before a race starts — a set, pre-planned strategy gets you nowhere. Racing changes by the minute — or even by the second — with caution flags coming out because of accidents, blown tires, lead changes, and mechanical failures. It would be silly to devise a plan before a race when that plan may be useless if something unexpected happens.

Strategy comes into play as the race unfolds. For example, when drivers take a pit stop near the end of the race, teams have to figure out whether to change two tires or four. Or if a race has *gone green* for a long time (the race has been under a green flag, without a caution flag coming out — see Chapter 5), teams may tell their drivers to conserve fuel by easing off the gas a little. They do that because they think their drivers may not have to make another pit stop before the race is over. Also, on superspeedways (see Chapter 13), drivers must know how to use the technique of drafting if they want to go fast and win.

In this chapter, I discuss a variety of these and other racing strategies.

The Art of Passing

One of the most obvious strategies in NASCAR racing is to pass as many cars as you can by coming up on either the right or left side of the car in front (see Figure 9-1). But passing during a race isn't like driving around a slow car on the highway. Even if the driver is trying to pass someone on the straight, wide part of the track, it may be difficult because that driver doesn't want anyone to pass him. And that driver will do anything he can to stay in front.

Making a pass is much more strenuous than it may seem, especially if the car a driver is trying to pass is on the lead lap or if he's battling for position. *Being on the lead lap* means that a driver has completed the same number of laps as the leader. (If the driver is a lap down, that means he has completed one less lap than the leader.) *Battling for position* means the car that the driver is trying to pass is on the same lap as the driver. For example, a driver is battling for position with a car ahead of him when he's in fourth place and that car is in third.

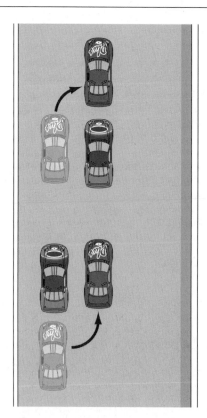

Figure 9-1:
Even on a straight-away, passing another car can be difficult.

Depending on the track and conditions, the easiest pass may be on the left (inside) or the right (outside).

If a driver is trying to pass a car that's on the lead lap or on the same lap he is, it's a good guess that driver isn't going to let another driver casually drive by. He's going to try to *block,* meaning he will try to put his car exactly where he thinks another driver is going to try to pass him. That requires plenty of concentration and plenty of glances into the rear-view mirror, but when a driver knows how to throw a good block, even the best cars can't get by him.

When a driver is trying to pass another car, he must be patient and stay right on the bumper of the car in front. He must also pay attention, especially going through the turns.

Passes frequently occur in the turns, where cars tend to become difficult to drive — and easy for other cars to pass — particularly if the car in front isn't prepared for the race correctly. If a driver can't zoom by and easily pass, he must wait for the driver ahead to make one mistake, even a small one, in order to get by. This could happen when the driver of the car in front takes a turn too wide (see Figure 9-2) and slides up the track when coming out of a turn. Or it could happen when that driver takes his car into a turn too quickly and loses control for a split-second. That's why drivers are more focused than usual when they go through the turns. They know they must capitalize on other drivers' errors and be ready to make a pass when the other driver slips up. Going through turns is a perfect place to take advantage of those situations and make a move.

Doing the bump

At short tracks, passing isn't as much of an art as it is a technique. Cars at short tracks are going relatively slowly and there is plenty of *downforce* — which means the cars stick to the track — so drivers can be very aggressive without causing a big accident. In order to pass a car in front, the driver doesn't necessarily have to go below him or above him on the track. All he has to do is give the car a healthy tap — called a *bump* — on the rear bumper, as shown in Figure 9-3. Most of the time that will cause the car to float up the track and give the driver enough room to pass by.

NASCAR frowns on this bump-and-pass technique, especially at bigger tracks where it would be a dangerous move. But at short tracks, it's tolerated some of the time. For example, when Dale Earnhardt smacked into the back of Terry Labonte on the last lap of the night race at Bristol in 1999, he moved Labonte out of the way to win. The problem was, he also spun out Labonte and sent him into the wall. NASCAR officials didn't think a penalty was necessary and let Earnhardt keep the win. The fans let Earnhardt know what they thought of his aggressive move, though. They vehemently booed him while he celebrated in Victory Lane.

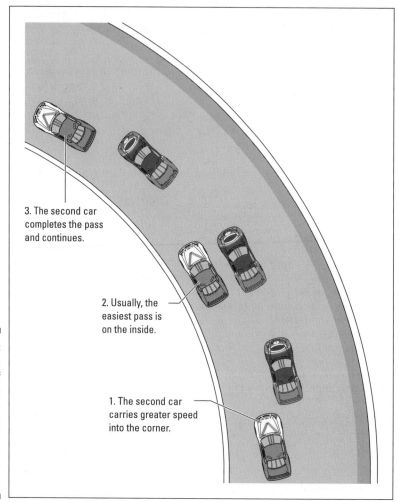

3. The second car completes the pass and continues.

2. Usually, the easiest pass is on the inside.

1. The second car carries greater speed into the corner.

Figure 9-2:
When the car ahead of you drifts up the race-track going through a turn, it's a perfect time to pass.

How other cars can slow you down

The driver in the lead wants to get as much space between him and the second-place car as possible. This becomes a problem — and a great, big pain in the neck — when that driver comes up on lapped traffic. *Lapped traffic* is made up of cars that aren't on the lead lap, which often are considerably slower than the leaders. So when the leader is trucking around the speedway, the last thing he needs is a bunch of slower cars getting in his way. It's sort of like driving in the fast lane on the highway and having to slow down when there's a slow car ahead of you that just won't switch lanes. Sure, you could pass on the right, but what if another slow car is in the right lane? You're stuck behind those cars until one or both of them decides to move out of the way. Drivers have the same problem in racing. When the lead car gets caught behind lapped traffic, the driver in second — who has no one ahead of him to slow him down — has more time to catch up to the leader's back bumper.

On the other hand, if the lead driver can pass the lapped car just before going into a turn, the second place car gets stuck behind the lapped car (see Figure 9-4).

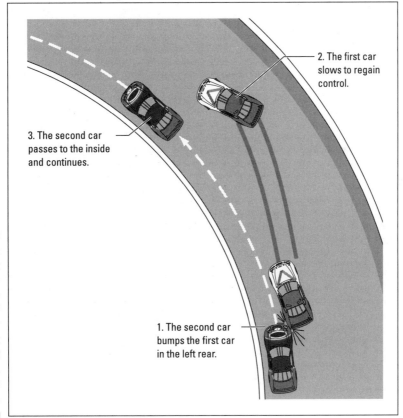

2. The first car slows to regain control.

3. The second car passes to the inside and continues.

1. The second car bumps the first car in the left rear.

Figure 9-3:
At short tracks, the technique is simple. If a driver doesn't move out of the way, someone moves him.

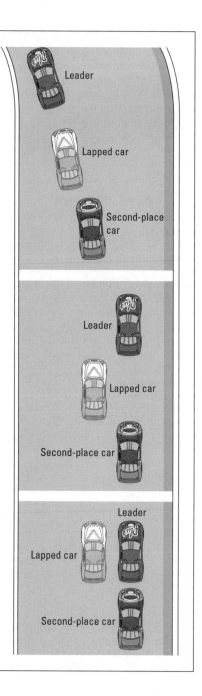

3. As the cars approach the turn, the second car must slow and fall behind the lapped car in order to get through the corner. The lead car can extend his lead.

2. The lead car moves to pass the lapped car.

1. The leaders approach a slower, lapped car.

Figure 9-4:
When lapped traffic gets in the way of a second-place car, the leader has a chance to gain ground.

Staying on the lead lap

Sometimes lapped cars aren't that much slower than the lead cars. They may be cars that blew a tire, spun out, or were penalized for speeding on pit road or doing something else illegal earlier in the race. Those drivers just want to get back on the lead lap so they can have a chance to win. If they get on the lead lap, those drivers have a chance at a good finish, especially if a caution flag comes out.

Under a caution flag (see Chapter 5), all the cars on the lead lap are bunched up single-file, almost bumper to bumper. They're brought together even if the lead car had a substantial lead over the second-place car; even if the last car on the lead lap was looking at the leader in his rear-view mirror and about to go one lap down. So look at it this way, if you're on the lead lap, there's always hope for you to get up near the front.

The problem is getting on the lead lap if you're a lap down, or even a couple laps down. Here are some ways a driver can get back on the lead lap:

- ✔ **Pass the leader under green-flag conditions.** Sometimes a driver may be a lap down only because his tire went flat or he ran out of gas — not because he has a slow car. In that case, that driver may be fast enough to pass the leaders and get back on the lead lap.

- ✔ **Stay on the track when the leaders make a pit stop, and then hope that something causes a caution flag so you don't have to pit under a green flag.** That way, you can pit under a caution flag, when cars are moving around the track slowly. That gives you enough time to make a pit stop, and then catch up to the tail end of the field. Otherwise, you'd still be a lap down if you pit when everybody else did.

- ✔ **After NASCAR officials call a caution, pass the leader by racing back to the start/finish line.** While NASCAR has no set rules for this behavior, it is a gentlemen's agreement that no one — except drivers trying to get their lap back — race back to the start/finish line to begin the first lap of caution. Drivers don't adhere to that agreement all the time, though. If a good driver with a good car is trying to get his lap back, you can bet the leaders aren't going to let him do it — because he may just steal the win from them if given the chance.

- ✔ **Have friends on the track.** Sometimes one driver lets another driver get his laps back by letting the driver who's a lap down pass the driver who's on the lead lap. It all depends on how the lead-lap driver feels about the other driver. If they're friends, teammates, or if they've worked well with each other in the past, the lead-lap driver will let the other driver pass. If they're not friends and have had previous on-track problems, you can bet that the driver who's down a lap isn't going to be able to pass. It's like stopping to let someone into your lane on the highway or on a road. You don't know why you do it. It kind of depends on what kind of mood you're in.

Listening to the Spotter

Unlike passenger cars, race cars don't have side-view mirrors. So it's not the easiest thing to pass another car when you're going 190 mph and running inches away from the car in front and behind you. That's why team members called spotters are perched high above the racetrack.

A *spotter* is a team member who watches a race from atop the press box or the grandstands so he can get a full view of the racetrack. His job is to be the driver's second set of eyes. As soon as the spotter sees there's enough room for a driver to pass another car, he tells the driver, "Clear high!" or "Clear low!" which means, "There are no cars on the high side of the track (the part closest to the grandstands)!" or "There are no cars on the low side of the track (the part closest to the infield)!" — a driver is clear to move around the track in those areas and pass cars.

While drivers use spotters at every racetrack, they are indispensable at certain tracks on the circuit. At short tracks, for example, drivers are lapping the track so fast, they can't even tell where they are at times — and they don't have a lot of time to avoid accidents. So, at places like the half-mile Bristol Motor Speedway where it takes cars only about 15 or 16 seconds to go around the track, spotters need to stay alert and notify their drivers of accidents as soon as they happen. If the spotters don't do that, their driver may become a part of the wreckage, too. The same thing goes for superspeedways, where cars run at almost 200 mph, just a few feet, or even inches, apart. For example, if there is an accident at the top of the racetrack coming out of turn 4, the spotter notifies the driver, and then tells him whether to go low or high on the track to avoid the wreck. (See Chapter 8 for an explanation of the turns on the track.)

At the bigger tracks, such as 2.5-mile Pocono Raceway or 2.66-mile Talladega Superspeedway, every team has more than one spotter. One spotter is usually positioned above the frontstretch and one above the backstretch because one spotter can't see the entire track, even from a high vantage point. They may even use more, with each spotter taking responsibility for a certain section of track. (Flip to Chapter 8 to find out more about the frontstretch, backstretch, and turns on a racetrack.)

From time to time, spotters communicate with people other than those on their team. If a spotter is working with a driver who is leading the race and coming up on a lapped car, a spotter may walk over to the lapped car's spotter and tell him to ask that driver to move over. The spotter then relays the other driver's request, but that driver doesn't necessarily have to move over if he doesn't want to. It all depends on the relationship between those two drivers. If they've worked well together before, maybe the lapped car will give the leader a break — possibly hoping the driver will remember the favor in the future. At superspeedways, where cars go faster when they work together than they do separately, a spotter may make a deal with another spotter to get two drivers to work together and draft to the front (see the "There's a Draft in Here" section, later in this chapter, or Chapter 13 for more information on drafting).

How's My Drivin'?

Not every driver is aggressive from the start of the race to the finish. Some like to zoom to the front as soon as the green flag drops; others like to hang behind the leaders. It all depends on the race they're in and the racetrack they're on. And it all depends on their race strategy.

Saving your engine

In a long race, such as the Coca-Cola 600 which is the longest NASCAR event, drivers don't like to push their cars and engines too hard at the beginning. They know it's wiser to conserve the car for when they'll need it most, which is 50 to 100 laps to go depending on how the race unfolds. If you push the car too hard, you're at risk of *blowing an engine* — which means you won't finish the race because your engine failed beyond immediate repair.

Taking care of your tires

One reason drivers don't go full-bore around a track all the time is that they must take care of their tires. No question — tires are sturdy: Goodyear Tire & Rubber Company has engineers whose job is to create tires for each racetrack. They're working hard to devise new tires that last longer during a race — and also ones that don't blister, pop, or go flat very easily. Also, throughout the year, Goodyear invites teams to tire tests to try out the new tires and tell the engineers how to improve them — if they need improving at all.

Still, tires aren't indestructible. Drivers must be careful not to wear out their tires too quickly during a race. This is called *tire management*. At sandpaper-rough tracks such as Darlington Raceway and North Carolina Speedway, drivers make sure not to push their cars too fast through the turns because the tires wear out more quickly. Even on less rough tracks, tires don't last very long, so drivers take it easy when they can. Otherwise, the tires may wear out and provide less traction, which means the car will be more difficult to control.

Drivers also run the risk of blowing a tire if they wear out their tires — and that may be dangerous if their car veers into a wall. See Figure 9-5.

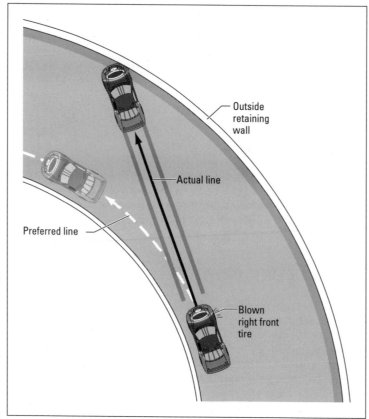

Outside retaining wall

Actual line

Preferred line

Blown right front tire

Figure 9-5:
When a car's right front tire blows, it's headed straight for the wall.

Give me a brake

Just as drivers take it easy on their tires at some tracks, they take it easy on their brakes at others, particularly at short tracks. Brakes can become a problem — a dangerous problem — at short tracks where cars don't spend much time on the straightaways because the tracks are so small. Cars spend just as much time going through the turns, causing drivers to press and release the brake a lot during a race.

If you drive into the turns hard, you have to jam on the brakes and that wears them down — especially at a track like Martinsville Speedway where races last 500 laps around the .526-mile oval. At short tracks, drivers make sure to conserve their brakes when they can — especially early in a race when driving aggressively usually doesn't pay off.

Pit-Stop Gambles

Pit stops play the greatest role in race strategy. When do you pit? When do you stay on the track? When should you come in for a gas-and-go? When should you make an air pressure adjustment in the tires — and which tires should you change — in order to get the car handling better? It's the crew chief's job to make those decisions, so that puts a lot of pressure on him, especially in the final laps when his driver is contending for the win. A good pit stop can get the driver out in front. A bad pit stop can cost the driver a victory.

The most important result of a pit stop is *track position* — where a car is in relation to the front of the pack. Teams can improve their cars' track position if they have a quicker pit stop than the teams who came into the pits ahead of them.

Tire gambles

Drivers can improve their track position if they change only two tires instead of four during a pit stop. That's because the driver advances ahead of other drivers who are still on pit road getting the extra two tires. There is a gamble with changing just two tires instead of all four, however. While a two-tire stop is several seconds shorter than a four-tire stop, a driver may not be as fast on the track as a driver who took four tires. Older tires don't provide as much traction — meaning the car won't stick to the track as much, so it will be slower. But how much slower will the car be? If you get out of the pit stop first after taking on two tires with ten laps left, and the driver who takes on four tires is tenth — perhaps those four new tires will make him so fast that he'll catch up to you before the race is over. Perhaps not. It's a guessing game that works both ways, depending on the track and how the team prepared the car for the race. Many times, crew chiefs won't commit to two or four tires until the last second. They watch other cars on pit road — only the cars contending for the lead — to see how many tires they're getting, before making their own decision.

Another question that arises is whether to use sticker tires or scuffs. *Sticker tires* are new tires that still have the manufacturer's sticker on them. *Scuffs* are tires that have been on the car during practice, used for only one or two laps. Both affect the handling of a race car in different ways, depending on the weather and the temperature of the racetrack.

Tires affect a race car's handling more than you may think. That's why drivers often complain during a race (over the in-car radio) that they don't like a particular set of tires. Those tires may make the car more difficult to turn or they may make the car feel all wiggly in its rear-end as it goes though the turns. The foremost thing on a driver's mind at that point is getting back into the pits for new, better tires.

Fuel and fuel mileage gambles

Fuel mileage isn't an issue in all races, only the ones where there aren't many caution flags. Long periods of green-flag racing mean that cars will be on the track until they need gas as opposed to staying on the track until there's an accident, which allows all drivers to make a pit stop while cars are slowed on the track during the clean-up.

Michigan Speedway and Dover Downs International Speedway are two tracks where fuel mileage is often an issue. It's where drivers try to get as many laps from one tank of fuel as they can, in order to utilize every last drop of gas in their tanks. If they consistently get good mileage out of each tank of gas, it may give them the opportunity to make fewer pit stops than the next driver — meaning they'll have a better chance at winning. Sometimes a driver may drive slower to conserve gas, pushing the fuel mileage as far as it will go and hoping he can make it to the finish without running out of gas. However, if a late-race caution flag goes up because of an accident or debris on the track, all that fuel mileage calculation goes out the window because all of the cars come into the pits for more gas.

Teams figure out their fuel mileage before a race begins, determining how many laps the car can make around the track before it runs out of gas. Then they decide on a *pit window,* which is when they'll need to make a pit stop to refuel. At some tracks, the pit window may be 55 to 60 laps, at others it may be 70 to 75, depending on the length of the track.

Obviously, teams don't want their cars to run out of gas — so they have a system of keeping tabs on the situation. To calculate their fuel mileage, they weigh the gas can when it's full, and then again after a pit stop to find out how much gas is left in the can and the catch can (which catches the overflow of gas) after a pit stop. (Flip to Chapter 10 for more on pit stops.) The gas in the cans reveals how much gas was dumped into the gas tank — which, in turn, reveals how long the car can go without sputtering and stopping. While this sounds like an exact science, it isn't. For one reason or another, cars can run out of gas in the final laps of a race, even when a team thinks it has enough gas to last much longer.

Tony Stewart was leading the Jiffy Lube 300 at New Hampshire International Speedway in 1999, looking as if he was about to win for the first time in his rookie year. What he didn't expect, though — especially after dominating the race — was his car to run out of gas with just two laps to go. Jeff Burton, my Roush Racing teammate, ended up winning instead. It happens to the best of us, including me a few times. After a while, though, you realize that you lose some races that way and you win some that way. For example, Jeff Gordon was leading the 1999 Winston all-star race by nearly a half of a lap at Lowe's Motor Speedway, but ran out of gas with one lap to go. I was in second place at the time, and couldn't have been happier to hear the news. The next thing I knew, I was in Victory Lane celebrating a surprise win while Gordon was steaming over the loss (and the lack of gas in his car).

Not running on empty

Even though crew chiefs, engineers, and team members figure out how many laps they can get out of one tank before a race begins, sometimes they make mistakes. In 1998, Dale Jarrett paid dearly for that. Jarrett was leading the Brickyard 400 and his team thought he could make just over the halfway point before making a pit stop. They thought they had enough gas to lead the race at halfway and pick up the $10,000 bonus for leading at halfway. The gamble wasn't worth the $10,000, though, when Jarrett ran out of gas on the backstretch of the huge, 2.5-mile track. Obviously, he lost his lead in a hurry while coast-ing back to pit road — but his car didn't make it all the way to his pit box. It stopped just at the entrance to pit road, which was quite an unfortunate place to come to a halt because his pit box was all the way at the other end of pit road. That's when his crew took off running down pit road to the car so they could push it back to their pit. They started out sprinting but, because it was a good half-mile to the car, the crew came back huffing and puffing. Jarrett lost several laps after that — as well as the $1 million bonus he could have won for finishing first — and then came back to finish 16th.

If a team thinks the race will be under a green flag until the end of the race, you may see a car dive onto pit road during a caution period just before the green flag is raised again. This is called a *gas-and-go stop* — a pit stop in which the pit crew doesn't change tires; instead, they just fill the gas tank with a smidgen of fuel before the driver peels back out onto the track. Teams do this when they think that small amount will be enough to get their car to the finish, while other cars will run out of fuel. Drivers also may come in for a gas-and-go at the end of the race, when they fear they will run out of gas.

There's a Draft in Here

Strategy on superspeedways and some of the larger intermediate tracks is different than at other tracks. The tracks are so large and the turns are so sweeping that *aerodynamics,* or the way air flows over a car, become a huge factor. (For more on aerodynamics and superspeedways, turn to Chapter 13.) Drafting is sort of like driving behind a semi-truck on the highway. When you're cruising behind it, you feel a slight pull from the truck if you drive a short distance behind it. But if you try to pass it, your car bounces all around because of the air flowing off the front, back, and sides of the truck, which causes turbulence.

Drafting is when drivers race in single file and share air flow among them. A driver tucks his car behind the driver in front of him, and then utilizes the air flowing over the car ahead of him to his advantage. Cars cut through the air faster together than they do separately. The line of cars racing down the track single file is known as the *draft*. The first group of cars going single file is called the *lead draft*. After a driver loses the draft and has to race by itself with no other cars around — or if he accidentally falls out of the single-file line — he's in big trouble because his car is so much slower. That goes to show you that, at superspeedways, drivers need help from other drivers so they can get around the track in the quickest way. Otherwise they're just wasting their time and riding around for nothing. See Figure 9-6.

Dale Earnhardt was known as the master of superspeedways because, as legend has it, he could "see" air flowing off the car ahead of him. It's exactly the sixth sense drivers need to make smart, thought-out moves on a superspeedway in order to win there.

The physics of drafting is this: Cars go faster when they travel together because the first car in line punches an imaginary hole in the air, and the cars behind it slip more easily through that hole. Thus, the engines don't have to work as hard to battle oncoming air. The car in front benefits, too. It gets "pushed" by the cars behind it.

Making a pass at a superspeedway takes a special skill because of the drafting aspect to the racing there. It also takes a little help. It's not like passing a car at a short track or shorter intermediate tracks, where you may roar past someone through a turn or tap the rear bumper of a car to try to move it up the track. Try that at a superspeedway, and you'll probably send that car flying into the wall or spinning around to cause a major accident — cars run too fast for that sort of trick. Instead, in order to pass someone, a driver has to team up with one or more other drivers, because two or more cars go faster together than they do separately. So passing becomes a challenge.

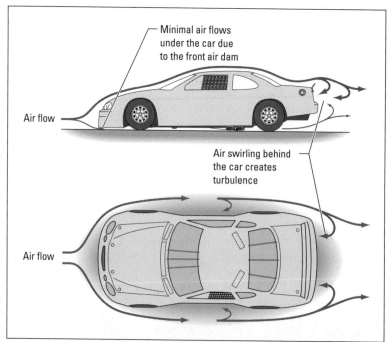

Figure 9-6:
Under-
standing
the way
that air
flows over
and under a
car is key
to success
at Super-
speedways.

Minimal air flows
under the car due
to the front air dam

Air flow

Air swirling behind
the car creates
turbulence

Air flow

Suppose a driver dives to the inside of the track to pass the leader, and the driver behind him follows. Both drivers most likely would draft past the leader because two cars go faster than one, particularly when the two drivers left the leader with no one directly behind him. So those cars trying to make the pass push and pull each other through the air and start gaining on the leader.

The tricky part of this scenario is that a driver can never be sure if someone is going to follow him when he makes a move. His spotter can make all the deals he wants with another spotter (see the "Listening to the Spotter" section, earlier in this chapter), in order to convince another driver to team up with his driver to pass the leader. The problem is, these impromptu deals are never guaranteed. The risk is that the driver dives to the inside and no one backs him up — this is called *getting hung out to dry,* racing slang for a driver running all by himself on the racetrack when he's out of the line of cars — and out of the draft. No car is ahead of him; no car is behind him. In turn, he's as slow as a fattened calf compared to the cars racing in groups on the track.

At superspeedways it's not unusual to see a driver go from first to tenth if he's hung out to dry. It's also not unusual to see drivers struggling to get back in line after they've fallen out of line and lost the draft. Cars run so close together, there isn't much room to squeeze in, and most of the time, your competitors show no mercy. Still, every driver tries desperately to get back into line and back into the draft. If he falls too far back, though, he may lose the lead draft altogether, meaning he's no longer running with the front-running pack of cars. He's out there on his own, not close to the lead draft at all. In that case, he's doomed unless he catches up to the pack (which isn't likely unless he has help from other cars) or a caution flag comes out to bunch the cars back together.

There is a special move drivers use to pass cars on superspeedways, but only experienced, superspeedway-savvy drivers have enough guts to try it and then enough talent to do it successfully. It's called a *slingshot move* and a driver has to utilize the air flowing off the car ahead of him very carefully, allowing his car to get sucked in by that car (see Figure 9-7). The driver then turns abruptly to one side or the other and gets shot through the air right by the car he was trying to pass. The catch is, the driver making the move has to know exactly where to position his car before before and as he makes the pass. For the move to work, he must use the air flowing off the opposing car and avoid the turbulent air at the same time. While the move doesn't work as well today as it did in the days before carburetor restrictor plates, which slow the cars down, Dale Earnhardt, the superspeedway guru, had been known to pull it off from time to time. (Turn to Chapter 13 for more on restrictor-plate racing.)

3. His momentum carries him around the first car as he completes the pass.

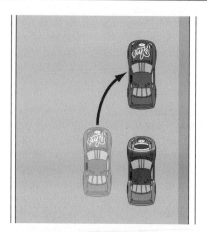

2. The second car uses the reserve power to accelerate behind the first car and slingshot out around.

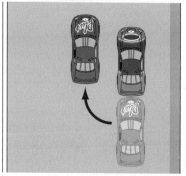

Figure 9-7:
Drivers can "slingshot" their way past a car in front of them by tucking behind that car, gaining speed, then ducking to the inside or outside.

1. The second car is able to go as fast as the first car while only using a portion of his available power due to the lower wind resistance.

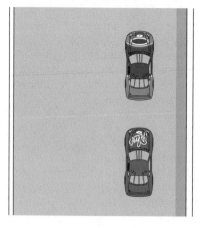

Accidents Happen

No matter how careful drivers are during a race, accidents happen. Sometimes drivers lose control of their cars. Sometimes they blow a tire. Sometimes they blow an engine — and the car behind them slips in the oil they dropped and spins out into the wall. Sometimes two cars inadvertently touch coming out of a turn and send each other reeling into incoming traffic. Sometimes a driver hits another car's back bumper and sends that car flying into the outside wall like a billiard ball. You can never tell when it will happen next. All you can do is hope you miss the mayhem.

Frequently, drivers avoid accidents by pure luck. Other times, the spotter alerts the driver of an accident, then tells him where to go on the track to avoid it. The spotter may say, "Go high!" or "Go low!" to tell the driver which part of the track is clear for him to move into, but even then that may not be right. When smoke is billowing into the air, the spotter can't see anything and the driver can't either. So the best technique in that situation is for a driver to grit his teeth and hope to make it through unscathed. While it's not failsafe, there's nothing else a driver can do.

Sometimes, though, drivers can see an accident in the making, and avoid it before it happens. Maybe a car isn't really stable as it comes out of the turns and its back end is wobbling around. Maybe a driver is taking too many chances by cutting off cars and coming close to the wall. Or maybe one car is riding too close to the back of another car and disturbing the air flow off the car in front. Instead of the air flowing onto the lead car's spoiler, which is the metal blade perched atop a car's truck that regulates air flowing over the car, it flows off the first car and onto the second car's front end. That leaves the lead car with little rear-end downforce, meaning it has little traction and little control of its back-end. This is called *taking the air off another car's spoiler* and it often ends in the lead car spinning out and getting into an accident — and sometimes taking out other cars with it (see Figure 9-8).

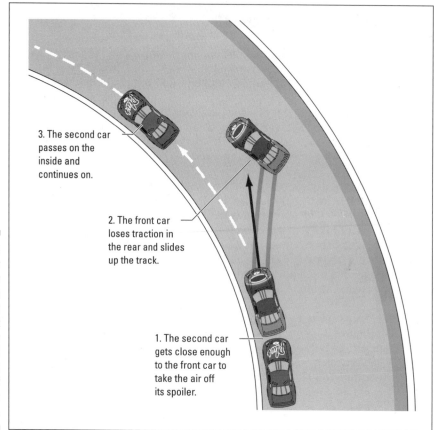

3. The second car passes on the inside and continues on.

2. The front car loses traction in the rear and slides up the track.

1. The second car gets close enough to the front car to take the air off its spoiler.

Figure 9-8:
When a car runs closely to the back of another car, it disturbs air flow and makes the back-end of that car unstable.

Chapter 10

Making Pit Stops

In This Chapter

▶ Understanding why pit stops are necessary

▶ Looking at the role of each pit crew member

▶ Knowing the rules of making a pit stop

▶ Finding out when drivers make pit stops

*T*he car that wins the race isn't necessarily the fastest one on the track. Many other factors — including pit stops — go into making it to Victory Lane. In fact, many people say that efficient pit stops are one of the most important components in winning a race.

A bad pit stop can cost a driver valuable time on the track. Wasting even one second during a pit stop can mean the difference between winning and losing, especially when races are frequently won by just fractions of a second.

Where Is Pit Road?

Pit road is a separate road inside a racetrack that usually runs parallel to a track's frontstretch between the final turn and the first turn. It's toward the infield, away from the grandstands. (For a description of a track's configuration, turn to Chapter 8.)

Pit road is where drivers go when they need their crews to service their cars, including changing the tires and filling the gas tank. It's kind of a safe haven, like the shoulder on a highway, where drivers can go to get out of the hectic action on the track. Along pit road, *pit boxes* of equal size are marked off for each of the 43 cars in the race. Yellow lines delineate the pit boxes and the drivers must pull into the box completely to avoid receiving a penalty. Some tracks have smaller pit boxes than others, depending on the size of the racetrack itself, so pulling into and out of a pit box can be difficult business, including for the crews who service the cars.

A wall, called the *pit wall*, separates the pit boxes from the area (called *pit stalls*) where teams keep their equipment and watch the race. Pit stalls are located just over the wall from the pit boxes so it's easy and convenient for crews to service their cars when they come in. Usually, the crew chief sits on top of a big box, called a *crash cart,* which is filled with equipment used for quick repairs, and the rest of the team hangs out in the area, monitoring lap times or listening to their two-way radio in order to hear their driver talk about the car and the race.

While most pit roads start before the final turn and end after the first turn, some are modified because of track size. Tracks that aren't big enough to fit 43 pit boxes down the frontstretch make modifications to fit their pit boxes around the track. For example, shorter tracks, like the half-mile Martinsville Speedway, have pit roads that start in turn 3 and end in turn 2, nearly all the way around the track. A few tracks even have pit roads on the frontstretch *and* backstretch (but not in the turns). This puts drivers pitting on the backstretch at a disadvantage, but I talk about that in "The backstretch blues" sidebar, later in this chapter.

What Is a Pit Stop?

A *pit stop* is when a driver pulls off the racetrack and onto pit road where members of his crew service his car. Pit stops happen when a car needs gas, fresh tires, mechanical repairs, or after it has been in an accident and needs to be fixed. Several factors go into how often a car comes in for a pit stop, including how quickly the tires wear down and what kind of fuel mileage the car is getting. While Goodyear, the company that manufacturers all the tires for NASCAR's top series, tries to manufacture racing tires that last a full tank of fuel, that's not always the case. Sometimes, the tires wear down more quickly than the fuel dwindles, so the teams have to make a pit stop before their gas tanks are empty. On the average, cars usually go about 100 miles per full tank of gas, which is 22 gallons. But their gas mileage varies from track to track and also depends on the driver's driving style. If a driver is rough and pumps the gas pedal frequently, he gets worse gas mileage than a driver who is smooth and steady with the gas pedal.

Going behind the wall

A driver also makes a pit stop whenever his team needs to repair his car after an accident or mechanical problem. If the team has to make major repairs to the car, including making substantial repairs to the engine or suspension, or replacing major pieces of sheet metal or parts, NASCAR rules say the team must perform those repairs behind the wall. *Going behind the wall* means leaving pit road and going into a safe area in the infield or garage where the crew can work on the car and repair it. For example, if a team needs to replace major pieces of sheet metal or parts, a car is brought behind the wall. Also, if the car is leaking fluids, a driver usually brings it behind the wall so that the car doesn't completely mess up pit road.

Besides filling the car with gas and changing the tires, members of a *pit crew* perform the following tasks:

- ✔ Repair the body of a car after an accident, but only if it didn't sustain major damage.
- ✔ Fix a broken component on the car if it doesn't require a major overhaul and doesn't need to be propped up onto stands so that crew members can work on the underside of the car.
- ✔ Clean the windshield and grille.
- ✔ Make adjustments on the car to improve the handling.
- ✔ Give the driver a bottle of water.

A pit crew accomplish a lot of tasks in a short time. A good pit stop can take as little as 15 seconds — not much time, considering the crew changes four tires and fills the gas tank with two 11-gallon cans. Pit stops range from 15 to 23 seconds, if the pit crew is completing a *four-tire stop,* during which all four tires are changed. But there are other types of pit stops besides a four-tire stop, including a *two-tire stop* when the team changes just two tires (the two on the left or the two on the right), a *gas-and-go* when the team adds gas to the car, but doesn't change any tires, and a *splash-and-go* when the team adds just enough gas to make it to the end or make it to the end without stopping for gas once again.

While an unlimited number of crew members are allowed in the pit stall during a race, only seven of them are allowed over the pit wall to work on the car during a pit stop. That's why the crew members who service the car are often called the *over-the-wall crew* or *over-the-wall guys.* The over-the-wall crew crouches atop the pit wall and waits for their car to come down pit road. Even before the car comes to a stop, the crew jumps off the wall and scrambles around the car to change tires, make adjustments, and fill the gas tank. They keep the equipment to do all those things in their pit stall.

Even though only seven crew members are allowed over the wall, other people can help service the car — as long as they don't step onto pit road. Those team members use a long pole with a squeegee or cloth on the end to wipe off any rubber or debris that has gathered on the car's grille (to keep the car from becoming overheated because air isn't getting through the grille and cooling its engine). Another team member may use a pole with a handy basket on the end to hand the driver a bottle of water.

The camera's watching

Most pit crews film their stops, using a camera attached to a pole that's extended above the pit box during a stop. By filming the stop, the crew can review what they did correctly and what they did wrong — even as soon as their car takes off down pit road. With a video monitor in every pit, the crew can review their stop immediately after their car rejoins the race.

The films can be useful in another way, too. Sometimes, if NASCAR fines a team for something the pit crew thinks it didn't do, the team refers to the video of the pit stop to prove their innocence.

Ballet without the tutus

While the pit crew performing a pit stop looks smooth and choreographed, it isn't easy. Crews spend as much as one hour a day practicing pit stops at their shop, sometimes with a pit crew coach who times and videotapes their stops and analyzes everyone's technique. Crews lift weights and get aerobically fit, usually with a personal trainer at a gym set up in their race shop, so that they can lift the tires with ease and scramble around the car quickly. Everybody knows that the faster the pit stop, the better chance their driver has of moving toward the front — and to Victory Lane.

Seven crew members (see Figure 10-1) have specific jobs to do after they leap over the wall:

- **Tire changers (2):** The crew has one tire changer for the front tires and one for the rear tires. They leap off the pit wall with air wrenches in their hands, and rush to the right side of the car (during a four-tire stop). They drop to their knees (wearing knee pads), and remove the five lug nuts holding the tire to the car. They take off the right tire and wheel, place a new tire and wheel on the car, tighten the lug nuts (which are previously glued onto the wheel), and then scurry to the left side to do the same thing.

- **Tire carriers (2):** Each tire carrier hands two 75-pound tires (already mounted onto wheels) at one time to the tire changers and takes the used tires away. When handing the fresh tire to the tire changer, the carrier is responsible for helping line up the tire onto the car, so that the changer can tighten the lug nuts right away, without having to lift the tire and wheel onto the axle. On the way to the left side, the tire carriers roll the used tire to a crew member who is waiting at the pit wall to take the tire away. Also, the front tire carrier sometimes cleans the grille as he goes past the nose of the car.

✔ **Jackman (1):** The jackman usually is one of the strongest people on the pit crew because he has to jump off the pit wall with a hydraulic jack in his arms that weighs about 35 pounds — and then use it to hoist a 3,400-pound car off the ground. His job is to run to the right side of the car, positioning the jack under a specific spot on each side (usually delineated by an arrow or a line), and use the jack to lift the car off the ground on that side. The job requires that the person be able to lift the car with one or two pumps of the handle, enough so the tires are off the ground — weaklings wouldn't fare too well. After raising the right side of the car, the jackman runs to the left side and does the same thing. The driver gets the signal to leave the pits when the jackman drops the jack and lowers the left side of the car.

✔ **Gas man (1):** The gas man doesn't have to be nimble, but he does have to be strong. He must step over the pit wall carrying a 90-pound, 11-gallon can of gas, and then fill the gas tank. When the first can empties, he usually gets a second can from the second gas man (who doesn't go over the wall), and fills the tank with that gas as well. Each can has a special valve on it and when it is placed into the opening to the car's gas tank, the gas shoots down into the gas tank quickly as gravity sucks the gas downward. You can recognize the gas man easily because he usually wears a helmet and a fireproof apron to protect him from fumes, spillage, and possible fires.

✔ **Catch can man (1):** The catch can man stands behind the car on the left side and holds a special container at the end of the car to collect gas that overflows from the gas tank. That keeps the gas from spilling onto the ground and possibly catching fire as the car takes off.

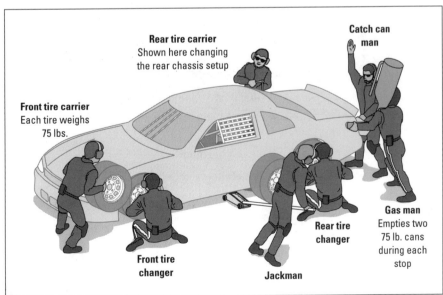

Figure 10-1:
The over-the-wall crew is a group of seven pit crew members who service a car during a pit stop. They change four tires and add gas in about 18 seconds.

Rear tire carrier
Shown here changing the rear chassis setup

Catch can man

Front tire carrier
Each tire weighs 75 lbs.

Gas man
Empties two 75 lb. cans during each stop

Rear tire changer

Front tire changer

Jackman

Making adjustments

When a driver says his car is handling terribly, the pit crew makes adjustments to the car during a pit stop. Usually you see the rear tire carrier insert a *ratchet,* which is a tool similar to a wrench, into a hole on the roof of the car to the front of the rear tires and crank the ratchet one way or the other. This is putting in or taking out *rounds of wedge*, which means he is adjusting the handling by changing the pressure on the rear springs. A team also can change a car's handling by adjusting the air pressure in the tires, raising or lowering the sway bar, or raising or lowering the track bar (see chapter 4 for descriptions of these parts of a car).

Pit Crews for Hire

Some over-the-wall pit crews are regular members of the team — mechanics, crew chiefs, car chiefs, or truck drivers. Others, however, are specially hired employees, who fly to the racetrack on race day solely to pit the car. Some team owners don't want to risk using regular team members to pit the car because those team members may be tired from working on the car all weekend, or because they just aren't athletic enough. Being a good pit crew member takes special skill, agility, and physical fitness, which makes them hot commodities in the garage. They have to try out and show their talents in order to get a job.

The following are some of the qualities that make a good candidate for a pit crew:

- Agility to maneuver around a car when six other pit crew members are trying to do the same thing.

- Strength to carry a jack or heavy tires, or to pump the jack handle and hoist the car off the ground.

- Fast reaction time to get lug nuts off a wheel without hesitation.

- Being able to remain calm under pressure, even when a race win is on the line.

- Excellent hand-eye coordination, especially for the tire changers.

- The ability to remain focused when people are screaming and cars are zooming by.

The importance of a good pit crew

Drivers never underestimate the power of a good, fast pit crew. At least I never have.

Suppose I've been running second to Jeff Gordon all day long and I've tried everything to pass him, but can't do it. I've gone into the pits in second place, and then have come out in second place. I've been about one second behind him all day and just can't catch him. In the next pit stop, though, the crew bangs out the fastest pit stop that's ever been, and I beat Gordon off pit road and take the lead. Gaining a second on pit road is much easier than gaining it on the track, especially in the final laps of a race when a driver doesn't have much time to make up ground with his car. That's why a good pit crew is invaluable, and that's why, many times, they're the first team members that I mention when I climb out of my car in Victory Lane.

The Rules of Pit Road

Just like everything else in NASCAR, there are rules, rules, and more rules governing pit stops. NASCAR officials, sitting above the track in the control tower, monitor cars as they travel down pit road. Each team also has an official standing in their pit, watching them as they perform a pit stop and making sure it's all done legally. If it's not, then the official penalizes them.

Speeding

While speeding on the racetrack goes with the territory, speeding on pit road doesn't. A driver can't just drive like a maniac coming off the racetrack and onto pit road. Although that's what drivers used to do, NASCAR now has a rule that limits the speed on pit road, to protect the crews working on the cars.

Safety isn't the pits

In 1999, my pit crew decided not to take any chances with their safety when they serviced my car on pit road. They decided to wear helmets during pit stops, which protects their heads in case another car or a piece of equipment hits them. The helmets are open-faced and light-weight, so the crew's visibility isn't obstructed as they dart from one side of the car to another to complete their tasks. While my crew is the only one in NASCAR to wear helmets during pit stops, crews in other motorsports, such as CART, are required to wear them.

The speed limit on pit road varies from track to track, depending on the size of the speedway. It ranges from 35 to 55 miles per hour, but drivers can't look at their speedometers to make sure they aren't speeding, because they don't have them — instead, they have *tachometers,* which measure the number of revolutions per minute that the engine is turning. During a pace lap, a pace car drives the pit road speed, while the drivers behind the pace car look at their tachometers to check how many rpm (revolutions per minute) they're turning. When a driver later crosses the line that begins pit road during a race, he checks his tachometer to make sure it reads the same as it did during the pace lap.

When a driver is caught speeding while coming down pit road, NASCAR officials hold him in his pit box for 15 seconds as a penalty. If NASCAR officials in the control tower catch him speeding *after* a pit stop, he has to come down pit road again for a *stop-and-go penalty,* which means that he has to come back to his pit box another time, stop, and then drive down pit road and back on the racetrack again. The worst penalty is when NASCAR docks a driver a lap or two, meaning they must stay in the pits while other drivers continue to complete laps around the track. If a driver is penalized one lap, he stays in the pits until the leaders have completed another lap. NASCAR then sends him back on the track.

Other no-nos

NASCAR has a list of other no-nos regarding pit stops during a race. If drivers disregard these, NASCAR penalizes them in some way:

- Drivers can't pass other drivers when under a caution flag (see Chapter 5) or when they're preparing to go onto pit road.

- When a driver pulls into his pit box, the car must be completely in the box with no part of it outside the box. A pit box is delineated by yellow lines just in front of a team's pit.

- Only seven crew members are allowed over the pit wall at once. After a pit crew member returns to the pit stall, no other pit crew member can replace him in order to work on the car.

- Teams may use only two air guns per stop. The air guns remove lug nuts from the wheel hub and tighten the lug nuts after a new tire and wheel are mounted on the car. If one of the air guns malfunctions, the team must complete the stop with the one working air gun. Teams must take both air guns back over the pit wall after they change the tires and before the car leaves the pit box.

- Teams may use only one jack per pit stop. If a car falls off the jack, however, team members can use a second jack to help raise the car back up.

- A catch can man must be on pit road to catch fuel overflow whenever gas is being added to the car.

- ✔ When a team changes tires, the tire changer must tighten all the lug nuts before the car leaves the pit.

- ✔ Teams can't let their tires roll across pit road or into another team's pit box.

- ✔ Drivers can't run over their air hoses or any other equipment when they exit the pit box.

When to Pit; When Not to Pit

A driver's crew chief stays in radio contact with him throughout the race, and tells him exactly when to make a pit stop. Teams always try to make a pit stop under a caution flag, which comes out an average of three or four times during a race during an accident, an oil spill, or debris accumulation on the track. A driver's goal is to make a pit stop and not lose a lap while he's on pit road and the rest of the field is zooming full speed around the track. So, if drivers duck onto pit road under a caution flag — when traffic is slow on the track behind the pace car — most of the time they don't lose a lap. That's because crews can bang out a pit stop and get the driver down pit road and onto the race-track before the rest of the field passes him to put him a lap down.

One of the big questions about making a pit stop is when to pit under green-flag conditions. In some cases, a driver can get himself into all sorts of trouble by pitting under a green flag, because a driver loses valuable laps on the track when he's sitting in the pits and not racing while the other cars are whizzing by. Pitting under a green flag is fine if everyone else pits with you because everyone is losing the same number of laps. But when a caution flag comes out and a driver is in the middle of or has just finished a pit stop, that driver has a big problem. He already lost laps while pitting, but the caution flag gives other drivers the opportunity to pit under caution — meaning they won't lose any laps because the field isn't driving top speed around the track. Instead, they are slowly circling the track behind a pace car, giving people on pit road time to change tires, get gas, and return to the track before they lose a lap.

Teams make it easy for drivers to find their pit box when they're driving down pit road by posting a big metal sign with the team name, logo, or car number above the pit. One of the crew members also holds out a long pole with a big, metal sign attached to it. He waves the sign up and down, so that his driver can see it, even through all the traffic. Sometimes, even with that sign, though, a driver needs help because of all the cars and activity on pit road. That's when a crew chief calls the driver on the radio and coaches him to his pit box, counting the seconds until he arrives at it. He says, "Five, four, three, two, one!" as the driver pulls closer to the pit box, just to give the driver an idea of how close he is.

The backstretch blues

Only two NASCAR Winston Cup Series tracks still have two pit roads — one on the frontstretch and one on the backstretch. Bristol Motor Speedway and Darlington Raceway are the last tracks to have these double pit roads which put teams pitting on the backstretch at a big disadvantage. Those teams are the ones that qualified at the back of the pack, and the ones who lose several positions every time teams make pit stops during a caution period.

Teams pitting on the backstretch can't dive onto pit road when everybody on the frontstretch does under a caution flag. When cars pitting on the frontstretch duck onto pit road, the cars pitting on the backstretch must follow the pace car all the way to the other side of the racetrack before heading down their pit road. It's an agonizing wait, because by the time they get there, the cars on the frontstretch may already be done with their pit stops and are headed back to the racetrack. Cars on the backstretch lose positions on the track, even when they have fast pit stops.

Chapter 11

Keeping Racing Safe

While nose-to-tail racing is fascinating because it's so competitive, it also creates a risk of accidents. Lucky for drivers, though, the cars are built for safety and to protect drivers.

Safety standards in NASCAR racing just didn't pop out of nowhere. They've evolved and improved as the sport has grown. In NASCAR's infancy, the cars weren't equipped as they are now to ensure drivers are able to walk away from a wreck. Back then, racing consisted of regular cars like the ones your parents drove to work, so when they collided, it wasn't pretty. Those cars didn't have the extra safety features they do now — safety features that save lives and protect drivers. I talk about these features in this chapter.

The Basics

NASCAR race cars are made to protect the drivers. Here are some of the most basic safety features on a stock car:

✔ It isn't made with any glass, which would shatter upon impact. That means no headlights, taillights, or side windows.

✔ The front and rear windshields are made of Lexan, a hard, shatterproof plastic.

✔ The doors can't swing open during an accident because there aren't any. That's why drivers squeeze through a window, which is an opening with no glass, to get into the driver's seat.

✔ Tires have an inner liner, so they don't explode when they run over or into something on the racetrack. The inner liner gives the drivers some time to notice that a tire is going flat, perhaps giving them enough time to make a pit stop for new tires.

Rusty's wild ride

While most drivers know firsthand how safe today's cars are, Rusty Wallace has perhaps the best story to tell after surviving one of the most spectacular accidents in NASCAR history. In 1993, he was racing at Talladega Superspeedway in Alabama, when Dale Earnhardt smacked into his back bumper and sent him flying. Literally. His car began spinning and was sliding backwards when air got under his car and lifted the rear end off the ground. That's when the roller-coaster ride began.

Wallace's car flipped about eight or nine times down the frontstretch before coming to a halt in the infield. Not much was left of his car — just the steel frame and a mangled heap of sheet metal and engine parts spewing onto the ground. "I just wanted it to stop," Wallace said. "I was thinking, man, this is going to be real bad."

Surprisingly, though, in a testament to how safe NASCAR stock cars are, Wallace ended up with only minor injuries. Examples like that keep racers from worrying as they climb into their race cars, knowing that drivers come away with only minor injuries.

Superior Seat Belts

Stock cars have added safety features that allow many drivers to walk away from accidents. Seat belts are one of the most obvious additions.

When a driver slides into his car, he doesn't have the luxury of one of those automatic seat belts strapping him in for safety. It's much more complicated that that, but when you're traveling at full speed with 42 other cars on the track, it has to be.

Drivers use *five-point seat belts,* which are five belts that come together at the center of a driver's chest, as shown in Figure 11-1. Each of the belts passes through a steel guide that is welded onto the car's frame. One belt goes over a driver's left shoulder, one goes over his right shoulder, another comes from the left side of the seat, one comes from the right side of the seat, and still another goes between a driver's legs. They're all latched on at a single point, where a quick-release buckle locks them into place. While it takes a little while to gather all the belts and buckle up, a driver can release the seat belts in a fraction of a second when he lifts up on the latch that holds all five belts in place. This is an important feature because drivers may need to exit their cars quickly (see the "Putting out fires" sidebar for information on how drivers handle fires).

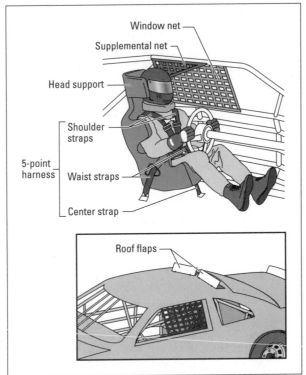

Window net

Supplemental net

Head support

Shoulder
straps

5-point
harness

Waist straps

Center strap

Roof flaps

Figure 11-1:
Stock cars
have safety
features
that protect
drivers.

Racing seat belts don't work the way the ones in a passenger car do. The ones in your regular car activate when the car jolts forward or stops abruptly. The seat belts in a race car are working at all times. Drivers get into their seats, lock their seat belts, and then give the belts an extra tug, making them as snug as possible. In case of an accident, a driver wants to be strapped in tightly because the less he moves around, the less likely he'll be injured.

If you're listening in on a radio scanner during a race, you may hear a crew chief tell his driver to "give one more tug" on his seat belts during a race. Why? No matter how cool it is outside, a driver's seat belts become looser and looser during a race because of the extreme heat inside the car. Drivers can lose as much as five to ten pounds during a race as they perspire, so they need to keep tightening their seat belts — during caution periods, not while going full speed — in order for the seat belts to provide optimum protection.

Putting out fires

In the early years of NASCAR racing, fires were a serious problem for drivers. So, to improve safety, NASCAR officials mandated that all drivers use rubber gas tanks — containers that wouldn't puncture, burst, or explode upon impact. Now fire is rarely a problem in NASCAR racing — cars are built with fire walls between the trunk, where the gas tank is located, and the driver's compartment, as well as between the driver and the engine.

According to NASCAR rules, every car must have a fire extinguisher installed within the driver's reach. NASCAR also recommends that the crewman who fuels the car wears fire-resistant gear — a suit, gloves, shoes, and helmet with face protection. (See Chapter 10 for more on gassing up a car during a pit stop.)

Extra Help with Window Nets

While seat belts keep a driver secured to the seat, they don't keep a driver's head and arms inside a race car when the car tumbles. That's exactly what Richard Petty found out when his car flipped over several times in May 1970 at Darlington Raceway in South Carolina. When his car began to flip, Petty's left arm and head came jutting out the window as the car flew through the air. Petty walked away from the accident with only a dislocated shoulder, but NASCAR officials made sure nobody else would have to endure the same situation by instituting the use of *window nets,* which are screens made of a nylon mesh material that cover the driver's side window (refer to Figure 11-1). They keep the driver's arms and head in the car in an accident.

Window nets are only used on the driver's side of the car. On the passenger side, there usually is a clear, shatterproof plastic window that protects the driver and provides for better aerodynamics — but only at tracks one and a half miles or more in length. This window doesn't roll down because it's just a shield that fits into and is secured in the window opening. On smaller tracks and on road courses, however, cars don't use the passenger-side window — there's just a big opening.

Drivers hook the window nets to the top of the window openings with a latch similar to the one used in their seat belts. It's a quick-release latch that takes only a second to unhook. During a race, drivers unhook the window net after an accident, which signals they aren't hurt badly. In a multi-car accident, that signal helps safety workers determine which driver needs help first.

Helmets and Head Protectors

Helmets are the number one piece of protective gear that drivers can't do without. Drivers don't just go to the local sporting goods store to buy their helmets. They get them from special manufacturers who fit the helmet specifically to a driver's head and put special padding inside the helmet to reduce impact during an accident. After an accident, these manufacturers examine the helmet and X-ray it to see if there are any internal cracks. If there are, the driver must replace the helmet.

In addition to helmets, *head protectors* on a driver's seat keep his head from snapping to the left or right during an accident (refer to Figure 11-1). They are custom-made to prevent neck injuries. Because every seat is customized to fit a driver's body, the head protectors vary, too.

Staying Grounded

Even when cars start spinning, they don't become airborne — despite being so aerodynamic. Cars have roof flaps on them designed to keep them on the ground. *Roof flaps* are rectangular pieces of metal attached to the roof of a car that are designed to lie flat when the car is moving forward, but pop into the air when a car spins backwards or sideways (refer to Figure 11-1). Roof flaps keep a car from lifting into the air.

A Protective Cage

Drivers walk away from accidents because a protective cage surrounds the driver, safeguarding him during impact. That cage is called the *roll cage,* which is protective tubing that keeps the driver from getting crushed if the car flips on its roof or side (see Figure 11-2). It also helps keep a driver safe from impact.

NASCAR officials make sure the *roll bars* that make up the roll cage are thick enough to keep a driver safe. During a routine inspection, they climb inside the car and use special instruments to determine the thickness of the steel. (Most of the roll bars are in plain view inside the car.) They also examine the roll bars to make sure teams haven't drilled holes in them to make the car lighter in those areas. Officials also make sure that roll bars are made of steel and not a lighter, softer, or less-durable metal. (See Chapter 5 for more information about inspections and ways teams get around the rules to gain an advantage.)

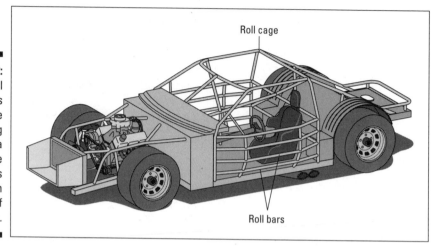

Figure 11-2: The roll cage is protective steel tubing that keeps a driver safe in case his car rolls on its roof or side.

Roll cage

Roll bars

While regular passenger cars have a simple frame, stock cars are much more complex, with protective bars surrounding the driver in almost every area. For example, the driver's side door is reinforced with roll bars installed to protect the driver from a driver's side impact. Another bar travels through the center of a car's windshield, going from the top of the dashboard to the roof of the car. It keeps the roof from collapsing on a driver. All the roll bars within a driver's reach inside the car are wrapped in padding. With protective bars and padding nearly overdone to ensure safety, drivers can survive crashes at full speed, sometimes even without a scrape.

Not Your Ordinary Sunday Outfit

Just like other professional athletes, NASCAR drivers have uniforms. But in racing, those uniforms are much more than just ways to identify who is who outside of the race car. Those uniforms have a special, protective use in case of a fire in the car.

Drivers wear a fire-resistant suit that's similar to a jumpsuit (see Figure 11-3). It covers their legs and their arms and zips up from their waist to their neck. Under those suits, drivers wear fire-retardant long underwear. While these suits make drivers hotter and more uncomfortable inside the car, the benefits are worth it. In the rare instance of a fire, the uniform can be a lifesaver by preventing burns.

In addition to their firesuits, drivers also wear special, space-age gloves and boots that protect their hands and feet from the heat and possible fires inside the car (see Figure 11-3). While the boots are specially-insulated to keep out heat, drivers wear heat shields over their boots because the floorboards and pedals get so hot that it's unbearable without special protection. Sometimes even those heat shields don't provide enough protection. Some of the more creative drivers cut out the bottom of Styrofoam cups and stick them on their heels inside their race car. But other drivers try to tough it out. Dave Marcis, who has driven for more than three decades, still hops in the car with his traditional wing-tip shoes — with no extra protection.

To give you an example of how hot the floorboards can get, Tony Stewart forgot to put on his heat shields for one race in 1999, then ended up with burns and blisters on his heels, which kept him out of commission for more than a week. Also, after one race in 1998, Johnny Benson gave his post-race interviews with his feet stuck inside a bucket of ice water.

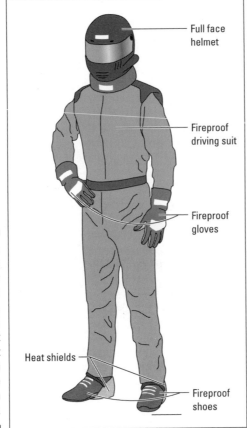

Full face helmet

Fireproof driving suit

Fireproof gloves

Heat shields

Fireproof shoes

Figure 11-3: Drivers wear special jumpsuits, shoes, and gloves that protect them from possible fires in the car.

Chapter 12

Winning It All

*W*inning a NASCAR Winston Cup Series race is every stock-car driver's goal. Most never get there, but those talented enough and lucky enough to win are certainly grateful when they finally reach the pinnacle of the sport. In some cases, that takes years; in other cases, just a few seasons. No matter how long it takes, though, the satisfaction of finally getting to Victory Lane makes the wait worthwhile — this chapter helps you understand how sweet victory tastes.

Going To Victory Lane

Victory Lane isn't really a lane — it's more like a circle or square in a fenced-in area somewhere near pit road — but it's where a driver goes to celebrate after winning a race. After the winner crosses the finish line, he circles the track one more time for a cool-down lap, and then drives down pit road toward Victory Lane. Before getting there, though, some drivers like to add some panache to their win by doing doughnuts — spinning the car in circles — in the infield or on the frontstretch. The car's wheels spin out, burn rubber, and send smoke into the air. What's left behind are a bunch of tire marks and a bunch of screaming fans.

Some drivers even go farther than just doing doughnuts as part of their celebration. The late Alan Kulwicki, who won the NASCAR Winston Cup Series championship in 1992, used to drive the opposite way around the track to celebrate a win. That way, his driver's side window would face the crowd, so the crowd could see him smile and pump his arm — and he could see the crowd cheer. It was Kulwicki's trademark victory lap before he died in a plane crash in April 1993. (See Chapter 16 for more on Kulwicki.)

Whatever unique celebration the driver thinks up, at some point he must start driving toward Victory Lane. On his way there, other crews may wait on pit road to give the winner a high-five, as they did in 1998 when Dale Earnhardt finally won the Daytona 500 on his 20th try. The winner's crew also usually waits just outside of Victory Lane to guide the driver in and greet their hero.

Who's in there?

Victory Lane is packed with all sorts of people. Of course, the winning team and the winning owner are in there, along with the winner's family, TV reporters, photographers, sponsor representatives, NASCAR media representatives, NASCAR officials, track officials, track public relations people, beauty queens, and anyone else who can manage to get in. To say it's a circus is an understatement. Everybody crams into that tiny area to get a glimpse at the winner.

Live network TV (and radio) coverage

Ever notice when you watch a race, you come back from a commercial and see the driver getting out of his car just in time for cameras to catch it on live TV? It's staged to be that way. A driver may drive into Victory Lane and pull his car up to the awaiting crowd, but he can't get out until the network TV crew tells him to. Even if he is about to burst with excitement about the win or is exhausted from the heat of the day, he must sit in the car and wait a few minutes until the commercial break is over. Then, and only then, can the driver dramatically emerge from his car, climb on the roof, and start spraying people with champagne or any other available, sprayable liquid.

After that, the winner has time only to give his crew chief or owner a quick handshake and his wife a quick peck on the cheek before he gets interviewed on live TV. After TV is done, then he gets interviewed on live radio, which most of the time is broadcast throughout the grandstands. After TV and radios interviews are done, the photo session begins.

Photos and the hectic hat dance

A hoard of photographers is positioned somewhere inside Victory Lane to take pictures of the winner, his crew, his family, and his sponsors. But it's not just a quick snap-and-go photo shoot as you may expect. A driver poses with the following people each time he wins:

- ✔ His team
- ✔ His car owner
- ✔ His family
- ✔ His car owner's family
- ✔ Each of his sponsors
- ✔ The event sponsors, such as employees from Coca-Cola at the Coca-Cola 600
- ✔ Representatives from his car manufacturer
- ✔ Beauty queens from various sponsors: In the old days, these beauty queens would give the driver a big smooch for the camera, but now all they give is a smile.

The photo shoot is especially complex because a driver has to do the *hat dance*. He must put on and take off dozens of baseball caps with different sponsor logos on them. Each time the driver puts on a cap, the photographers snap photos to send or sell to the sponsor. Those photos are one of the perks a sponsor gets for being involved with the team and in the sport. While a driver appreciates all the sponsors' involvement, you can bet he is hardly able to smile at the end of the hat dance. Still, he does what he can do to look genuinely happy after posing for his 45th picture!

Where'd everybody go?

The post-win activities run so late that a driver hardly ever gets time to congratulate his crew for the win. By the time the driver is done taking pictures and talking to reporters, most of the time his crew already has loaded up the car and left. That takes some of the fun out of winning because the driver wants to share it with the people on his team who got him to Victory Lane in the first place. When a driver talks to his crew a day later, it's just not the same.

Local TV, newspaper, and magazine reporters

The Victory Lane proceedings may last more than an hour, depending on the race, but even then the driver isn't free to go celebrate with his crew. He must stay put in order for local TV reporters to interview him. After that's done, track public relations representatives whisk the driver away to the press box where he and his crew chief or car owner talk to newspaper and magazine reporters for about a half hour. There's always a question-and-answer session in front of the group, and often another session in which reporters get to ask the driver questions in a small group.

Stopping by the suites

After that's done, the afternoon or night still isn't over. All winners go to suites where employees from big-wig companies await them. The winner goes to the Union 76 Gasoline suite — a tradition because the company has been involved in the sport for such a long time. After he gets there, he answers a few questions, then signs autographs for about 30 people in the suite. Champagne flows freely for everyone there, too, in order to celebrate the victory some more. Winners may also visit other suites, where employees and guests of the various sponsors watch the race and gather to meet and congratulate the driver. At some tracks, the driver also may go to the track owner's suite or a NASCAR suite after winning.

Growing Money

NASCAR racing has become more and more lucrative over the years. Just look at how much today's drivers win each season. In the years that NASCAR legend Richard Petty raced, from 1958 through 1992, he won 200 races, seven NASCAR Winston Cup Series championships, seven Daytona 500s, and $7,755,409 — making him the most successful NASCAR driver in history. That means he averaged about $221,583 per season for 35 years.

Today, even the non-winning drivers average much more than that every year:

- From 1994 to 1998, Ward Burton won one race and averaged $866,820 per season.

- In that same time, Ward's brother, Jeff, won five races and averaged $1,407,774 per season.

✔ In 1997 and 1998, David Green competed in 41 NASCAR Winston Cup Series races — finishing only 30 of them and failing to record any top-ten finishes. Still, he averaged $476,852 each season.

✔ Jeff Gordon tops everyone. From 1993 to 1998, he won 42 races, three NASCAR Winston Cup Series championships, and $26,002,761. That's an average of $4,333,793 per season. In 1998 alone, he won $9,306,584 — more than Richard Petty won in a 35-year career.

When a driver wins a race, NASCAR publishes the amount they've won. That's the number you see in the newspaper the next day. But drivers don't leave the racetrack with all that cash stuffed into their driver's suit. They have to share the winnings. Depending on their contract with their team owner, drivers get about 40 or 50 percent of the money they win.

Winning a race can be very lucrative, but so can just starting a race. For example, Jeff Gordon won $2,194,246 for winning the 1999 Daytona 500 — but John Andretti didn't go home empty-handed after crashing and finishing last. He won a purse of $91,751 just for starting the event. Not all races are as financially rewarding as the Daytona 500, though. A *race purse*, which is the money the track pays to drivers who start the race, varies from race to race and from track to track. Some of the bigger races, such as the Brickyard 400 at Indianapolis Motor Speedway, pay the biggest purses because they have the largest crowds and get the most money from TV networks. Some of the smaller races at the smaller racetracks pay much less.

Contingency awards

A team may also receive money from STP oil filters, for example, which it wins only if it uses that brand of filters and only if the car has the STP decal on the front quarter-panel on the car. This kind of prize money is called a *contingency award* — see Table 12-1 — and not all drivers participate in all the available awards. (See Chapter 2 for more on contingency awards.) For example, I don't get an STP contingency award when I win a race because my sponsor is Valvoline, another motor oil company. I have to use and endorse Valvoline, so I can't advertise for or take money from a competitor.

Table 12-1	Contingency Awards*
Sponsor	*Award*
3M	$700
AE Clevite	$1,200
Aeroquip	$1,300

(continued)

Table 12-1 *(continued)*

Sponsor	Award
Bowman	$900
Competition Cams	$1,400
Edlebrock	$900
Goodyear Belts & Hoses	$1,500
Holley Carburetors	$2,000
Hurst Shifters	$950
MCI "Fast Pace" Award (for posting the fastest lap of the race)	$5,000
Moog	$1,000
Nomex	$2,000
Plasti-Kote	$3,000
Prestone	$2,000
Raybestos	$2,000
Spicer	$1,400
STP Oil Filters	$1,000
True Value "Man of the Race" Award	$2,000
76 Race Gasoline Award	$1,000

*Given by companies whose products a driver uses or whose decals a driver displays on his car.

A breakdown of winnings

Ever wonder where all the prize money comes from when a driver wins a race? Table 12-2 shows a breakdown of the purse that Jeff Gordon won when he earned $1,637,625 at the 1998 Brickyard 400 at Indianapolis Motor Speedway. It was one of the highest payouts in auto racing history.

Table 12-2 **Jeff Gordon's $1.6 Million Purse**

Source	Amount
Race purse and TV money (both from the track)	$270,875

Mark Martin is known as one of the most focused and successful drivers in NASCAR racing.

Drivers look like astronauts when they're inside the car. Their high-tech helmets have maximum padding to absorb shock, reflective shields to minimize glare, and attached tubing to ventilate air.

Fans know exactly where the drivers will be, so they position themselves to get a glimpse of — and maybe even an autograph from — their heroes.

Source	Amount
NASCAR car owners "Winner's Circle" award (The ten most recent winners qualify for this program)	$10,200
NASCAR car owners "Plan 1" award (The top 30 teams from the prior season qualify for this program)	$7,000
Winston Leader Bonus (Awarded to any driver who wins a race and leads the series point standings at the conclusion of that event. The bonus starts out at $10,000, then increases $10,000 for each race it goes unclaimed. Jeff Gordon won $160,000, the record pay-out for this award, when he won the DieHard 500 at Talladega Superspeedway in 1996. Two years later, Gordon won $290,000 of a possible $330,000 after winning the bonus 11 times.)	$10,000
Third place qualifying award	$2,500
Defending NASCAR Winston Cup Series Champion Award (Given to the defending NASCAR Winston Cup Series champion each time he starts a race)	$5,000
PPG "Winner's Trophy" Award (from the track)	$225,000
Lap leader bonus (for leading the most laps)	$10,000
Kodak "Photo Finish" Award (to winner)	$10,000
Herff Jones "Champion of Champions" Award (to winner)	$10,000
Ameritech "Youngest Driver" Award	$5,000
Premier Farnell Corp. Race Team Excellence Award (to winner)	$5,000
Premier Farnell Corp. Mechanical Excellence Award (to winner)	$5,000
Snap-On Tools "Top Five" Award (for drivers finishing in the top 5)	$2,500
"No Bull" 5 $1 Million Bonus (see the "Bonus program" section for more information)	$1,000,000

Bonus program

Each year the series sponsor, Winston, gives drivers (and a lucky fan) a chance at winning a $1 million bonus through the Winston "No Bull 5" program. Drivers become eligible for the program by finishing in the top five at one of five "No Bull 5" races. If one of those drivers wins the next race in the program, they win the $1 million bonus. And, because the five drivers who are eligible to win are matched with five different fans, a fan could win $1 million, too! The five "No Bull 5" lineup varies somewhat from year to year, but always includes the Daytona 500, which is the first race of the season.

The Winston Million

The "No Bull 5" program hasn't been around forever — it replaced the Winston Million, which was Winston's first incentive program offering a million-dollar paycheck.

The Winston Million program, which began in 1985 and ended in 1997, offered $1 million to the driver who could win three of NASCAR's crown jewel races. Those premier races were the Daytona 500 at Daytona International Speedway, the Coca-Cola 600 at Lowe's Motor Speedway, the Winston 500 at Talladega Superspeedway, and the Southern 500 at Darlington Raceway.

Bill Elliott didn't waste any time when it came to the Winston Million. In the first year of its existence in 1985, Elliott won the Daytona 500, the Winston 500, and the Southern 500 to pocket the million-dollar prize. The feat landed him on the cover of *Sports Illustrated* magazine. Even though Elliott won the million in the program's first year, it took a dozen more years for another driver to win the Winston Million. Jeff Gordon did it in 1997 when he was on his way to his second NASCAR Winston Cup Series championship.

Going for the "No Bull 5" million-dollar bonus can be stressful on a driver and a team throughout race weekend. Print reporters want to interview you about your million-dollar effort. TV reporters want to talk to you on-camera about your chances. Your team walks around with "No Bull 5" T-shirts and hats, just to remind everyone you're in the running for a million bucks. Even the number on top of your car is different. That number is highlighted with a Day-Glo red, so fans in the stands can see which cars are in the "No Bull 5" program.

After the race starts, though, the hype is over. Every driver in the program races just as he always does — at least in the beginning of the event. The closer the finish line gets, the more exciting it gets, especially if one or more "No Bull 5" drivers are in contention for the win. If a driver going for the million is battling with another driver at the end, you can bet he's going to make some daring moves to get across that finish line first and collect the hefty jackpot.

The Points System

After every event, points are given to drivers and their car owners, depending on where they finish in a race. The system used today was put into place in 1975, so that drivers and teams could vie for a series championship.

The formula for doling out points was designed to reward teams and drivers who support the series by racing in it on a consistent basis. The winner of a race gets 175 points, and the next five drivers each get five fewer points (second gets 170 points, third gets 165 points, and so on).

From positions six through 11, the points decrease by four each position. Sixth gets 150 points, seventh gets 146, and so on. From 11th to 43rd, the points decrease by three each position. That gives the last-place finisher (the 43rd-place driver and team) 34 points. So, you can see how somebody can lose a lot of ground in the championship if he blows an engine and finishes last.

Here is a breakdown of each finishing position and how many points the driver and car owner earn for that race:

- First place — 175 points
- Second place — 170 points
- Third place — 165 points
- Fourth place — 160 points
- Fifth place — 155 points
- Sixth place — 150 points
- Seventh place — 146 points
- Eighth place — 142 points
- Ninth place — 138 points
- Tenth place — 134 points
- 11th place — 130 points
- 12th place — 127 points
- 13th place — 124 points
- 14th place — 121 points
- 15th place — 118 points
- 16th place — 115 points
- 17th place — 112 points
- 18th place — 109 points
- 19th place — 106 points
- 20th place — 103 points
- 21st place — 100 points
- 22nd place — 97 points
- 23rd place — 94 points
- 24th place — 91 points
- 25th place — 88 points
- 26th place — 85 points

- 27th place — 82 points
- 28th place — 79 points
- 29th place — 76 points
- 30th place — 73 points
- 31st place — 70 points
- 32nd place — 67 points
- 33rd place — 64 points
- 34th place — 61 points
- 35th place — 58 points
- 36th place — 55 points
- 37th place — 52 points
- 38th place — 49 points
- 39th place — 46 points
- 40th place — 43 points
- 41st place — 40 points
- 42nd place — 37 points
- 43rd place — 34 points

Bonus points

In addition to the regular points that drivers and teams get for competing in a race, they also can earn bonus points in a couple of different ways:

- **Any driver who leads a lap gets five extra points.** That means he must be in front of the field when crossing the start/finish line. So, a race winner gets a minimum of 180 points for winning a race because, at the very least, he led the final lap. Sometimes, a driver stays out when the rest of the field makes a pit stop just so he can lead one lap and pick up those five extra points. This happens when the driver is scrounging for points, sometimes because he is in the chase for the championship — and sometimes because he is fighting to get in the top 25 in the standings so he can get unlimited provisionals.

- **The driver who leads the most laps gets five bonus points.** A race winner potentially can earn 185 points for winning — 175 for the win, five for leading a lap, and five more for leading the most laps. Sometimes, though, it doesn't work that way, and a race winner leads only one lap — the last one.

Earning points

You may have seen drivers with the flu, broken bones, or other maladies slide into their cars on race day, just to complete one lap. They don't do that because they love pain, but because a driver needs to complete one lap of a race in order to earn points. NASCAR awards points to the driver who starts the race. So a driver gets himself into his car for at least a lap in order to get those points. Then, after that lap (or after he can't take the pain anymore), he pulls onto pit road where a relief driver replaces him.

The *relief driver* may be a driver who had mechanical problems with his car and retired from the race early. Or, it could be a NASCAR Busch Series driver who just happens to be at the race that day. Regardless of the relief driver's experience, he's someone who gets in the car because the primary driver isn't healthy enough to finish racing 500 miles. He may hop in the car for free or may charge a one-day fee for his services, depending on how well the driver and team owner know the relief driver and whether that relief driver is willing to do the team a favor. Whatever it costs, though, the injured driver or the team owner is happy to pay. If that relief driver finishes well, the injured driver ends up with the championship points because he started the race. And the car owner accumulated those points, too, no matter who drives his car.

Car owner points are different than driver points. A driver accrues points (called *driver points*) for the races he competes in, whatever car he drives. But a car owner accrues points — called *car owner points* — whenever his car is in a race, no matter who's driving it. This ensures that teams reap benefits from running in a race and investing in the sport. Driver points accumulate toward the championship, while owner points accumulate to help teams obtain provisional qualifying entries (see Chapter 8).

Winning the Championship

To win the championship, a driver has to collect more points than any other driver during that season. The point system, described in "The Points System" section, later in this chapter, doles out points to every driver who starts a race, with the winner getting the most points and the last-place car getting the fewest points. Throughout the season, every driver, crew member, and owner dreams about those points — and collecting a gazillion of them so they can win the NASCAR Winston Cup Series championship — stock-car racing's version of winning the World Series, the Stanley Cup, or an Olympic gold medal.

The following are some of the many perks that accompany winning the NASCAR Winston Cup Series title:

✔ **Money:** The champion takes home more money from the point fund than anyone else. The point fund contains money contributed by Winston, the series sponsor, to the drivers that finish in the top 25 each year. In 1998, for example, Jeff Gordon received a $2,000,000 check for winning the championship. The second-place driver, who just happened to be me, received $630,000. While that's still a lot of money, it isn't even half of what Gordon won. In addition, drivers and teams get all sorts of other monetary awards for winning the title, including cash from sponsors.

✔ **Media exposure:** After winning the NASCAR Winston Cup Series championship, the driver goes on a whirlwind media tour. Reporters from newspapers and magazines interview him, and their photographers snap hundreds of photos of him. He gets to be on national television programs such as *Late Night with David Letterman* and *Live! With Regis & Kathie Lee*. It's a thrill from the moment he wins until the end of the next season when his reign ends (unless he wins the title again). Of course, the driver's sponsors are ecstatic about the media blitz, because that gives them even more exposure than usual.

✔ **Prestige:** Winning the championship means that you're the best stock-car driver on the best team that year. And no matter how your career unfolds after you win NASCAR's top honor, you'll always be known as a former champion. Fans and other drivers never forget it — and the record books don't erase it.

✔ **Respect:** When you win a championship, other drivers and teams look at you differently. It doesn't matter whether they like you as a person, they still have to respect you for your accomplishment. They know how good a team must be *throughout* the season — not just *part* of a season — to win the title. Drivers can't just win ten races and expect to win the championship. They have to record good finishes week after week, and finish every race — or nearly every race. For example, if a driver wins half the races in a year, but gets into accidents and fails to finish the other half — which are called *DNFs* because a driver *did not finish* those races — he isn't going to win the championship. To win the title, a driver must be consistent — Terry Labonte is a perfect example of that. He only won two races when he won the 1984 championship, and then only two when he won it again in 1996, proving race wins don't win championships. Consistency does.

✔ **A great parking spot:** The reigning champion always gets to park his team hauler in the No. 1 spot and also uses the best garage stall at each track for the entire year. The rest of the teams line up their haulers and use garage stalls according to where they rank in the points championship.

The race for the championship is hectic, nerve-wracking business. In 1997, the championship came down to the very last race of the season, the NAPA 500 at Atlanta Motor Speedway. Before the race began, nobody knew who would be the champion — Jeff Gordon, Dale Jarrett, or me. Gordon had to finish 18th or better to win the title, otherwise Dale or I would have had a chance. As it turned out — unfortunately for me — Gordon finished 17th in the race and won his second title. Jarrett finished second in the championship, just 14 points behind Gordon. I finished third in the championship, just 29 points out of first. It was the closest three-way battle in NASCAR Winston Cup Series history.

A driver doesn't always clinch the championship at the final race of the season, though. Sometimes, if his lead is big enough, he clinches the title with two or three races to go. That means he gained enough points that the driver in second has no mathematical chance at catching him. The first-place driver could finish last in the remaining races — and sometimes not even start those races — and he still would walk away the champion.

New York, New York

Of all the perks a driver gets for winning the NASCAR Winston Cup Series championship, the end-of-the-year banquet may be the most fun. Each year, during the first weekend in December, NASCAR holds an award banquet at the luxurious Waldorf-Astoria hotel in New York City. That's where NASCAR pays tribute to the champion and his team. It's also where Winston doles out the checks from the points fund.

In the days preceding the banquet, the champion is carted around the city in a limousine. He goes to photo shoots, newspaper interviews, and live TV shows. And he gets to stay in the nicest, most glamorous, suite in the Waldorf, which costs upwards of $7,000 per night.

After the driver finishes his media tour of New York City, he settles down, dresses up, then heads for the banquet. It's a black-tie function where everybody gets spiffed up and celebrates the end of the season. It's where drivers and crew members wear tuxedos instead of their driving suits or uniforms, and where wives and girlfriends get dolled up in fancy gowns. It's also where drivers who finish in the top ten in points get to give a speech in front of the crowd packed into the Grand Ballroom. That's one reason why there's a big difference between finishing tenth and 11th in points. Giving a speech at the banquet is prestigious, and drivers battle to finish in the top ten not only because it means they've had a good season, but also to get a chance to walk onto that stage at the Waldorf.

Rookie of the Year Award

The Rookie of the Year Award is one of the awards given out at the NASCAR Winston Cup Series banquet. All the drivers running their first full season on the circuit are eligible, unless they've run more than five races in the series during another year. Some of the best drivers in NASCAR history are former Rookies of the Year, including former NASCAR Winston Cup Series champions Dale Earnhardt, Jeff Gordon, and Rusty Wallace.

NASCAR awards rookie of the year honors to the first-year driver whose best 15 finishes are higher than any other first-year driver in a complex scoring system that gives one point to every rookie who makes a race, ten points to the highest finishing rookie, and nine points to the next highest finishing rookie, and so on. Top ten finishes are awarded extra points.

Rookies get bonus points three times a season, which NASCAR awards after the tenth race, 20th race, and the season's last race. The highest rookie at those times gets ten bonus points, the next highest one gets nine bonus points, and so on.

NASCAR also doles out discretionary points at the end of the year that are based on how a driver conducts himself with the fans, the media, and his fellow competitors. This way, NASCAR officials have the final word on which rookie wins the award.

Part IV
Keeping Up with NASCAR Events

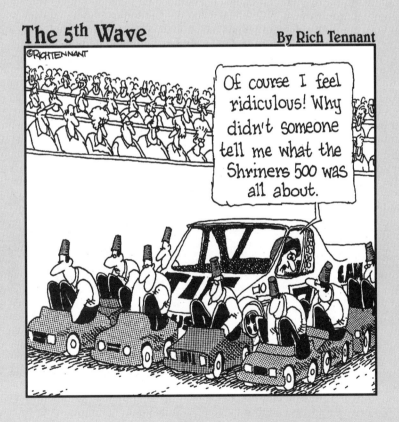

The 5th Wave   By Rich Tennant

Of course I feel ridiculous! Why didn't someone tell me what the Shriners 500 was all about.

In this part . . .

This part is completely dedicated to budding NASCAR fans — and even some of the fans who have been around a while and want to be on the cutting edge of fandom. Whether you're a NASCAR novice or a NASCAR expert, you'll find this part handy because it tells you all about each of the tracks that host NASCAR Winston Cup Series races, which are the top races in NASCAR. The rest of this part tells you the do's and don'ts for NASCAR fans: what to wear, what not to wear; what to bring, what not to bring; which driver to root for (me), which driver not to root for (anyone but me)! You can also find listings of NASCAR TV shows, radio programs, and Web sites, so that you can explore and discover the sport from the comforts of your own home.

Chapter 13

Understanding NASCAR Tracks

● ●

In This Chapter

▶ Understanding the characteristics of tracks — from superspeedways to road courses

▶ Discovering the allure of night races

▶ Meeting the track owners

▶ Taking a look at each NASCAR Winston Cup Series track

● ●

*N*ASCAR drivers are sometimes depicted as people who get into cars, go fast, and turn left — doing the same thing week after week without any variance or scenery changes. That, thank goodness, couldn't be farther from the truth.

Racing is always different, even though drivers do go fast and turn left most of the time. It's hard to tell from the grandstands, but each track has its own characteristics that make it challenging. One track may be *high-banked* — which means the racing surface is steeply-sloped — while another track may be flat. One may have a smooth surface, while another has plenty of bumps. One may have a wide *straightaway*, which is the long section of track between the turns, while another may have a narrow straightaway.

NASCAR drivers must adapt because each weekend the tracks are different in many ways. Not only does each track feel different to drive on, but each looks different, too. You can find superspeedways (the longest of all NASCAR tracks), intermediate tracks, short tracks, and road courses. All have different sizes and shapes — and if a driver wants to be successful, he must be able to negotiate every track with skill. A driver who is masterful on superspeedways but slow on short tracks won't make it to Victory Lane. Drivers must be versatile and able to quickly adapt to different tracks each week.

NASCAR's wide range of racetracks does more than pose a challenge for the drivers — it also gives fans variety. If watching the bump-and-pass moves on a short track doesn't thrill you, perhaps you're drawn to the high speeds and danger of a superspeedway. Or maybe you find watching a racer's agility on a road course more thrilling. Whatever your taste, the NASCAR Winston Cup

Series, NASCAR's top level, has a track for you. Each track also has a seat for you, too. Many racetracks seat more than 100,000 fans, not including the infield, which is filled with fans perched atop motorhomes and cars to get a glimpse of the action.

Superspeedways Are Super-Fast

If you're looking for high-speed thrills, you'll love superspeedways. Drivers race at close to 200 mph down the straightaways while just inches apart, and long conga lines of cars zoom past the start/finish line in a blur of color.

In NASCAR Winston Cup Series racing, only two tracks are considered superspeedways. While the technical definition of a superspeedway is any track one mile or more in length, that has changed now that NASCAR has introduced bigger, faster, and higher-banked tracks into its series. Right now, drivers and crew members consider only two tracks in NASCAR as superspeedways: Daytona International Speedway and Talladega Superspeedway. They fall into that category because of their size (2½ miles or more), because they're high-banked (at least 31 degrees), and because they require use of carburetor restrictor plates.

A *carburetor restrictor plate* is a metal plate with four holes drilled into it that NASCAR officials place atop an engine's carburetor, lining up the plate's four holes with the four holes at the bottom of the carburetor. The holes in the plate restrict the amount of fuel and air that flows through the carburetor and into the intake manifold, on its way to the combustion chamber. The fuel and air mixture must squeeze through the four small holes before flowing more quickly through the four larger holes in the carburetor.

In short, the plate chokes the flow of air into the engine, which reduces its horsepower. So, instead of cars roaring around the monster tracks with about 750 horsepower, they have about 450. And less horsepower means less speed (see Chapter 3 for more on horsepower). They're used at the two following tracks:

✔ Daytona International Speedway, a 2.5-mile tri-oval located in NASCAR's hometown of Daytona Beach, Florida. A *tri-oval* is a modified oval racetrack with an extra turn to it (albeit a slight turn) instead of just four turns. Usually that turn is located mid-way down the frontstretch, which is the section of a racetrack between the last turn and the first turn. The start/finish line is located on the frontstretch.

✔ Talladega Superspeedway, a 2.66-mile tri-oval located in Talladega, Alabama.

In the past, cars used to average speeds of more than 210 miles per hour circling these tracks, but in 1988, NASCAR officials decided to slow the cars down to make races safer. They did so by requiring that all cars use carburetor restrictor plates in their engines.

Restrictor-plate racing

While fans may be safer because of restrictor plates, drivers certainly don't feel the same way when the NASCAR Winston Cup Series circuit heads to superspeedways, which is four times each year — two times at each superspeedway.

Drivers feel a little queasy when showing up at Daytona and Talladega because the restrictor plates put them in a compromising position. While the plates keep speeds down and fans safe, they also cause the cars to run in packs, with each car dangerously close to several others. Drivers use a racing technique called *drafting* to go faster around the racetrack, which requires cars to race nose to tail in order for them to cut through the air faster. (Flip to Chapter 9 to get the lowdown on drafting.) Cars also race in packs because the restrictor plates choke an engine to the point where throttle response is slow and sluggish. So, instead of cars being able to accelerate away from each other, they drive around the track in packs. And that leaves drivers feeling less in control of their cars.

Unlike other tracks, where drivers decide when to accelerate and when to brake, at superspeedways those decisions are easy: they always have their foot to the floor and rarely brake (unless they see an accident). In racing, that is called *running wide open* because the accelerator is wide open the entire time. Drivers can do this at superspeedways because the engines are choked down so much. If the engine didn't have a restrictor plate, the car would be running well over 200 miles an hour even through the corners — and it would be nearly out of control. But with the plates, the drivers are much gutsier because they feel as if they're going as fast as a riding lawnmower.

Even though the restrictor plates cause cars to bunch in packs, many times you see a group of cars breaking away from the main pack to form a lead pack. But even then, that may mean a dozen cars are running bumper-to-bumper at breakneck speeds. If one driver makes even the slightest mistake going 200 miles an hour with a train of ten cars behind him, he may inadvertently cause an 11-car pileup in no time.

At those speeds, drivers sometimes are able to react quickly to avoid an accident just ahead of them. Sometimes they miss a wreck by just a few feet. But most of the time, unfortunately, drivers can do nothing if a car just inches ahead of them blows a tire and veers wildly to one side.

The thrill of superspeedways

I'm one of the few drivers in the NASCAR Winston Cup Series garage who knows how it feels to drive a car on a superspeedway without a restricted engine. That's a feeling a driver never forgets. I drove in an Automobile Racing Club of America (ARCA) race in 1981 at Talladega and averaged more than 200 mph per lap. We didn't race in packs back then because we didn't use carburetor restrictor plates and drivers had control over whether they were going to run wide open or not. A driver could go so fast that he needed to brake in certain situations (or else, he crashed) — so a driver and his skill were integral in performing well in the event.

At that time, no one dared run an inch off someone else's bumper because it was frightening. The cars ran fast and drivers knew they were going fast. Now, though, it's like driving down the highway going 40 mph. Drivers aren't afraid of driving an inch behind the car ahead of them because they don't feel as if they're going fast at all. Drivers feel totally in control. But in a NASCAR Winston Cup Series car, that feeling is deceiving. While we are driving slower, we're still going pretty darn fast. And if a driver crashes, it still hurts pretty darn bad.

Aerodynamics: Feel the wind in your hair

Race teams spend many long days, even longer than their usual long days, working on their cars before arriving at superspeedways. That's because *aerodynamics,* or the airflow over the surfaces of a car, is crucial at those big, high-speed tracks. The long straightaways and wide, sweeping turns provide a perfect arena for cars to go their fastest — even though carburetor restrictor plates limit their speeds. Even with restricted engines, the cars still exceed more than 200 mph on the straightaways. That means they're cutting through the air pretty fast.

Why is aerodynamics so important at superspeedways? At those tracks, a driver never takes his foot off the gas pedal, so one of the only ways to get an advantage over the competition is to have a car that slips through the air with a minimum of resistance. A sleeker car means a faster car. That's why race teams are forever banging on, pulling at, and reworking the bodies of their cars in preparation for a superspeedway race.

Preparing for races on superspeedways is different than preparing for races on any other type of racetrack because of how flawless a car's body must be in order for it to go fast. While a winning car at a short track may have a banged up side or a crumpled bumper, even the tiniest imperfections on a car costs precious speed on superspeedways — and can cost a win, too.

A physics lesson

Aerodynamics and superspeedways go hand in hand. In fact, you can see a good example of the effect of aerodynamics when you stick your hand out of a car window. When you cup your hand, you feel resistance from the air and you have trouble keeping your hand still. But when you keep your hand flat like a knife or a wing, the air flows over your hand more easily and much of that pressure from the air is gone. That's the same way that race cars work. The shape of the car is critical when designing for improved aerodynamics. Teams want to make their car as sleek as possible, so that it slips through the air.

Wind tunnels: Laboratories for race cars

In preparation for a superspeedway race, such as the Daytona 500 that kicks off the NASCAR Winston Cup Series season each February, teams take their cars to the wind tunnel to figure out how well air is flowing over their car. A *wind tunnel* is just what it sounds like: a tunnel that shoots wind at a car from all different angles. It's like taking their car to a laboratory and conducting highly-detailed tests in an enclosed, monitored area. Just like other kinds of scientific testing, it's a slow and tedious process to get all the data from the wind tunnel, but the information is invaluable. Teams may make one change to the body of the car, and then go to the wind tunnel and compare the results to the last time they went to the tunnel. If the results are worse, then they know the change wasn't a good one and that they must go back a step and rethink their methods. During one day at a wind tunnel, a team may change the car 20 times before coming up with an aerodynamic shape that works for them.

The trip to the wind tunnel never is a cozy one, and only a few team members go along to conduct the tests. It's a big deal that involves engineers from the manufacturer, wind tunnel engineers, and team owners. In fact, from time to time, NASCAR officials impound several NASCAR Winston Cup Series cars after a race and take them to the wind tunnel themselves. They'll make sure to bring at least one car from each manufacturer — which means at least one Chevy, one Ford, and one Pontiac. These NASCAR tests are different than the private tests teams conduct in the wind tunnel. In private tests, the teams and the manufacturer are the only ones to see the data — and they pay for that right, too. Wind tunnel time is very expensive, costing about $16,000 for an eight-hour test.

In the group tests, though, NASCAR foots the bill and shares the data with all three manufacturers, just to give them information on whether they're ahead or behind in the area of aerodynamics. It also helps NASCAR keep the three cars in the same ballpark so they can maintain parity among the cars. If one car has great aerodynamics and another one doesn't, the sleeker car would win technically all the superspeedway races — and that wouldn't excite fans very much.

The following are some of the measurements taken at a wind tunnel:

✔ **Drag:** When a car moves through the air, the air causes different kinds of pressure on the surfaces of the vehicle. Drag is one of them. Drag also is something race teams can't stand because it slows the car down tremendously. Basically, drag is a major drag.

Drag is caused by several things, including a high amount of air pressure pushing on the front of the car and low air pressure pulling on the back of the car. Both of these things make moving forward more difficult for the car, so if a car has a lot of drag, it's not as fast in comparison to cars with less drag. Other things cause drag, such as air flowing through the cooling system, ducts in the body, and open windows. Air travels into these openings instead of smoothly sliding over the car. Also, friction between a car's body and the air flowing over it causes drag.

With less drag, a car can accelerate faster, especially at higher speeds, because you need less horsepower to move the car forward through the air.

✔ **Downforce:** While drag is bad, one type of air pressure is actually good for a race car — and that's downforce. *Downforce* is the air pressure that pushes a car onto the track, causing it to stick on the track even at high speeds. It provides better traction and keeps cars from losing traction at high speeds, especially going through the turns. When the air pressure on the top of the body is greater than the air pressure on the bottom of the body, you have downforce.

Even if a car isn't engineered to have a lot of downforce, NASCAR has implemented a few rules to provide for it. These rules allow cars to have front air dams and rear spoilers, which help create downforce and are defined as follows:

• A *front air dam* is a special extension that goes from the bottom of the front bumper and extends nearly to the ground. (See Chapter 4 for an illustration and further explanation.) Most of the time, passenger cars don't have them, but race cars do in order to control the amount of air flowing under the car and the amount of air pressure pushing the front end to the ground. The air dam reduces drag because air has less space to flow beneath the car; instead, the air slides over the car. The air dam also increases downforce because more air is flowing over the car, so more air is pushing down on the car, giving it more traction.

- A *rear spoiler* is a blade that is perched at the back of a car's trunk lid. (Turn to Chapter 4 to for an illustration and more explanation.) Its main purpose is to create downforce on the back end of the car. When air flows over a car and along the sides of a car, it hits the rear spoiler and gathers in front of it, increasing the pressure on the top of the body. At a superspeedway, the spoiler angle must be 45 degrees, but at other tracks, each team determines the spoiler angle (from 60 to 70 degrees) so their car reaches its optimum speed. (That spoiler angle is one of the elements that teams test for when spending time at a wind tunnel test. They move the spoiler up and down, searching for the best combination of drag and downforce at a specific kind of track. The trick is finding a way to increase downforce while minimizing the resulting increase in drag.)

Testing at the racetrack

With all of the pressures and forces affecting the way a car drives, NASCAR drivers and teams have to know a lot about physics. They use that knowledge during wind tunnel tests and also at track tests where teams test different body shapes and spoiler heights in order to find a car's maximum speed and best aerodynamic setup. At superspeedways, though, the tests are the most nerve-wracking because they know how crucial a role aerodynamics plays there. Teams gather information such as lap times, corner speeds, and suspension settings to figure out how to make their cars faster. While the body has to be nearly perfect for the car to cut through the air efficiently, the suspension package must be nearly perfect, too, so that the car can hug the ground as much as possible.

MARK SAYS

Rule changes make things equal

The heights of the spoiler and air dam don't stay the same throughout the year, necessarily. NASCAR officials constantly monitor if one car make has more downforce than another or if it has an aerodynamic advantage over another make. For instance, in 1998, NASCAR officials decided the new Ford Taurus had too much downforce because it was performing better on intermediate tracks than other cars — it could go faster on those tracks because it was sticking to the racing surface better, which allowed Taurus drivers to race through corners without slowing down much, while other drivers had to slow down in order to stay in control of their vehicle. Because NASCAR is forever searching to keep the three car makes as equal as possible (see Chapter 1), it changed the rules and required a smaller spoiler on every Taurus. The smaller spoiler gives the car less downforce and less drag, which makes the car less stable on the track, harder to drive, and slower, too.

Short Tracks

While cars must be nearly impeccable to win a superspeedway race, the opposite applies to short track races. They can, and they have, limped into Victory Lane battered and banged up but still victorious.

Short tracks are racetracks shorter than one mile in length, where aerodynamics and horsepower aren't particularly important in winning the race. That's because the track is so short, there's not much room to accelerate and get into open air, so sometimes, drivers are on the brake almost as much as they're on the gas. Also, with little room for cars to move around, short-track races are filled with bumping and banging because of the small size of the racetrack. Many times, you see the winning race car roll into Victory Lane with a bunch of dents, scratches, and tire marks on it. Even though the car may look pretty sad, it was still strong enough to survive a short-track race — and surviving is the key to winning.

The following speedways are the short tracks on the NASCAR Winston Cup Series circuit. They are the places where cars are bound to get a beating before the race is over:

- Bristol Motor Speedway, a high-banked, .533-mile oval located in Bristol, Tennessee

- Martinsville Speedway, a nearly-flat, .526-mile oval located in Martinsville, Virginia

- Richmond International Raceway, a ¾-mile, D-shaped track located in Richmond, Virginia

Short tracks create short tempers

The shorter the track, the less room the cars have to maneuver. And less room invites more contact among cars. So at short tracks, the etiquette changes a bit. Instead of passing someone on the outside or inside, some drivers opt for the bump-and-pass move. They nudge the car ahead of them out of the way by bumping its rear bumper so it moves up the track. Sometimes, though, that technique can go a little too far. For example, Dale Earnhardt rammed into the back of Terry Labonte in the August 1999 night race at Bristol on the last lap of the race. Instead of just nudging Labonte up the track to create a passing lane, Earnhardt spun Labonte out and sent him careening into the inside wall. That gave Earnhardt the opportunity to run off with the win.

NASCAR officials saw the whole thing but opted not to penalize Earnhardt because they reviewed the tape and deemed it inconclusive. Sometimes, spinning someone out is reckless driving and sometimes it's "just racing."

Where stock-car drivers start out

Most NASCAR drivers started their careers driving on short tracks in the nation's smaller stock-car series, so short tracks are places many of us can call home. People just don't grow up learning how to drive on a 2.5-mile paved superspeedway or a high-banked intermediate track. There aren't many around — and that's probably a good thing because a driver needs to have certain skills before he or she drives on those tracks, anyway.

So, beginning racers learn how to drive on small dirt tracks, where they hone their skills and improve their reaction times, and then move up to bigger tracks through the years. Still, that doesn't mean that short tracks are easier to drive — in fact, in many cases, they're more difficult. Just because a driver has a good, fast car doesn't necessarily mean he'll be in Victory Lane at the end of the race. Short tracks require keen driving skills to pass or to stay in front, so they're a great place to learn the basics.

Sometimes cars get penalized and sometimes they don't. That's the nature of short-track racing. It's high-contact, high-temper, and high-action crammed into one tiny track. What makes it all possible is that nothing in the rule book says exactly what's against the rules.

If you have infield passes for Bristol or Martinsville, don't expect to saunter in during mid-morning practice. Those tracks don't have tunnels to let pedestrians and vehicular traffic into the infield while cars are on the track, so you have to wait until practice is over for the gates to open. At Dover Downs International Speedway, an intermediate track, there's no tunnel, either, but the track does have an overpass that people can use to get to and from the infield.

Short tracks mean big headaches

While short track racing is a lot of fun, there's a big drawback. There are many accidents because there's not much room to move around and all the cars are bunched up together. If one car spins out or loses control, cars behind it can end up getting collected by the wreck because they have no where else to go. Accidents happen really quickly at short tracks because the speeds are so fast and the tracks are so small. At Bristol, for example, a car can circle the track in about 15 seconds. So, when an accident happens, the cars behind the wreck can become a part of it in a fraction of a second.

Qualifying is particularly important at short tracks because it's difficult to pass on tracks so small. So, even if a driver qualifies a decent 15th, he may be stuck there if he can't find a way around the cars ahead of him. Most race winners at these tracks come from the top-ten qualifiers. Most drivers who don't qualify in the top ten are cranky.

Short tracks are NASCAR's roots

Short tracks are special places in NASCAR history because racing started there and many racers started their careers there. Way before NASCAR formed in 1948, short tracks ruled the racing world. There was no such thing as superspeedways or even 1½-mile tracks. (In fact, I don't even think asphalt was that popular back then.) Those bigger tracks were too expensive to build, so track owners went with the plain and simple dirt track to get by — and those were the only tracks around. Sure, people always raced on the hard-packed sands of Daytona Beach, but in most parts of the nation, short tracks were all that racers had. Drivers either raced on a short track or they didn't race at all. That's how short tracks became so popular and how they provided a strong foundation for stock-car racing in America.

Intermediate Tracks Are Middle-of-the-Road

Not all racetracks in NASCAR Winston Cup Series racing are superspeedways or short tracks. There are plenty of tracks that fall into a category between those two extremes, combining a diluted version of a superspeedway's high speeds with the rubbing-and-bumping kind of racing found on a short track. Those combination tracks are called *intermediate tracks*, which are oval tracks at least one mile but less than two miles long. (Keep in mind that NASCAR technically considers tracks one mile or more in length as superspeedways, but that technical definition isn't what drivers and teams go by.)

The following are the intermediate tracks on the NASCAR Winston Cup Series circuit:

- Atlanta Motor Speedway, a 1.54-mile oval located in Hampton, Georgia, just outside of Atlanta.
- California Speedway, a 2-mile oval located in Fontana, California, near Los Angeles.
- Darlington Raceway, a 1.366-mile, egg-shaped oval located in Darlington, South Carolina.
- Dover Downs International Speedway, a 1-mile oval located in Dover, Delaware.

✔ Homestead Miami Speedway, a 1.5-mile oval located in Homestead, Florida, near Miami.

✔ Indianapolis Motor Speedway, a 2.5-mile oval located in Indianapolis, Indiana.

✔ Las Vegas Motor Speedway, a 1.5-mile oval located in Las Vegas.

✔ Lowe's Motor Speedway (formerly Charlotte Motor Speedway), a 1.5-mile oval located in Concord, North Carolina, just north of Charlotte.

✔ New Hampshire International Speedway, a 1.058-mile oval located in Loudon, New Hampshire.

✔ Michigan Speedway, a 2-mile oval located in Brooklyn, Michigan, just outside of Detroit.

✔ North Carolina Speedway, a 1.017-mile oval located in Rockingham, North Carolina.

✔ Phoenix International Raceway, a 1-mile oval located in Phoenix, Arizona.

✔ Pocono Raceway, a 2.5-mile triangular track located in Long Pond, Pennsylvania.

✔ Texas Motor Speedway, a 1.5-mile oval located in Fort Worth, Texas.

Even though NASCAR's intermediate tracks are all comparable in size, that doesn't mean they host the same kind of races and are the same to drive on. Each racetrack has its own characteristics, such as high *banking* (when the racing surface is at an angle), bumpy racing surfaces or difficult-to-negotiate turns. That's what makes each intermediate track unique. And that's what makes it challenging for drivers and interesting for fans.

The Dreaded Road Courses

It's not an exaggeration to say most NASCAR Winston Cup Series drivers would rather call in sick than drive on a road course. It's just not what they're used to. *Road courses* aren't simply-shaped, the way ovals are, with four turns and two straightaways. They're complex configurations of left and right turns at all sorts of angles. While some may be sweeping, gradual turns, others may be *hairpin turns* — which are drastic, sharply-angled turns that prompt drivers to slow down to a crawl. (These turns are shaped like a hairpin where drivers go into the turn traveling one way and exit the turn going the opposite way. Those difficult-to-negotiate turns are just one of the many tricky parts of road racing.) The whole point of it is that there's no consistency to the course — sometimes drivers feel as though they're driving through a great, big, hilly field; other times, they think they're racing through a maze.

Road course skills

Racing on road courses is a specialized skill for NASCAR drivers because they are so used to racing on circular tracks like the ones they raced on as beginning drivers. So it's understandable to see stock-car drivers freak out a bit when they show up at a track without four turns and two straightaways. A road course's long straightaways, short straightaways, wide turns, sharp turns, dips, and slopes make stock-car drivers uneasy, especially because drivers have to turn left *and* right during the race. It's just not what drivers were trained to do. For me, though, driving on a road course comes more easily than for most stock-car drivers. In fact, it's almost second nature.

I learned how to drive a car — not a go-kart, but a real car — when I was just 14. I drove my car as fast as it would go, not only on paved road, but also on the hilly, curvy dirt roads of Arkansas. That's where I fine-tuned my driving skills, such as how to control a car going through turns and how not to run into ditches (which was important because there were plenty of ditches around to run into).Those lessons have helped me through the years on all tracks, but particularly on road courses. I won three consecutive races at Watkins Glen International from 1993 to 1995, so I can't complain much. Other drivers can't stand them.

Instead of holding the throttle wide open the whole way around the track as a driver does on a superspeedway, racing on a road course entails a lot of shifts in speed — and a lot of shifting gears. Pocono Raceway, which isn't a road course, is the only other track on the NASCAR Winston Cup Series circuit where drivers shift gears during the race. They shift at least two times per lap because of the sharp turns at the triangular track — but the road courses require much more shifting than that because of the many turns and elevation changes during an event.

NASCAR travels to only two road courses every year, with one race at each of the tracks:

- Sears Point Raceway, a 1.95-mile, 11-turn road course in Sonoma, California.
- Watkins Glen International, a 2.45-mile, 11-turn road course in Watkins Glen, New York.

Night Racing Under the Lights

While each NASCAR Winston Cup Series track has its own appeal, some of the tracks have a special allure: night racing. While cars circle the track the same way and race the same way, the show they put on for fans is much different. When cars bottom out or crash against each other, sparks shoot into the air like fireworks. It's quite a spectacle.

More and more tracks are installing lighting systems so that they can host night races, or so that rain-delayed events can be held at night, if need be. Currently, four speedways host night NASCAR Winston Cup Series events:

- ✔ Bristol Motor Speedway hosts night racing each summer at its second NASCAR Winston Cup Series event of the season.
- ✔ Daytona International Speedway has a night race every July.
- ✔ Lowe's Motor Speedway hosts the Winston all-star race in mid-May, and then holds the Coca-Cola 600 on Memorial Day weekend, which begins in the late afternoon and ends at night.
- ✔ Richmond International Raceway holds night races every time NASCAR comes to the track.

For the drivers, night racing has a slightly different feel than racing during the day. The lighting systems have become so good that drivers actually can see more of the track, including many of the bumps and dips of the racing surface. Also, night races are cooler than daytime racing, especially in the summertime — and comfort means a lot when you're racing in (or watching) a three-hour race in the steambath of central Florida in July. The fans love night racing, too, for the same reasons.

Night moves

Night races often provide plenty of excitement, with all the sparks flying off the cars and the blur of colors racing by. But drivers and crews also find racing under the lights thrilling for another reason. Racing on Saturday nights gives us Sunday off. So, we don't mind that night races last until nearly midnight. After the races, we rush to our planes to get home as soon as possible, so we can go to sleep in our own beds and sleep late the next day. That gives us an extra day to spend with our families, go to our family church, run errands, or do things normal people do on weekends. It's kind of weird waking up on Sunday with no race to drive in, but drivers relish the moment, especially because our schedules are so packed during the week. So, it's no wonder my wife and son love Saturday night races, too!

For a fan, night racing isn't too bad, either. After the race, you don't have to drive home or fly home early the next morning to be at work on time. Instead of hurrying back, you can relax in your hotel or campground for one more night, then leisurely get up the next morning and mosey all the way home without any stress.

Who Owns the Tracks?

In the old days of stock-car racing, big-wig companies didn't own racetracks — people did. Families or individuals with money or land built small tracks in their communities so that people could enjoy racing there and watching races there. Now, though, individually-owned racetracks, at least on the NASCAR Winston Cup Series level, aren't common. The big companies have taken over.

Two large companies, both publicly-owned with stock traded on the New York Stock Exchange, own most of the 21 tracks hosting NASCAR Winston Cup Series races:

✔ International Speedway Corporation, or ISC, as it's known in the racing world, is the company that owns most of the tracks that host NASCAR Winston Cup Series races. ISC is based in Daytona Beach, Florida. Bill France Jr. — who is NASCAR's president — is the company's chief executive officer. His father, Bill France Sr., founded the company and also founded NASCAR. In addition to the tracks ISC already owns, it is building more tracks. ISC is building a speedway in Kansas City and developing tracks in New York City, Chicago, and Denver. For now, though, ISC owns the following NASCAR Winston Cup Series racetracks: California Speedway, Darlington Raceway, Daytona International Speedway, Homestead Miami Speedway, Michigan Speedway, North Carolina Speedway, Phoenix International Raceway, Talladega Superspeedway, and Watkins Glen International.

✔ Speedway Motorsports Inc., or SMI, is NASCAR's second-largest speedway owner. It is based in Concord, North Carolina, and O. Bruton Smith is the CEO. Smith also heads the nation's sixth-largest car dealership conglomerate. SMI owns the following NASCAR Winston Cup Series tracks: Atlanta Motor Speedway, Bristol Motor Speedway, Las Vegas Motor Speedway, Lowe's Motor Speedway, Sears Point Raceway, and Texas Motor Speedway.

✔ The rest of the NASCAR Winston Cup Series tracks are owned by individuals, except for Dover Downs, which is run by Dover Downs Entertainment, LLP, a relatively small public company that runs different forms of entertainment, such as a horseracing track and a gambling establishment.

✔ Some families have held onto their tracks and haven't sold out to huge companies yet:

- Indianapolis Motor Speedway is owned by the Hulman-George family.

- New Hampshire International Speedway is owned by the Bahre family.

- Richmond International Raceway is owned by the Sawyer family.

- Pocono Raceway is owned by the Mattioli family.

So you see, even though big companies have elbowed their way into the speedway ownership business, some die-hard families have resisted the pressure to sell out.

A Snapshot of Each NASCAR Winston Cup Series Track

Suppose you've saved up enough money to attend a NASCAR race. With 21 tracks on the NASCAR Winston Cup Series circuit, how do you choose which one to go to? Because NASCAR weekends aren't inexpensive (including tickets, travel, food, and lodging), you should consider your options carefully.

Do you like the bumping and banging of a short track? Do the high speeds of a superspeedway get you pumped up? Do the thrills of a night race on an intermediate track get your heart pumping? If you're not sure, watch a few races on television before you decide which track to go to. This section tells you which track is which.

After you decide which track you like the best, call for tickets right away. Many times, races are sold out months — or even a year — in advance! The same goes for making hotel reservations. Race fans tend to stay at the same hotel year after year, renewing their reservations before they leave to ensure they have a place to stay the next year. So, if you're looking for lodging, start planning way in advance, perhaps by calling the local tourist bureau or chamber of commerce to see what's available. Also, if you want to camp out at the track (in the infield or adjacent to the track), many facilities require reservations — call the track for information.

Atlanta Motor Speedway

The track hosts two NASCAR Winston Cup Series events each year, one in the spring and one in the fall. Both those events are lightning-fast because the track is high-banked and was repaved and reconfigured in 1997. The newly-paved track causes cars to stick to the track more so drivers can go faster through the turns without worrying about losing control. For example, Geoffrey Bodine set the track qualifying record for the NAPA 500 in 1997, the first NASCAR Winston Cup Series race after the track was repaved. He went a blistering 197.498 mph, which is ultra-fast and ultra-scary for a driver on a 1.54-mile track.

Track specs

- **Shape:** Quad-oval, which is a modified oval with two extra, very slight turns. Those turns are located part-way down the frontstretch, one on each side of the start/finish line.

✔ **Length:** 1.54 miles

✔ **Banking:** 24 degrees in the turns and 5 degrees in the straightaways, which are the frontstretch and the backstretch. The frontstretch is the part of the track between the first and last turns. The backstretch is the part of the track between the second and third turns.

Dates to watch

Mid-March and late November.

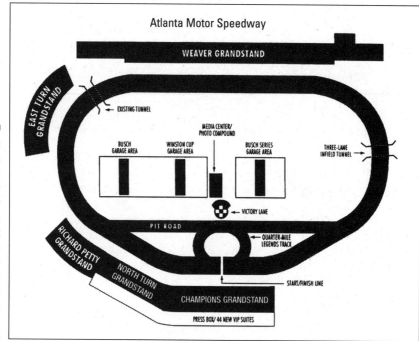

Figure 13-1:
Despite its size, Atlanta Motor Speedway is one of the fastest tracks on the NASCAR Winston Cup Series circuit.

Getting to the track

The track is located at highways 19 and 41 in Hampton, Ga., about 30 miles south of Atlanta. To get there from I-75 south, take exit 77 south, and go 15 miles to the track. From I-75 north, take exit 70, and follow Georgia 20 for eight miles to get to the track.

Getting tickets

For tickets or information, call 770-946-4211 or check out the track's Web site at www.gospeedway.com.

Finding lodging

▮ ✔ Henry County Chamber of Commerce: 770-957-5786

▮ ✔ Atlanta Convention and Visitor's Bureau: 404-521-6600

The key to enjoying a race at Atlanta Motor Speedway is avoiding the traffic. Get to the racetrack extra early if you want to see the green flag fall, otherwise you may be listening to the beginning of the race on your car radio. Also, make sure to bring a raincoat to the spring race because it tends to rain — or even snow! — at some point during the weekend.

Bristol Motor Speedway

Even though Bristol is one of NASCAR Winston Cup Series' tiniest tracks at a half-mile around, it doesn't lack action. The track has a concrete racing surface and the steepest banks on the circuit, with a neck-straining 36-degree banking in the turns. People liken it to a Roman coliseum because more than 147,000 seats tower above the small track. Drivers describe racing at the track by comparing it to flying a Learjet around a clothes dryer or maneuvering a speed boat around a toilet. There's not much room on the track, but there's a whole lot of noise in the place — particularly with 43 NASCAR Winston Cup Series cars circling the track and the roar of the engines reverberating off the aluminum grandstands.

Bristol is nicknamed "The World's Fastest Half-Mile" for a reason — cars lap the track in about 15 seconds. Blink a few times, and you've already missed the lead cars go by. The track hosts two NASCAR Winston Cup Series events each year, one in the spring and another in late summer. The late summer event is held at night and is one of racing's hottest tickets.

Track specs

▮ ✔ **Shape:** Oval

▮ ✔ **Length:** .533 miles

▮ ✔ **Banking:** 36 degrees in the turns and 16 degrees in the straightaways

Dates to watch

End of March and late August.

Getting to the track

The track is located on Volunteer Parkway, Highway 11E, about five miles south of Bristol, Tennessee. To get there, take Virginia exit 3 off I-81 and follow Volunteer Parkway to the track. Or take Tennessee exit 69 off I-81 and follow Highway 37 to Highway 11E.

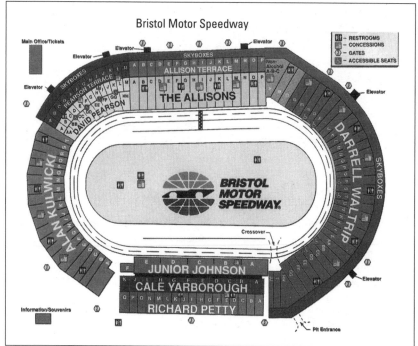

Figure 13-2:
Bristol
Motor
Speedway
isn't a track
for the faint-
hearted
because
of all the
accidents
and
bumping
during races
there.

Getting tickets

For tickets or information, call 423-764-1161 or check out the track's Web site at www.bristolmotorspeedway.com.

Finding lodging

✔ Bristol Chamber of Commerce: 423-989-4850

✔ Bristol Convention and Visitor's Bureau: 423-989-4850

✔ Camping at the track: 423-764-1161

If you want to go to a race at Bristol, getting tickets may be a difficult task. Events are sold out years in advance, with most ticketholders keeping their seats from year to year. You can get to a race, though, if you scour the classified section in racing magazines or newspapers for somebody selling tickets. Also, you can take your chances and head to Bristol without tickets, hoping to bump into somebody hawking tickets near the track. Another option is calling the track to find out when tickets go on sale for new seats, which are added from time to time. Don't hold your breath, though. If you're in your 20s now, you may be collecting social security before you can get your hands on tickets.

California Speedway

You'll find only two NASCAR Winston Cup Series tracks on the west coast, and California Speedway is one of them. The track was built by legendary IndyCar driver Roger Penske and is one of the snazziest tracks around. Drivers love it because we think it's laid out the way a track should be: It's a regular, simple oval, not shaped like a dog's hind leg. Also, the racing surface is nice and smooth, making it a dream to drive on. In fact, the entire facility is a dream, too. It has meticulously groomed grounds along with neat parking lots and grandstands. The track workers smile and wave, even when they have to get up at 4 a.m. and direct traffic all day. The traffic flow to and from the speedway isn't too bad, either. The one problem about California Speedway is that it tends to host uneventful races because the track is so easy to drive on. Other than that, it's a great place to incorporate into a family vacation to Disneyland. The track hosts one NASCAR Winston Cup Series event every season.

Figure 13-3:
California Speedway is one of the newest tracks on the NASCAR Winston Cup Series circuit, located about one hour east of Los Angeles.

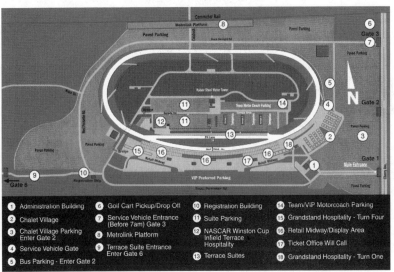

California Speedway

Track specs

- ✓ **Shape:** Tri-oval
- ✓ **Length:** 2 miles
- ✓ **Banking:** 14 degrees in the turns, 11 degrees on the frontstretch and 3 degrees on the backstretch

Date to watch

End of April or early May.

Getting to the track

The track is in Fontana, California, about 40 miles east of Los Angeles. To get there, follow I-10 east from Los Angeles and take the exit for Cherry Avenue. Head north to the speedway.

Getting tickets

For tickets or information, call 800-944-RACE or check out the track's Web site at www.iscmotorsports.com and click on California Speedway.

Finding lodging

- ✔ City of Fontana Chamber of Commerce: 909-822-4433
- ✔ City of Ontario Chamber of Commerce: 909-984-2458

California Speedway is just about an hour east of Los Angeles and Hollywood, the movie-star mecca. If you're in the mood for some people-watching, make this trip. Just give yourselves plenty of time to get there and get back. The traffic in Los Angeles is even worse than the traffic on race mornings — but it lasts the whole day, not just a few hours.

Darlington Raceway

Darlington is one of NASCAR's oldest and most ornery tracks. It was built in 1950 and is NASCAR's original superspeedway, which back then was any paved track a mile or longer. Over the years, it earned a nickname as "The Track Too Tough to Tame" and there's a good reason for that. Most drivers can't tame it — and many drivers have trouble driving it.

The speedway is egg shaped, meaning one end of it has tighter turns than the other. Also, the banking on the end with the tighter turns is two degrees steeper than the other end. So, drivers must pay attention in the turns nearly every second of every lap, in order to keep from smacking into the wall. Then again, smacking the wall at a storied place like Darlington is part of a driver's initiation. Driving close to the wall is mandatory — but not by choice. Your car drifts up the groove on the racetrack and ends up only inches from the wall, many times scraping it and leaving a stripe on the car from the wall's paint. Over the years, that stripe has become known as the Darlington Stripe — and every driver who has raced there has gotten one at one time or another.

Rumors of Darlington losing one of its two annual NASCAR Winston Cup Series events surface every year. Yet, although Darlington isn't near a big city like California Speedway and doesn't have the rows and rows of sky boxes like Bristol Motor Speedway — it does have history. It hosts the Southern 500 each Labor Day weekend, a race drivers consider one of NASCAR's most prized victories. In 1999, the track held the 50th annual running of the race. The track also holds another race each spring.

Figure 13-4:
Darlington
Raceway,
NASCAR's
original
speedway is
one of the
toughest
tracks in
NASCAR
Winston
Cup Series
racing.

Track specs

- **Shape:** Egg-shaped oval

- **Length:** 1.366 miles

- **Banking:** 25 degrees in turns 1 and 2; 23 degrees in turns 3 and 4; and 2 degrees on the straightaways

Dates to watch

Mid-March and the Sunday of Labor Day weekend in September.

Getting to the track

The track is in Darlington, South Carolina, about 75 miles east of Columbia, South Carolina, and ten miles north of Florence, South Carolina. To get there from I-95, take Highway 52 to Darlington. From I-20, take 401 east to Darlington. The track is on Highway 151/34, two miles west of Darlington.

MARK SAYS

A preponderance of pond

Why is Darlington shaped so strangely? Well, at first it wasn't to make the track challenging for drivers. When building the track, the original owner, Harold Brasington, wanted his speedway to have sweeping turns all the way around, but a local farmer's stubbornness kept him from doing that. That local farmer refused to sell his fish pond — the one that sat right in the way of one end of the proposed track — so Brasington had to squeeze that end of the track to fit it in the allocated spot. He also had to make the banking steeper on that end to make the turn easier for drivers to negotiate. Years later, the fish pond is still there and the track still boasts its weird shape. Good for the fish, bad for the drivers.

Getting tickets

For tickets or information, call 843-395-8499 or check out the track's Web site at www.darlingtonraceway.com.

Finding lodging

- Darlington County Chamber of Commerce: 843-393-2641
- Florence Chamber of Commerce: 843-665-0515
- Pee Dee Tourism Commission: 800-325-9005
- Camping at the track: 843-395-8499

When buying tickets to a Darlington race, try to get seats close to the turns because a lot of the action happens there. You also may want to plan a trip to the beach during your weekend at Darlington: Myrtle Beach is only 70 miles away, where you can play mini-golf, body surf, or even continue your race-filled weekend and head to NASCAR Speedpark, where you can race go-karts.

Daytona International Speedway

Daytona International Speedway is the most famous track in NASCAR racing, mostly because Daytona Beach is where NASCAR began. Even before NASCAR was founded, racers would flock to Daytona's hard-packed sand beaches to go head-to-head against each other while trying to avoid the incoming tide. Now, though, those racers and millions of fans each year flock to the 2.5-mile superspeedway a few miles inland from where NASCAR stock-car racing started.

The high-banked, high-speed track hosts two official NASCAR Winston Cup Series races each year — the Daytona 500 and the Pepsi 400, formerly known as the Firecracker 400. The track also holds the Bud Shootout, which is a non-points race about a week before the Daytona 500 consisting of pole winners from the previous year and one wildcard entry.

For the most part, race fans just don't show up in Daytona Beach the day before the Daytona 500 — because there's plenty to see before the big event. The track hosts more than two weeks of racing each February, a time of the year known as *Speedweeks.* The annual series of events starts out with the Rolex 24 at Daytona, a sports-car endurance race. The stock-car portion kicks off with pole qualifying and the Bud Shootout. The track also features lower-tier stock-car races, such as an Automobile Racing Club of America (ARCA) race and a NASCAR Goody's Dash Series race. Also during those hectic two weeks, the track hosts an International Race of Champions (IROC) race, where 12 of the best drivers in the world compete against each other in equally-prepared stock cars. Then, the NASCAR Craftsman Truck Series and the NASCAR Busch Series have their season-opening events — followed by the Daytona 500 the next day as the Speedweeks highlight.

In the summer, the Pepsi 400 is less hectic because it's the only event going on at the track. For years, the 400-mile Fourth of July race was held in the steaming, sweltering midday heat — when temperatures on the racetrack would reach more than 150 degrees. In the race cars and in the grandstands, it wasn't that much cooler, so in 1997 the track decided to do something about it. For a mere $5 million, the speedway installed lights around the gigantic track, just in time for the 1997 Pepsi 400 — the first race held under the lights at the track. That historic race was postponed from July to October because of wildfires in Florida, but the event was a hit nevertheless.

Track specs

- ✔ **Shape:** Tri-oval
- ✔ **Length:** 2.5 miles
- ✔ **Banking:** 31 degrees in the turns; 18 in the tri-oval (frontstretch) and 3 degrees in the back straightaway

Dates to watch

Mid-February and Fourth of July weekend.

Getting to the track

The track is in Daytona Beach, Florida, about 70 miles northeast of Orlando. From Orlando, take I-4 East to Daytona and exit on U.S. 92 or West International Speedway Boulevard. From I-95, take the U.S. 92 exit toward Daytona Beach.

NASCAR's Super Bowl

The Daytona 500, held at Daytona International Speedway each February, is the most famous stock-car race in the world. It's NASCAR's Super Bowl and is the race every driver dreams of winning. Why is it such a big deal? Well, not only does it pay the most money, but it also has the most prestige.

Some of the most legendary drivers in the world have won the event, including Richard Petty (a record seven times!), Cale Yarborough, and even Indy 500 winners Mario Andretti and A.J. Foyt. But if you win the Daytona 500, not only do you join that elite group of drivers — but you also get loads of fame. The winner goes on a whirlwind media tour the week after making it to the famed Victory Lane, making appearances on national TV shows like *Late Night with David Letterman* or the *Tonight Show*. So, if you're not famous when you win it, you will be by the time the week is over.

Sure, winning the Daytona 500 is quite an accomplishment because about 200,000 fans watch it in person and millions of people watch it on TV, but there's something even more special about winning the 500-mile race. The driver who wins it feels pretty darn good about his upcoming season — the Daytona 500 kicks off the NASCAR Winston Cup Series season every year and doing well in the race boosts a driver's (and his team's) confidence heading into the rest of the season.

Figure 13-5:
Daytona International Speedway hosts the Daytona 500 each year, one of the most famous auto races in the world.

Getting tickets

For tickets or information, call 904-253-RACE or check out the track's Web site at www.daytonaintlspeedway.com.

Finding lodging

 ✔ Daytona Beach Chamber of Commerce: 904-255-7311

 ✔ Daytona Beach Area Convention and Visitor's Bureau: 800-854-1234

 ✔ Camping at the track: 904-253-RACE

If you plan on bringing your family to Daytona Beach for the races, you'll find there are plenty of things to do in the area. Orlando, and its attractions such as Walt Disney World and Universal Studios, is just an hour away. The beach is just east of the speedway. But if you're in town, you really don't want to miss Daytona USA, a motorsports attraction that's part NASCAR museum, part interactive funhouse. You can watch movies, play video games, and even participate in a real pit stop. Tours of the speedway also are available, so even if you don't get into the infield on race day, you can see everything up close beforehand. Call 904-947-6800. Just down the street from Daytona USA and the speedway is Mark Martin's Klassix Auto Museum, which displays American classic cars and motorcycles. Also another great side trip — and not just because I own it! Call 904-252-3800 for details.

Dover Downs International Speedway

There's nothing prim or proper about Dover Downs International Speedway. It's loud (with noise reverberating off the aluminum seats) and dirty (with dust kicked up everywhere), and it's good, hard racing (with fast cars running close together). For drivers, though, it's not quite relaxing enough. The racing surface used to be asphalt, but it's concrete now, making the ride bumpier than usual. Imagine driving down a concrete highway and hearing the "Thump-thump! Thump-thump!" of the wheels riding over the concrete seams on the road. Well, that's how drivers feel as their car travels over the rough concrete — and 400 miles of that thump-thumping isn't what I call a mellow afternoon. Most of the time, though, fans get their money's worth at the track dubbed the "Monster Mile," even though the drivers are exhausted and cranky when the day is over. While there's not much passing, the cars go frighteningly fast down the straightaways and into the high-banked turns.

Track specs

 ✔ **Shape:** Oval

 ✔ **Length:** 1 mile

 ✔ **Banking:** 24 degrees in the turns and 9 degrees on the straightaways

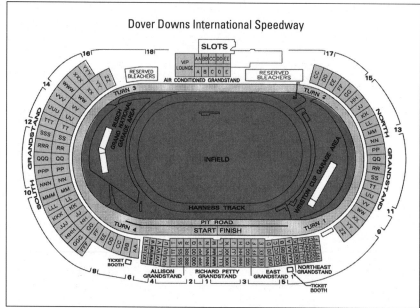

Figure 13-6:
Dover
Downs isn't
a driver
favorite, but
the grand-
stands sell
out nearly
every time.

Dates to watch

Early June and late September.

Getting to the track

The track is in Dover, Delaware, about 65 miles south of Philadelphia and 75 miles away from Baltimore. From New Jersey, take the N.J. Turnpike south across the Delaware Memorial Bridge and follow U.S. 13 south to the track. From Philadelphia, take I-95 south to I-495 south to U.S. 13. From Baltimore or Washington, take U.S. 50/301 east across the Bay Bridge, and then take U.S. 301 north to Maryland 302 east. After that, turn right on Maryland 454 at Templeville, which becomes Delaware 8, and turn left on U.S. 13.

Getting tickets

For tickets or information, call 302-674-4600 or check out the track's Web site at www.doverdowns.com.

Finding lodging

✔ Central Delaware Chamber of Commerce: 302-734-7514

✔ Delaware Tourism Office: 800-441-8846

Dover isn't the biggest town around and lodging is scarce and expensive, with race teams taking up the rooms at most of the hotels near the track. So when looking for a place to stay, try Newark or Wilmington, two cities north of the track. While the drive may be a bit longer, you'll have a better chance there than with the ones closer to the track.

Homestead Miami Speedway

The 1.5-mile track south of Miami used to be called the Metro-Dade Homestead Motorsports Complex, but it was renamed the Homestead Miami Speedway in mid-1998. The track was crowned with the new name — much less of a mouthful than the old one — before NASCAR Winston Cup Series' first race there in November 1999. When NASCAR hit south Florida, it was quite a culture clash. NASCAR has a distinctly southern, old-fashioned twinge to it. South Florida, on the other hand, is known for its international flair and the cutting-edge fashion (and nearly naked beach-goers) of the South Beach area. But NASCAR racers and fans seemed to enjoy the trip south anyway, especially because of the weather in Homestead, which is normally mild in late November. Many NASCAR Busch Series competitors stay there for vacations after they're done racing because the series' season finale is there.

Homestead Miami Speedway

Figure 13-7:
Homestead Miami Speedway hosted its first NASCAR Winston Cup Series event in 1999 and is now a regular part of the schedule.

Track specs

- ✔ **Shape:** Oval
- ✔ **Length:** 1.5 miles
- ✔ **Banking:** 6 degrees in the turns and 3 degrees in the straightaways

Dates to watch

Mid-November.

Getting to the track

The track is located in Homestead, Florida, 25 miles south of Miami. To get there from the north, take Florida's Turnpike to Speedway Blvd (SW 137th Avenue) and go south. From the south, take U.S. 1 to Palm Dr., then go east for 2½ miles. Turn left on SW 142nd Avenue.

Getting tickets

For tickets or information, call 305-230-RACE or check out the track's Web site at `www.racemiami.com`.

Finding lodging

- ✔ Greater Miami Convention and Visitor's Bureau: 800-933-8448
- ✔ Homestead/Florida City Chamber of Commerce: 305-247-2332

When booking a hotel in the Homestead area, you may be tempted to search in and around Miami, but don't forget to look south of the speedway, too. The Florida Keys are just over 45 minutes south of the track, and staying there gives you the opportunity to enjoy gorgeous blue ocean waters and white sand beaches while still staying relatively close to the track. Also, after the race most of the traffic flows north to Miami, so by staying in the Keys, your trip back may be easier.

Indianapolis Motor Speedway

Indianapolis Motor Speedway, nicknamed the "Brickyard" because its racing surface used to be paved with bricks, is hallowed grounds for IndyCar racing. It was built in 1909 and is the oldest continuously operating track in the world. The Brickyard became legendary for hosting the Indianapolis 500, the nation's marquee event for Indy cars, where more than 400,000 fans pack into the grandstands and infield. Because the track is such an Indy car racing icon, many people thought hell would freeze over before stock cars raced on (and desecrated) the track.

Well, as it turned out, hell did freeze over. In 1994, the NASCAR Winston Cup Series competed at the Brickyard for the first time, breaking tradition at the 2½-mile track. Now, the Brickyard 400 is one of NASCAR's most prestigious races.

When NASCAR comes to the Brickyard, the race is technically a sell-out, but no infield tickets are sold. Even so, there are almost 400,000 fans in the grandstands to see the Brickyard 400 — which makes it the biggest race, in terms of fan attendance, on the NASCAR circuit. Drivers get to see those fans, too. The turns are nearly 90 degrees, making it seem as if you're going to drive right into the grandstands before easing off the throttle to turn drastically left. It's scary, especially for rookies who aren't used to the sharp turns, high speeds on the straightaways, and racing in on the narrow speedway. As a driver, you just have to get used to it before you feel comfortable, which may take a few years because NASCAR only races once a year at the speedway.

Track specs

- ✔ **Shape:** Four-cornered oval, which is nearly a rectangle because the turns are almost at 90-degree angles.

- ✔ **Length:** 2.5 miles

- ✔ **Banking:** 9 degrees in the turns and flat straightaways

Dates to watch

Early August.

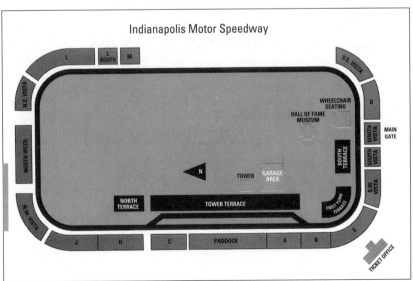

Figure 13-8:
Indianapolis Motor Speedway is the home of the famed Indianapolis 500 — but also the Brickyard 400 NASCAR Winston Cup Series race.

Getting to the track

The track is in Indianapolis, Indiana (technically in a town called Speedway), and is located about seven miles northwest of downtown Indianapolis. To get there, take Exit 16A (the Speedway/Clermont exit) off I-465 west, then go east on 16th Street to the track.

Getting tickets

Tickets for the Brickyard 400 are sold by mail order only. Call 317-484-6700 for an order form or write to P.O. Box 24152, Speedway, IN 46224. The race sells out quickly, so you must call or write for an order form at least one month before the August race if you want to get tickets before they're sold out.

Finding lodging

- Indianapolis City Center: 317-237-5200

- Indianapolis Convention and Visitors Association: 317-639-4282

- Indianapolis Chamber of Commerce: 317-464-2200

- Indianapolis Hotel Information Line: 800-323-INDY

No matter how high you get in the grandstands, your view of Indy's huge 2½-mile track is limited. When buying tickets, your best bet is to sit somewhere in the frontstretch section where you can see cars come out of turn four, race down the straightaway, then barrel through turn 1. But get the seats facing the infield, not the ones in the infield, if you want to have the best vantage point.

Las Vegas Motor Speedway

If you're a race fan who loves nightlife, the Las Vegas Motor Speedway is your mecca for NASCAR racing. You get to watch great racing during the day on a track that drivers love because there's plenty of room to drive on. Drivers can run on the bottom, in the middle or on top — which is great because, as you've probably figured out, racers love having a lot of room to work with so they can pass the cars in front of them. While you're watching the racing, you can't help but notice the track's breathtaking surroundings. The McCullough Mountain Range is in the distance, plus Nellis Air Force Base isn't far, either, often providing a free air show of F-14s flying in formation.

After you're done watching racing, you can get out of your racetrack duds, put on some fancy-schmancy outfit, and explore the town. Las Vegas is nick-named "the entertainment capital of the world" because of its dozens of casinos, hundreds of restaurants, and smorgasbord of shows (and smorgasbords) to choose from. But don't stay out too late the night before the race, because traffic to the track is a nightmare. You'll have to get there early to avoid starting your day with congestion on the roads — and avoid a headache, too. Also, make sure to get your fill of Vegas before the weekend is through. So far, NASCAR Winston Cup Series only stops there once a year.

Track specs

- ✔ **Shape:** Tri-oval
- ✔ **Length:** 1.5 miles
- ✔ **Banking:** 12 degrees in the turns, 9 degrees on the frontstretch and 3 degrees on the backstretch

Dates to watch

Early March.

Getting to the track

The track is located in Las Vegas, 11 miles from the heart of the Vegas Strip. To get there, take I-15 north to Exit 54 for Speedway Boulevard.

Getting tickets

For tickets or information, call 702-644-4443 or 800-644-4444. Also, check out the track's Web site at www.lvms.com.

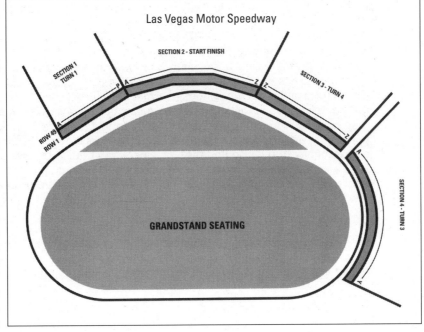

Figure 13-9: Las Vegas Motor Speedway made its NASCAR Winston Cup Series debut in 1998 and quickly has become one of the drivers' favorite tracks.

Finding lodging

- ✔ Las Vegas Visitor's Information: 702-892-7576
- ✔ Las Vegas Tourist Bureau: 702-739-1482

When Vegas nightlife gets too cheesy, perhaps a more down-to-earth option is sticking around the speedway. There's a dirt track around the corner from the track, where you can see even more racing after the NASCAR garages close for the evening. Those races, held under the lights, don't host NASCAR cars. They have other cars and other series, including the World of Outlaws Series, which features sprint cars with a large wing on top. The wing helps the cars — which are fast, light cars with no fenders — stick to the track more. Otherwise, they'd become airborne.

Lowe's Motor Speedway

Most NASCAR Winston Cup Series drivers live in the Charlotte area, so it's no wonder they love racing at Lowe's Motor Speedway. Two times per year, many drivers get to sleep in their own beds on race weekends instead of holing up in a hotel or their motorhomes. Drivers also like the track because you can pass on it and go very fast. For those reasons, many drivers list Charlotte Motor Speedway as one of their favorite tracks in the NASCAR Winston Cup Series.

The 1½-mile track, formerly known as Charlotte Motor Speedway, is the first NASCAR track to change its name after owners sold its naming rights. Expect many more tracks to change their names in the future because Lowe's Motor Speedway paved the way. But, whatever the name of the track, the facility hasn't lost any of its glitz. It has many luxury sky boxes just as other tracks do, but it also has two condominiums built at one end of the track, where many drivers and fans own condos overlooking the racetrack. How exciting it must be to wake up in the morning and glance out your window to see a group of gritty race teams testing their cars. Or just think, you can have a dinner party and watch races while nibbling on hors d'oeuvres and sipping on chardonnay. You'll also find the ritzy Speedway Club at the track, which is racing's version of a country club. It's a concept dreamed up by Speedway Motorsports CEO Bruton Smith and speedway president H.A. "Humpy" Wheeler, two of the most innovative, creative promoters in the sport.

Besides hosting The Winston all-star event each May, Lowe's Motor Speedway hosts two NASCAR Winston Cup Series events each year, including the annual Coca-Cola 600 on Memorial Day weekend which has grown quite popular and rivals the Indy 500 in importance.

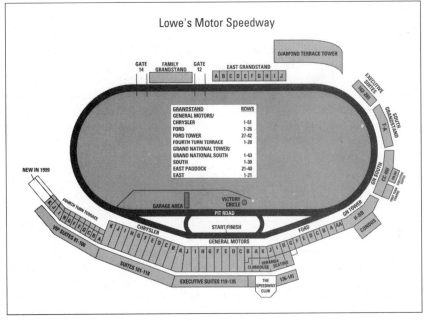

Lowe's Motor Speedway

GRANDSTAND	ROWS
GENERAL MOTORS/	
CHRYSLER	1-51
FORD	1-26
FORD TOWER	27-42
FOURTH TURN TERRACE	1-28
GRAND NATIONAL TOWER/	
GRAND NATIONAL SOUTH	1-43
SOUTH	1-30
EAST PADDOCK	21-40
EAST	1-21

Figure 13-10:
Most drivers
live near
Lowe's
Motor
Speedway,
so drivers
love to race
there.

Track specs

✔ **Shape:** Tri-oval

✔ **Length:** 1.5 miles

✔ **Banking:** 24 degrees in the turns and 5 degrees in the straightaways

Dates to watch

Mid-to-late May and early October.

Getting to the track

The track is located in Concord, North Carolina, about 12 miles northeast of Charlotte. To get there, take I-85 north from Charlotte, and take exit 49 for Speedway Boulevard. The speedway is on Highway 29.

Getting tickets

For tickets or information, call 704-455-3200 or check out the track's Web site at www.lowesmotorspeedway.com.

Finding lodging

✔ Charlotte Convention & Visitors Bureau: 800-231-4636

✔ Camping at the track: 704-455-4445

If you want to see race teams up close and personal, you can drive to some (or even all, if you're so inclined) of the race shops in the Charlotte area. You won't have a hard time finding one because they're everywhere. The best place to see a group of shops in one visit is Mooresville, about 20 miles north of the track. Take exit 36 off I-77 North, go over the highway and turn left at your first light. Drive down that group of streets, including Rolling Hills Road and Knob Hill Road, and you'll find more race shops than you can visit in one day, including Roush Racing, Penske-Kranefuss Racing, and Team SABCO. Most race shops have a free visitors' area, where you can take a peek at the race teams preparing cars.

Martinsville Speedway

Martinsville's .526-mile oval is the tiniest track in NASCAR Winston Cup Series racing and also is one of the oldest. It was built in 1947 and even pre-dates NASCAR itself. Good old Martinsville is a typical short track with not much room to pass and a bumpy racing surface. The tricky part is, it's concrete through the turns and asphalt in the straightaways. Some drivers lovingly call it two drag strips attached by two U-turns. Some just call it frustrating, mostly because it's so small and there isn't much room to pass. With little room to get by the car in front of you, drivers know they must qualify well to have a decent finish. But qualifying well doesn't exempt you from finishing the race unscathed. Even though Martinsville isn't high banked the way Bristol is, cars still get bumped and banged during the race. There just isn't anywhere to hide, especially when somebody spins out or wrecks just in front of you.

Track specs

- **Shape:** Oval
- **Length:** .526 miles
- **Banking:** 12 degrees in the turns and zero in the straightaways

---

Humpy's pre-race festivities

Humpy Wheeler is known especially for his pre-race festivities, which border on the ridiculous. Nevertheless, they are unforgettable. For instance, before the Coca-Cola 600 (formerly the World 600) each year, he calls in the National Guard to perform a military exercise, filled with loud booms and plenty of billowing smoke. But Wheeler has had some brilliant ideas over the years, including The Winston all-star event each May, which features NASCAR Winston Cup Series' winners. The race has strange rules and is not an official points event. It's a 70-lap shootout in the middle of which the field is inverted just to make things interesting.

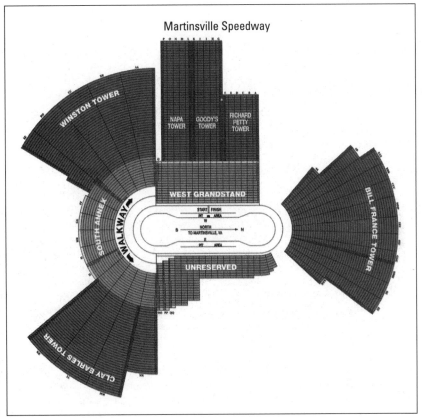

Figure 13-11:
Martinsville is the only track on the NASCAR Winston Cup Series circuit that has hosted races before NASCAR began.

Dates to watch

Early April and late September or early October.

Getting to the track

The track is located two miles south of Martinsville, Virginia, and about 50 miles south of Roanoke, Virginia. To get there, take U.S. 220 South Business. From Greensboro Airport, take Route 68 North to U.S. 220 North to the track.

Getting tickets

For tickets or information, call 540-956-3151 or check out the track's Web site at www.martinsvillespeedway.com.

Finding lodging

To reach the Martinsville-Henry County Chamber of Commerce, call 540-632-6401.

A trip to Martinsville is a trip into NASCAR's history, but it also can be a culinary thrill. While at the track, it's imperative that you try one of the track's famous (or infamous, depending on who you ask) Jesse Jones brand hot dogs. On the outside, they are regular-looking hot dogs, which you can get with all sorts of toppings, including chili and cheese, but after you bite into them, you'll notice they have an extraterrestrial pink glow in the middle. Rumor has it, that's what makes them taste so unique. If you have a weak stomach, however, you may want to steer clear.

Michigan Speedway

With Detroit just about an hour away, executives from the car companies don't have to travel far to see some of the best racing in the sport. That's because many racers deem Michigan Speedway as one of the best tracks they drive on. There's plenty of room to race on the speedway's wide straightaways and turns, making it easy for drivers to take the low route, the high route, or any route they choose to get by somebody in front of them. Michigan is also one of the fastest tracks on the NASCAR Winston Cup Series circuit because of the long straightaways and the relatively high banking. The catch is, unlike cars at Daytona and Talladega, cars at Michigan don't have to use restricted motors which cut down on horsepower and speed.

While drivers love the 2-mile oval, fans may wonder why the track is so alluring. Sure, the wide, fast racing surface is easy to negotiate, but that makes for few accidents and cautions. Many times, races at Michigan come down to a battle of which team gets the best fuel mileage or which team pumps out the fastest pit stop — not which driver makes the most dramatic, thrilling moves on the track to take the lead.

Track specs

- **Shape:** D-shaped oval
- **Length:** 2 miles
- **Banking:** 18 degrees in the turns, 12 degrees on the frontstretch and 5 degrees on the backstretch

Dates to watch

Early June and late August.

Getting to the track

The track is located in Brooklyn, Michigan, about 70 miles southwest of Detroit. From Detroit, take I-94 West to Highway 12 West (Exit 181A). The track is one mile west of U.S. 12 and M-50.

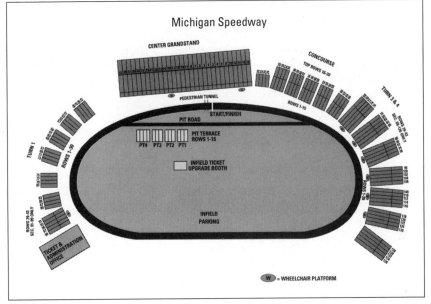

Figure 13-12:
Michigan
Speedway's
wide
straight-
aways and
high banking
make it fun
to drive on.

Getting tickets

For tickets or information, call 800-354-1010 or check out the track's Web site at www.michiganspeedway.com.

Finding lodging

✔ Greater Jackson Chamber of Commerce: 517-782-8222

✔ Brooklyn-Irish Hills Chamber of Commerce: 517-592-8907

✔ Brooklyn Tourist Bureau: 800-354-1010 or 800-543-2937

Races at Michigan Speedway don't have many cautions and accidents, so the best place to see the most action is from the north grandstands. Sitting there will give you a good vantage point to see the cars exit turn 3 and enter turn 4, then barrel down the frontstretch.

New Hampshire International Speedway

Yes, there's hope for North Englanders who want to see a NASCAR Winston Cup Series race but don't want to drive all over creation to do it — a 1-mile track in Loudon, New Hampshire. The speedway is a huge version of the Martinsville Speedway. It has sharp turns, a slick racing surface, long straight-aways, and not enough room in the corners to pass the cars in front, even if the car in back is much faster. In fact, there isn't much room to pass any-where on the track, which is why qualifying up front is so important.

The NASCAR Winston Cup Series races at the track twice a year, once in the summer when the nights are much cooler and crisper than in the steamy south, and once in the fall just as leaves on the trees start to turn colors. Oh, and racers never call the track New Hampshire International Speedway. It's just called "Loudon," short and sweet. (There are too many syllables in New Hampshire International Speedway, so it takes too long to say. And racers are always in a rush, rush, rush.)

Track specs

- **Shape:** Oval
- **Length:** 1.058 miles
- **Banking:** 12 degrees in the turns and 5 degrees in the straightaways

Dates to watch

Early July and mid-September.

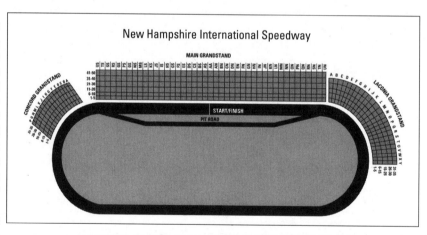

Figure 13-13: New Hampshire International Speedway is the only NASCAR Winston Cup Series track in New England.

Getting to the track

The track is located in Loudon, New Hampshire, about 70 miles north of Boston, and ten miles north of Concord, New Hampshire. To get there, take I-93 north to I-393 east, and then follow Route 106 to the track.

Getting tickets

For tickets or information, call 603-783-4931 or check out the track's Web site at www.nhis.com.

Finding lodging

- Greater Concord Chamber of Commerce: 603-224-2508
- Southern New Hampshire Visitor's Bureau: 800-932-4282

While lodging is available in the nearby towns of Manchester and Concord, race weekend in Loudon is the perfect opportunity to check out small, cozy inns and bed and breakfasts in the New Hampshire Lakes region not far from the track.

North Carolina Speedway

Like New Hampshire International Speedway, North Carolina Speedway is never called North Carolina Speedway, at least in the NASCAR garage. It's called "Rockingham" or "The Rock" because it's located in Rockingham, North Carolina. Rockingham is usually the second race of the season, held the weekend after the season-opening Daytona 500. It's where drivers come to vent their frustrations over a poor showing — or boast about a good performance — in the 500. But whatever they have to complain about or gloat over, drivers soon forget the 500 all together, especially when tackling Rockingham's rough racing surface, tight turns, and long straightaways. The track is extremely tough on tires, so drivers must stay aware of tire wear or risk getting a flat and crashing. (See Chapter 9 for information on tire wear.)

Track specs

- ✔ **Shape:** Oval
- ✔ **Length:** 1.017 miles
- ✔ **Banking:** 23 degrees in turns 1 and 2; 25 degrees in turns 3 and 4; and 8 degrees on the straightaways

Figure 13-14: North Carolina Speedway is called Rockingham by everybody in the NASCAR garage.

MARK SAYS

My first win

Rockingham is a special place for me. I won my first NASCAR Winston Cup Series race there on October 22, 1989, and felt as if I had accomplished one of the biggest goals in my life. "I can't believe it," I said from Victory Lane that day. "My life is fulfilled. I feel like I'm the luckiest man alive." Even though that was an unforgettable moment for me in my career, I don't get nostalgic when I go to Rockingham twice a year.

Race car drivers just don't get mushy like that — if they do, they may lose their concentration, then crash and hurt themselves or someone else. So, even though my first win was a monumental moment in my career, I'll have to wait until I'm an old man to enjoy those memories. Then I can tell my grandkids all about Rockingham and my first win there, while sitting on my front porch relaxing in my rocking chair.

Dates to watch

Late February and late October.

Getting to the track

The track is located in Rockingham, North Carolina, about 75 miles east of Charlotte. To get there from Charlotte, take Highway 74 East to U.S. 1. From Raleigh, take U.S. 1 south. From Greensboro, take Highway 220 to Highway 74 east to U.S. 1 north.

Getting tickets

For tickets or information, call 910-582-2861 or check out the track's Web site at www.iscmotorsports.com.

Finding lodging

- Richmond County Tourist Development Authority: 800-858-1688
- Pinehurst Area Convention and Visitor's Bureau: 800-346-5362

TIP

Have a few free hours during your trip to Rockingham? Then by all means, bring your golf clubs. The area around the track has some of the nation's best golf courses, including Pinehurst Resort & Country Club, which hosted the men's U.S. Open Golf Championship in 1999 and will host the women's U.S. Open in 2001. Many golf resorts in the area offer packages where you stay in a nice room, get every meal served to you in the dining room, and then play golf all day. You may have to wake up darn early to get in 18 holes on race day, but the sacrifice may be worth it.

Phoenix International Raceway

With the majestic Sierra Estrella Mountains in the background, Phoenix International Raceway is one of the most picturesque tracks in NASCAR racing. It's also one of the most oddly shaped tracks. Instead of being a plain, old oval, Phoenix is shaped like a "D" because the track's owner didn't want to alter the facility's road course to accommodate an oval.

Phoenix isn't a high-banked track and the turns are tricky because there are different degrees of banking in turns 1 and 2 than in turns 3 and 4. Each turn is challenging. Turns 1 and 2 are tight, with the wall coming out of nowhere as you come out of turn 2. Turns 3 and 4 are more sweeping, with a quick, crooked turn (or *dogleg*) just before turn 3 just to make things more interesting. But NASCAR Winston Cup Series drivers don't have to fret over those turns too much. The series races at the 1-mile track only once per year.

Track specs

- **Shape:** D-shaped oval
- **Length:** 1 mile
- **Banking:** 11 degrees in turns 1 and 2; 9 degrees in turns 3 and 4; and zero degrees on the straightaways

Dates to watch

Mid-November.

Getting to the track

The track is located in Phoenix, Arizona, about 15 miles southwest of downtown. To get there, take I-10 west to the 115th Avenue exit. Follow the road south for six miles.

Getting tickets

For tickets or information, call 602-252-2227 or check out the track's Web site at www.phoenixintlraceway.com.

Finding lodging

To reach the Phoenix & Valley of the Sun Convention & Visitors Bureau, call 602-254-6500.

The track sells general admission tickets for seating on the hillside above turns 3 and 4 — and those may be the best seats at the speedway. It's relatively inexpensive and parking is nearby, which makes hillside seating the best buy at the raceway. Bring a blanket and binoculars if you plan to park yourself on the hill, though, because it's no luxury box. It's a bit rougher than more-expensive seats, but it's a great way to watch a race.

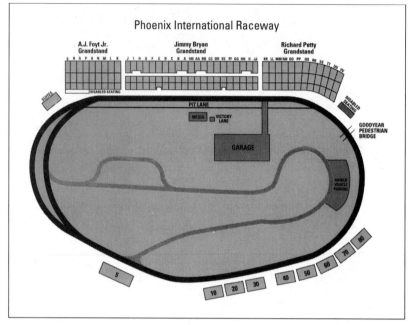

Figure 13-15:
Phoenix's
odd shape
makes it
challenging
for drivers.

Pocono Raceway

Pocono's triangular racetrack, tucked into the Pocono Mountains (a haven for honeymooners in the northeast) may very well be the most difficult and frustrating track in NASCAR. It isn't a regular oval, a D-shaped oval, a road course, or a superspeedway. It's a combination of those tracks. It's part superspeedway because of its long front straightaway, which is the longest straight stretch of road in NASCAR Winston Cup Series racing. Cars can reach 200 mph as they barrel down that straight. Going into the turns, though, cars aren't going that fast. That's where Pocono the superspeedway turns into Pocono the road course because the turns are so drastic. In fact, drivers must downshift and upshift at least two times per lap.

The most heartstopping turn at Pocono is turn 2, known as the "tunnel turn" because the tunnel into the infield is beneath the turn. It's also known as the toughest turn in racing. The tunnel turn is extremely narrow, so cars must negotiate the turn single file. If they don't, they'll end up smacking into the wall. Drivers must travel through turn 1 the same way, also close to the bottom of the track, or suffer the same fate. Turn 3, though, is relatively easier. It's a wider turn with more racing room.

With those three very different turns on the same course, drivers and teams must set up their cars carefully. They must learn to make compromises in order to get the best out of their vehicles through each lap. Sometimes, though, teams choose to set up their cars for turn 3 so the driver is better equipped to make a pass there and carry some momentum down the long stretch. But remember, that means that going through turns 1 and 2 could be a difficult experience.

Track specs

- ✔ **Shape:** Triangle
- ✔ **Length:** 2.5 miles
- ✔ **Banking:** 14 degrees in turn 1; 8 degrees in turn 2; 6 degrees in turn 3; and no banking in the straightaways

Dates to watch

Mid-June and late July.

Getting to the track

The track is located in Long Pond, Pennsylvania, tucked into the Pocono Mountains about 80 miles northwest of Philadelphia. To get there, take exit 43 off I-80, then go south for three miles.

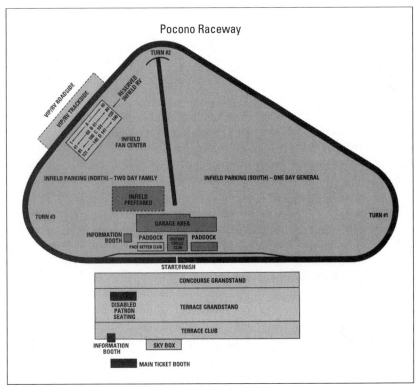

Figure 13-16:
Pocono Raceway is a road course combined with a super-speedway because of its unique shape and challenging turns.

Getting tickets

For tickets or information, call 800-RACEWAY or check out the track's Web site at www.poconoraceway.com.

Finding lodging

- ✔ Pocono Mountains Vacation Bureau: 800-646-2300
- ✔ Monroe County Chamber of Commerce: 717-421-4433
- ✔ Camping at the track: 800-RACEWAY

Looking for an autograph of your favorite driver? On the way from the garage to pit road, there's a small grandstand where fans with pit passes can sit and wait for a glimpse of drivers and crews. It's called "autograph alley" because there are a few windows built into the fence in front of the stands, where fans can hand drivers hats, T-shirts, programs, and other souvenirs to sign. Sit there long enough and a driver is bound to come by and oblige you.

Richmond International Raceway

Many drivers deem Richmond International Raceway the best short track in NASCAR. Even though it's only three-quarters of a mile long, there's still enough room for you to race up high, down low, or in the middle. If drivers want to make a pass, they can do it anywhere you want instead of waiting for a wide enough spot on the racetrack. While drivers love the place, fans don't think it's too shabby, either. It hosts two nighttime NASCAR Winston Cup Series races every year — and the place becomes electric with those cars circling the racetrack under the lights. When fans snap photographs, the flashbulbs make the grandstand look as if it's filled with fireflies. And when the drivers race, their cars throw sparks into the air to electrify the night even more.

Track specs

- ✔ **Shape:** D-shaped oval
- ✔ **Length:** .750 miles
- ✔ **Banking:** 14 degrees in the turns; 8 degrees in the frontstretch; and 2 degrees in the backstretch

Dates to watch

Mid-May and mid-September.

Getting to the track

The track is located near downtown Richmond on the Virginia State Fairgrounds. To get there, follow signs from I-64 or I-95 for the fairgrounds. The address is 602 East Laburnum Avenue.

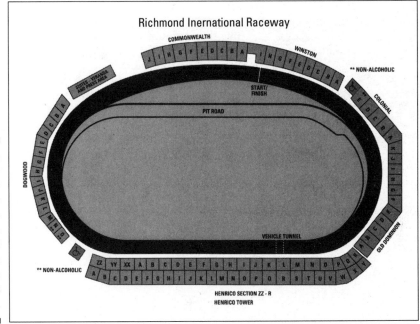

Figure 13-17:
Richmond
International
Raceway
holds two
nighttime
NASCAR
Winston
Cup Series
events
each year.

Getting tickets

For tickets or information, call 804-345-7223 or check out the track's Web site at `www.rir.com`.

Finding lodging

The speedway publishes its own fan guide, which includes information on local hotels and restaurants. To receive a guide, send a self-addressed, stamped, business-sized envelope (with 78 cents postage) to Fan Friendly Guide, P.O. Box 9257, Richmond, VA 23227-9257.

To reach the Richmond Convention and Visitors Bureau, call 800-365-7272.

The best seats at Richmond are in the turns, but it's hard to be picky about where you sit when tickets are so hard to come by. The track holds a lottery to handle requests for tickets, so take what you can get. But if you have a choice, pick the Dogwood grandstands or the Old Dominion grandstands where you can get a good view of the cars going through the turns.

Sears Point Raceway

For those mellow, wine-drinking race fans, Sears Point Raceway in Sonoma, California, may be the quintessential venue. The track, located in the heart of

Sonoma Valley's wine country, is a twisting, turning road course with as many elevation changes as there are wineries nearby. Drivers have to deal with sharp turns, dips, and hills throughout the race, so it's exhausting as much as it is demanding.

Fans have it all together different. They are spread throughout the hills surrounding the track, drinking wine, snacking, and cavorting while watching the race. You can find some grandstand seating, but not much, so be prepared to bring a blanket and food so you can chill out while your wine chills. Then you can watch the race and enjoy the spectacular scenery of the valley. The track hosts one NASCAR Winston Cup Series race each year.

Track specs

- ✔ **Shape:** 11-turn road course
- ✔ **Length:** 1.95 miles

Dates to watch

Late June.

Getting to the track

The track is located in Sonoma, California, about 40 miles north of San Francisco. To get there, take Highway 101 North to Route 37, and then take Route 121 to the track.

Getting tickets

For tickets or information, call 800-870-RACE or check out the track's Web site at www.searspoint.com.

Finding lodging

- ✔ Sonoma Valley Visitors Bureau: 707-996-1090
- ✔ Sonoma Valley Chamber of Commerce: 800-899-2623

Don't expect to see the entire racetrack if you're going to an event at Sears Point. The track is so big and has so many dips and turns, that there's just no way to see the whole thing. So, when hunkering down to watch the race from the hillside, try to pick a place where you'll see at least one of the turns. That's where you'll find a lot of the action on a road course because a lot of passing is done there.

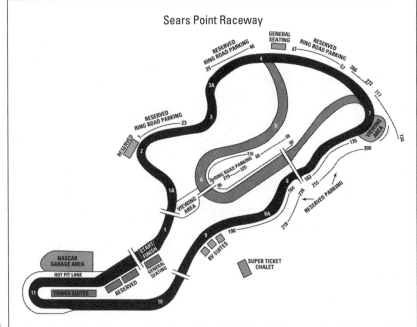

Figure 13-18:
Sears Point
Raceway is
one of two
road
courses in
NASCAR
Winston
Cup Series
racing.

Talladega Superspeedway

According to legend, Talladega stands on an old Native American burial
ground in Alabama, and that's why so many strange things have happened
there, like when Bobby Isaac was leading the race one year, pulled over on
the frontstretch, and walked away from his car after voices in his head told
him to get out. Still, despite several odd happenings, there's no doubt that
Talladega is the biggest, meanest, and fastest track in NASCAR racing. Bill
Elliott set the speed record for stock cars in 1987 when he won the pole for
the Winston 500 with a 212.809 mph lap. Obviously, that was before NASCAR
mandated carburetor restrictor plates (see Chapter 5) to slow down the cars.

Talladega is Daytona International Speedway's sister track, built almost to the
same specifications although, at 2.66-miles around, it is slightly bigger. And it
is slightly scarier, too, with cars coming off turn 4 three-, four-, and even five-
wide when they race down the frontstretch.

Track specs

✔ **Shape:** Tri-oval

✔ **Length:** 2.66 miles

✔ **Banking:** 33 degrees in the turns and 18 degrees through the tri-oval

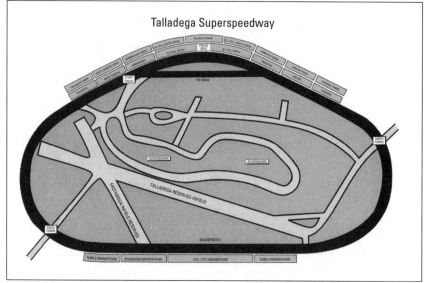

Figure 13-19:
Talladega
Superspeed-
way is
NASCAR
racing's
longest
track.

Dates to watch

Late April and mid-October.

Getting to the track

The track is located in Talladega, Alabama, about 40 miles east of Birmingham. To get there from the west, take I-20 east to exit 169 to Speedway Boulevard, and then go about three miles to the track. From the east, take I-20 west to exit 173.

Getting tickets

For tickets or information, call 256-362-RACE or check out the track's Web site at www.talladegasuperspeedway.com.

Finding lodging

  ✔ Greater Birmingham Convention and Visitors Bureau: 800-458-9064

  ✔ Calhoun County Chamber of Commerce: 256-237-3536

Even at the highest point in the grandstands, it is impossible to get a good view of the entire track because it is so big. Don't get upset if you can see only part of the racetrack. Odds are, you'll see plenty of bumper-to-bumper racing to make your trip exciting.

Texas Motor Speedway

When Texas Motor Speedway opened in 1997, drivers couldn't stand it because the transitions into and out of the turns were too drastic and the racing surface was falling apart. But after millions of dollars of renovations and reconfigurations, the track has become popular among drivers. While the racing surface is smoother and the turns are friendlier, fans have noticed other improved parts of the speedway, such as the Speedway Club and condos at one end of the track. The club houses a gourmet restaurant with dinner and dancing after the race, and also holds a state-of-the-art gym for locals to work out in. All that has made the facility one of the most innovative tracks in racing.

Track specs

- **Shape:** Quad-oval
- **Length:** 1.5 miles
- **Banking:** 24 degrees in the turns and 5 degrees in the straightaways

Dates to watch

Late March/early April.

Getting to the track

The track is located in Fort Worth, Texas. To get there, take I-35 West, north of downtown Fort Worth, and then take the exit for Highway 114.

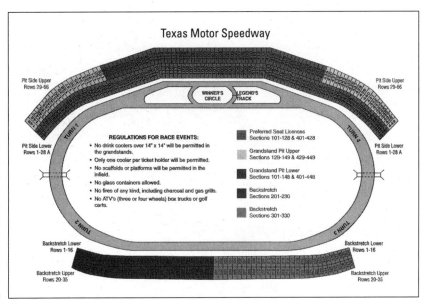

Figure 13-20: Texas Motor Speedway is one of the newest tracks in NASCAR. It opened in 1997.

Getting tickets

For tickets or information, call 817-215-8500 or check out the track's Web site at www.texasmotorspeedway.com.

Finding lodging

- Fort Worth Convention & Visitors Bureau: 800-433-5747
- Dallas Convention & Visitors Bureau: 800-232-5527

Despite numerous moves to alleviate traffic at the speedway, expect to spend a good part of your evening — several hours — in your car after the race. For some reason, improving traffic flow has stumped speedway officials and state troopers — so bring food in the car and a couple of relaxing CDs or cassette tapes.

Watkins Glen International

Unlike Sears Point, Watkins Glen is more of a modified oval with mostly right turns instead of left turns. It also doesn't have the drastic sharp turns Sears Point has, so cars can lap the track much faster. One of the best things about "the Glen," as it's affectionately called, is that fans can get a great view of the track by perching themselves at various points around the speedway. Still, you can't see the entire track because it sprawls so much. The track hosted Formula One racing's U.S. Grand Prix from 1961 to 1980, but now its biggest race is when NASCAR comes to the tiny town in the Finger Lakes region of upstate New York.

Figure 13-21: Watkins Glen International hosts one of the two NASCAR Winston Cup Series road course races a year.

Track specs

- ✔ **Shape:** 11-turn road course
- ✔ **Length:** 2.45 miles

Dates to watch

Mid-August.

Getting to the track

The track is located five miles southwest of the village of Watkins Glen, New York, about 80 miles southwest of Syracuse and 18 miles northeast of Corning. Going south, take Route 414 to County Route 16 and go three miles to the track.

Getting tickets

For tickets or information, call 607-535-2481 or check out the track's Web site at www.theglen.com.

Finding lodging

- ✔ Schuyler County Chamber of Commerce: 800-607-4552
- ✔ Corning Chamber of Commerce: 607-936-4686

Just like at Sears Point, the best seats at Watkins Glen are near the turns where drivers most often make their moves. The *esses* is a part of the track where cars snake through the course in a series of turns, and it's an especially good part of the track to watch from because they snake right up a hill. Sit at the top of the hill and you'll see plenty of action.

Chapter 14

Going to a Race

Going to a NASCAR race isn't like going to a professional basketball game. It's more like going to Woodstock. Fans make pilgrimages to NASCAR races, sometimes driving across the country to their favorite tracks. And when they get there, they enter a unique universe.

From 70,000 to 400,000 fans descend on NASCAR tracks during race weekends. They bring their NASCAR hats, NASCAR T-shirts, NASCAR flags, and NASCAR bumper stickers. But most of all, they bring their loyalties for their favorite NASCAR drivers. While fans at basketball games cheer for one team or the other, fans at NASCAR races cheer for one of 43 drivers. It's a meld of different fans with different allegiances coming together to have a good time.

Often, NASCAR fans camp out on speedway grounds or near the speedway before going to an event. They bring their tents, motorhomes, campers, and vans to the track, then party like there's no tomorrow. You think tailgating before a college football game is a blast? Well, you haven't seen anything unless you've trekked to a NASCAR race. Fans don't (usually) run around naked and roll in the mud as they did at Woodstock, but they do have fun and make race weekend unforgettable.

Buying Tickets for a Race

Before you head to a NASCAR race, it's best to have tickets for the event in hand. Most races sell out weeks or months before the event, so tickets are hard to come by. They can also be quite pricey, ranging in cost from $25 to more than $250. Keep in mind that some tracks sell discounted tickets for children. (See Chapter 13 for information on how to get tickets at the 21 NASCAR Winston Cup Series tracks.) Here are some tips for getting tickets to events:

✔ Call the track ticket office as soon as possible, even a year before an event, to get information on securing tickets for the race you want to see. Tickets for races go on sale long before the event, so if you call early, you increase your chances of going to an event (and getting the best seats). If the race is sold out, some tracks can put you on a waiting list just in case more seats open up. Or you can stay on the waiting list until a season-ticket holder decides to give up his or her tickets.

✔ If you're computer-savvy, you can get on the Internet and check to see if a track sells tickets on its Web site (see Chapter 13 for Web site addresses). Sometimes, tracks reserve a chunk of seats and save them for Internet-based customers. Check the Web sites for details.

✔ Flip through the classified section of your local newspaper or national racing publication. Fans often sell tickets to sold-out races all the time, so if you keep your eyes open for tickets to the race or racetrack of your dreams, then you may get lucky.

✔ Drive or walk around a racetrack to find fans selling their unused tickets or scalpers who are selling tickets to make money. (But first see the following caution.) Sometimes, fans buy too many tickets and have extras on race day. Other times, tickets are sold by ticket scalpers who charge too much, and you also risk buying counterfeit tickets — see Figure 14-1.

Whenever you buy tickets from a place other than the racetrack, you're taking your chances. You may buy a fake ticket. You may pay exorbitant prices for tickets, which are much more expensive than the face value. Be aware that in some states, it is illegal for someone to sell tickets to an event if they aren't properly licensed. In other states, it is illegal for someone to charge more than face value for tickets. Still more states have laws about how much a scalper can boost the ticket price over face value. It may be a pain to find out what the local laws are regarding scalping tickets, but it's beneficial. Depending on the jurisdiction, you can get fined or even arrested for buying tickets illegally. Consider the consequences before you buy tickets off the street.

Figure 14-1:
Beware of buying tickets from people hawking them outside a track. Make sure they look like the real thing. Even if they do, you're still taking a chance.

What a suite deal

Way above the grandstands, you'll see a row of boxes encased in glass where people gather to watch races. These are called *suites* and you can't get tickets to sit in them. They're for corporations or people with enough money to rent them out. Usually, companies rent the suites for thousands of dollars each race, and then invite employees, colleagues, clients, friends, or family members to watch the race. Many suites have TVs, so you can see all the action, including replays of big wrecks or key passes. Most also have catered lunches or dinners, so you can dine while the drivers bump and bang on the track. It's a luxurious way to watch a race and a great way to entertain a group.

Grandstands or infield?

When buying NASCAR tickets, you have the option of getting tickets for the grandstands or for the infield (for some tracks). Each location gives you a different feel of NASCAR racing, and neither one is better than the other — it just depends what you want to get out of your trip to the racetrack.

- ✔ **Grandstands:** Most fans watch races from the grandstands. It's the traditional way to do things. It's just like sitting in the stands at a football game, but much louder — not because of the people around you, but because of the roar of the engines as the cars go around the track. Sitting in the grandstands, you get to see most of the track. You get to make friends with the person you're sitting next to, whether you like it or not, because the seats are so close together. When buying grandstand tickets, you purchase tickets for specific seats.

  Keep in mind the best seats are the highest seats, which isn't the case in most sporting events. Sitting up higher gives you a better view of the entire track, while sitting lower gives you a perfect view of cars zooming by — and that's about it. All you see is a blur. So this is one sporting event where you don't want to be in the front row.

- ✔ **Infield:** Not all tracks, particularly the smaller ones, allow fans in the infield. The ones that do offer infield tickets, however, are packed with people not only on race day, but also throughout the weekend. The tickets are general admission, because there are no seats in the infield, so don't expect luxury when you get there. Watching a race from the infield isn't anything like watching a race from the grandstands. It's an acquired taste, somewhat like caviar, El Dorados, or plaid pants. It's a big party from the time the people stream in to the time the people trickle out. Sometimes, you wonder if they even notice if the race is going on.

  Fans usually drive their cars, motorhomes, pick-up trucks, or even overhauled school buses into the infield, then sit on top of them to get a glimpse of the track. Still, from those vantage points, fans usually can't see the entire racetrack. You may see a bit of the frontstretch or a turn or two, but that's it. The rest is up to your imagination. Sometimes, though, fans don't have a choice. When the grandstands are sold-out, tickets for the infield usually are still available.

Before you get your heart set on camping in the infield of a track, contact the track. Many parking spaces and camping spaces in the infield are reserved in advance and sold out before the race comes to town. At Daytona International Speedway, for example, motorhome spaces are reserved so that you have an exact place to set up camp. The track also has unreserved places, which are doled out on a first-come, first-served basis. As you can guess, the reserved spaces are more expensive and are in a better spot inside the track than the unreserved spaces. Also, be prepared to spend money on an infield pass for each person in your party, because buying a parking spot in the infield doesn't grant you admission. If you have eight people stuffed in your Winnebago, you need eight tickets. The best part about bringing your motorhome, camper, or tent into the infield is that you get to sleep in it, so you'll save money on lodging. While staying at a hotel may cost $200 a night (especially on race weekends when hotels tend to hike up their prices), staying in the infield may cost $250 for two nights. The prices for infield camping vary widely, though, depending on whether you get a reserved spot (which is more expensive) and how many spaces are available. So check with the track before driving down in your pop-up camper and $20 in your pocket.

Camping out in the infield isn't for everyone. I'd put it this way — bring your children at your own risk because you may see behavior that Barney or Captain Kangaroo would frown upon. While nooks of the infield can be children-friendly, most of it is an adult playground — especially at night when everyone gets restless. If you do want to bring the family and make a weekend out of it, many tracks have staked out camping areas for families, complete with curfews and noise limits.

Make sure to bring a gas grill if you want to cook out in the infield. Many tracks don't allow open fires in the camping areas.

Fans in the infield aren't the types to show up on race day, watch the race, then head dutifully home right after the checkered flag falls. They usually get to the racetrack two or three days in advance to set up their campers, motorhomes, or tents, then slip into their pre-race partying mode. They bring their gas grills, coolers filled with beverages, and lawn chairs, and then cavort like mad. Some cavort more during the race, and keep cavorting even when the race is done. So, if you're a serious race-watcher who doesn't like distractions during an event, the grandstands may be a better place for you.

Finding Lodging Well in Advance

Suppose you have tickets to a NASCAR race and are ready to head to the event. If you're making a day trip out of it, the only thing you need to worry about is traffic. If you need to stay over a night or two, you have a bigger challenge on your hands.

Finding a place to stay near a racetrack during a NASCAR race weekend is not easy. Most racetracks aren't in metropolitan cities with hotels on every corner. They're in smaller towns away from cities, like Talladega, Alabama, or Dover, Delaware. So, by nature, there aren't many hotels around. Imagine 100,000 or so race fans streaming into town and looking for a place to stay. As you can guess, there aren't enough hotels to go around.

Before taking off for a race with your spouse and children, call beforehand to make hotel reservations. The simplest way to find out what hotels have vacancies is to call the chamber of commerce in the town where the race-track is located. They usually have a list of hotels with available rooms, and can also suggest hotels in your price range. (Turn to Chapter 13 for phone numbers of the chamber of commerce in each town with a NASCAR Winston Cup Series race.)

Because the demand for lodging is so high, hotel rooms during race week-ends aren't cheap. Expect to pay from $100 to $250 for a hotel room close to the track. But don't expect to stay in luxury, even at those prices. Even the dumpiest hotel can jack up its prices when so many race fans are looking for so few rooms.

Be aware that most hotels ask for three- or four-night minimums and many ask for a one-night deposit when you make the reservation. Of course, the far-ther away the hotel, the cheaper the room, so if you can't bear to part with all that cash, just get in your car and drive an hour or so away from the track.

Leaving Early to Make the Race

Going to a NASCAR race is an all-day excursion. You can thank the heavy traf-fic for that. Because racetracks aren't in the biggest towns, the roads leading to them aren't six-lane highways. The roads can't accommodate the hoards of fans driving to a race, especially when everybody drives to the racetrack at the same time.

If you like sitting in traffic, you're in luck. Feel free to leave a couple hours before the race starts, and listen to the event on your radio while you're stuck behind some exhaust-spewing '76 Ford Pinto. A trip that normally takes an hour can turn into a four-hour ordeal on race morning.

If you have an aversion to traffic, prepare to leave early for the race: I'm talk-ing about at the crack of dawn if the race is at noon. If you do this, you'll avoid the bumper-to-bumper traffic that clogs up roadways two hours or so before the race. After you get to the track, you can sleep in your car or walk around the grounds of the racetrack to check out what the vendors are sell-ing as souvenirs. You can also grab breakfast, and then head to your seat early to watch the pre-race activities. NASCAR hands out awards before each race, and introduces each driver to the crowd. Be in your seat at least 45 min-utes before the race if you don't want to miss it.

Another way to avoid race-day traffic jams is to show up at the track a few minutes before the event begins, because most fans have already arrived and taken their seats. You're taking a chance if you do this, though, because leav-ing just in time for a race may leave you in traffic until the final laps if there's an unexpected tie-up on the road.

The Do's and Don'ts

There are certain things NASCAR fans should and shouldn't do. But if you haven't been to a race before, how do you know what those things are? Here's a handy list of do's and don'ts for you to follow:

- ✔ *Do* bring binoculars to a race, no matter where you're sitting. Even if you have the best seats in the house, it's difficult to see the teams, cars, and drivers up close, especially at a big track.

- ✔ *Do* bring a camera with a telephoto lens (which brings the action closer to you) if you want a good picture of the cars on the track.

- ✔ *Do* bring earplugs, especially for children. NASCAR races are loud, with decibel levels that can rival the roar of an airplane engine. The best kinds of noise deterrents are headsets that actually muffle the sound. You also can use foam earplugs that you roll with your fingers and stick into your ears, but make sure to pull back your outer ear and properly insert the earplugs. If you don't, they won't be effective. If you're the macho type who doesn't want to wear earplugs, your ears may ring and your head may hurt the next day.

- ✔ *Do* bring a raincoat. Umbrellas aren't allowed in the grandstands because they get in the way of other fans' views of the track.

- ✔ *Do* dress for the weather. It can be steamy and sweltering at races held in the summer, but cold, damp, and windy at races held in the spring or fall. Be prepared and check the weather forecast before you leave for a race.

- ✔ *Do* wear sunscreen. You're a perfect candidate for sunburn when you watch a race. You sit in aluminum grandstands for four hours in the middle of the day. Sunscreen protects you from an uncomfortable ride home.

TIP

Buying a program

If you're a novice NASCAR fan, buying a race program helps guide you through your afternoon or evening. Programs usually contain stories about the top drivers or teams. They also have a list of drivers, which may contain biographical information, car number, team affiliation, and *paint scheme,* the design on a car. While some paint schemes, such as Dale Earnhardt's legendary black No. 3 Chevy, stay virtually the same from year to year, some teams have ever-changing paint schemes. Keep that in mind when you're looking for a car on the speedway. Sometimes looking for the car number, not the car color, is a better move.

Programs also may have race records, NASCAR records, and charts that translate lap times into miles per hour. As a beginner fan, all that information, for the price of about $10, can help you become a savvy NASCAR devotee.

✔ *Do* bring a seat cushion if you want a more comfortable perch in the stands.

✔ *Do* bring a radio or scanner (which I discuss in the "Riding Along with the Driver" section, later in this chapter) if you want to keep track of what's going on during a race. Wear headphones, though, because other fans don't want to hear what you're listening to.

✔ *Do* stay hydrated on hot days. Just like drivers and crews, fans need to drink plenty of liquids to keep themselves from dehydrating. You wouldn't believe the number of fans who are taken to the hospital with heat stroke or exhaustion.

✔ *Do* pack food if you don't want to spend money on concessions at the track, which, like at all stadiums, are usually overpriced.

✔ *Don't* bring any glass containers into the grandstands.

✔ *Don't* bring any coolers that are bigger than 14 x 14 x 14 inches.

✔ *Don't* throw anything onto the racetrack or in the grandstands. If you do, security guards will kick you out of the speedway with no refund.

✔ *Don't* drink too much and do crazy things. If you do, you'll be kicked out before you know it — which will most likely sober you up.

✔ *Don't* curse and carry on. The people around you paid good money for their seats and don't want to hear you ranting about how much you hate Bobby Labonte. Also, remember that kids are in the stands and their parents don't want them to be corrupted at the racetrack. (They'll leave it to TV and movies to do that.)

Fitting Into the Crowd

If you're sitting at your first NASCAR with a bunch of veteran fans, what do you do in order to fit in? Well, if you don't know much, the best plan is to keep quiet, watch the race, and learn. If you want to join in on the fun, though, you can cheer for your favorite driver and take part in some of the conversations around you.

First aid at the track

Every track has first aid centers set up throughout the grounds, as well as a central medical care center in the infield. Experienced medical personnel are on hand to help you if you fall and scrape your leg, hurt your back, break your wrist, or even have a serious medical emergency such as a heart attack. If you're too hurt to walk to a first aid center, send a friend to get help, or contact one of the ushers in the grandstands. Everyone is connected via two-way radio, so help will arrive shortly.

The same goes for fans in the infield. At many tracks with motorhomes parked inside them, emergency workers rove through the grounds on four-wheelers. The infield care center also is available for fans who need medical assistance.

One sure-fire way of sounding like a longtime NASCAR fan is to refer to teams by their car numbers. So, when talking about Dale Earnhardt's team, you can say, "The 3 is really kicking butt today." Or, if someone asks which teams you like, you can say, "Oh, I like the 88." An educated fan would immediately know that you're a Dale Jarrett supporter. If you really want to dazzle the fans around you, you can use a multi-numeric scheme such as, "Wow, did you see the 33 pass the 25 on the inside? I thought he was going to spin out the 22 or at least smack into the 8 when he did that."

You can fit also into the crowd at NASCAR races quite well if you dress the part. That means you should at least have a T-shirt or hat with a driver's or team's logo on it. You rarely see fans at a NASCAR race with plain, button-down shirts and khakis on. If you wear an outfit like this, you'll stick out like — well, like a prepster at a Metallica concert. NASCAR fans are loyal and love to support their drivers — and are proud to show it.

Going Behind the Scenes

While grandstand tickets and infield passes give fans a great view of NASCAR races, *garage passes* provide fans with a behind-the-scenes look at the sport. Garage passes allow fans to go into the pits and the garages before the race starts. Unfortunately, track fans can't buy garage passes at most tracks, particularly for NASCAR Winston Cup Series races. Those passes are reserved for sponsors, friends and family of race teams, or people who are affiliated with the sport in some way. Fans who get garage passes are people who know someone who knows someone in NASCAR or at the racetrack. But the bottom line is that an everyday fan usually can't get a garage pass to get close to the drivers. Call a track ahead of time, though, to see if passes are for sale for other races, especially for NASCAR Busch Series races or NASCAR Craftsman Truck Series races, which may be less restrictive than NASCAR Winston Cup Series races. You may get lucky.

Following the rules

If you're lucky enough to get a garage pass, you get a unique view of the drivers and the crews preparing for a NASCAR race. You can walk through the garage area and look at crews working on their cars. You can hang out outside team haulers (see Chapter 6 for a description) to get a glimpse of drivers as they walk to their cars. You can take all the photos you want to remember your day. But remember the following no-no's before heading into the garage:

- You need to stay on your toes in the NASCAR garage because you really are in the middle of the action. Practice time is precious for NASCAR teams, so the cars often zoom in and out of their garages to get as much track time as possible. The drivers are focused on making their cars just right, meaning they aren't necessarily watching out for people strolling through the garage like tourists at Walt Disney World. So, for goodness sake, watch where you're going and look both ways before you cross from one side of the garage to the other. Take a tip from team members, who always stay to one side of the garage when they walk — or scurry across the areas where cars may drive. Remember, drivers sometimes shut off their engines and coast into the garage, so an oncoming car may be silent. Looking where you're going is the only way to get through the garage unscathed.

- When in the garage, revert to the wise words of advice your mom gave you when the two of you took a trip to the china store when you were six: *Look, but don't touch.* You should feel fortunate to get a peek at NASCAR teams at work, so don't get uppity when someone tells you to stop touching a piece of equipment or stand back from a car. The drivers and crew members are at work and don't want to be disturbed — and they don't want their equipment to be disturbed, either. So walk through the garage with respect.

- You must adhere to the following dress code if you want to step foot in the garage area — no ifs, ands, or buts about it:

  - You must wear long pants. No shorts, culottes, clam diggers, Bermuda shorts, capris, and so on are allowed because your pants must cover your legs entirely.

  - Your shirt must cover your shoulders. No tank tops, tube tops, or sleeveless shirts allowed.

  - You can't wear open toed shoes such as sandals, flip-flops, or strappy stiletto high heels.

✔ Stay clear of the garage during Happy Hour, which is the final hour of practice before the race. It's dangerous to linger in the garage because cars are rushing in and out of the garage while teams make last-minute changes.

✔ Don't bring any alcoholic beverages into the garage. They aren't allowed.

✔ You must keep your garage pass visible at all times, and a form of identification in your possession; otherwise, you will be asked to leave.

Getting autographs in the garage

Usually, you can find autograph cards outside each team hauler, where drivers and crews congregate when not working on their cars. An *autograph card* is a sheet of heavy-duty paper with a driver's picture on the front and his vital statistics on the reverse side. It's for — you guessed it — getting autographs. Some people take them for souvenirs, though, because they're free. (It's not good form to take more than one.)

If you want to use the autograph card to get an autograph, you can try to corner a driver in the garage area to get him to sign it. This can be tricky business because drivers are so focused while they're in the garage — because they're at work. The garage is their office. But if you insist on getting autographs or getting your picture taken with a driver, try to use a little courtesy.

Here are some hints:

✔ **Wait outside a team hauler to catch a driver.** He isn't around his car, so he isn't going to be as distracted. But don't dare go *into* the hauler. It's off-limits to fans because that's where drivers and teams have meetings.

✔ **Don't bother drivers just before qualifying.** They may be nervous about their fast lap. If you approach them, they may be cranky and scrawl an autograph that's barely legible. They may scowl in your photo.

✔ **Pay attention to whether a driver is running well during practice if you want his autograph.** If he isn't, he probably won't be in the mood to sign autographs. If you do approach him for an autograph or photo, at least have something positive to say.

✔ **Keep sponsor loyalty in mind.** Think twice before asking Jeff Gordon (a Chevy driver) to sign a Ford hat, or before asking Tony Stewart (who drives for The Home Depot) to sign a Lowe's Home Improvement Warehouse T-shirt. Remember that loyalty runs deep in NASCAR. You don't want to put a driver in an awkward position.

✔ **Bring your own pen.** A black felt-tipped marker, such as an indelible Sharpie, is best.

✔ **Be prepared to walk with a driver as he signs your item.** Most drivers know that if they stop, they'll soon be mobbed by fans. They use the walk-and-sign technique, so be prepared to stride alongside them.

✔ **Don't expect to have a full-blown conversation with a driver.** They're on the job and trying to concentrate. If you want to chat with your favorite driver, go to a pre-scheduled appearance he's making in the area (see Chapter 7 for more on drivers making appearances). Bill Elliott may sit down and sign autographs at a local McDonald's because he is sponsored by McDonald's. No doubt he'll be more relaxed in that atmosphere than he is at the track.

✔ **Even if you've been waiting all day in the sun, don't chastise a driver if he walks out to his car without stopping to give you his autograph.** Maybe he's in a rush to get somewhere. Maybe his car isn't running well. Maybe he doesn't feel well. Maybe he has personal things on his mind. Remember: A garage pass doesn't guarantee you autographs, but it does guarantee you a rare look at drivers and teams at work — a look that most people aren't fortunate enough to get.

✔ **Saying "thank you" always helps.**

Riding Along with the Driver

Whether you're watching a race from the grandstands or the infield, there are ways for you to be even closer to the action. For example, if you bring a stopwatch, you can time your favorite driver's lap, and then compare it to the leader. That'll let you know if your driver is making up any ground on the leader. Or, if you bring a radio with a headset, you can listen to the radio broadcast of a race while you watch it in person. This helps you tremendously because radio announcers offer analysis, race statistics, and play-by-play commentary of what's going on during a race. They tell you what's going on in turn 2, when you can only see the cars coming out of turn 4. They'll also let you know what kinds of problems different cars are experiencing. You may see Ken Schrader slow down on the track, but unless you're tuned into the broadcast, you won't know why.

While many fans listen to the radio during a race, a good number of fans have hand-held *radio frequency scanners* — Walkman-sized instruments that pick up pre-selected radio channels in the immediate area. They allow you to listen in on conversations between drivers and their crews during practice, qualifying, and races. You also can hear NASCAR officials talk among themselves and with the teams, and team members talking to other team members. It's sort of like a legal way to eavesdrop — and it's really fun.

You can rent a scanner at the racetrack (at booths set up on the grounds) for about $25 to $45 a day. They should come with headphones and a list of all the frequencies you need to listen in on everybody involved in a race. Many times, the scanners are pre-programmed, so you don't have to fuss with inputting all those numbers. If it's pre-programmed, just make sure to get a list of the frequencies so you can tune into a specific team when you want.

If you attend NASCAR races often, you may want to invest in your own scanner. You can buy one at your local electronics store such as Radio Shack or at radio companies that have booths at the racetrack. The scanners cost from $100 to $350, depending on their features. Look for a scanner that scans at least 100 channels per second, and one that scans VHF and UHF high and low bands. Really, you don't need a scanner much fancier than that when you're at a NASCAR race — you just need the correct frequencies of the drivers, teams, officials, and radio broadcast to get your money's worth. You can buy updated scanner lists outside the racetrack where souvenirs are sold.

Here are some companies you can call to buy scanners or get information on obtaining frequency lists:

- **Racecomm of Virginia:** 775-599-TALK or www.racecommofvirginia.com on the Web.

- **Race-Scan:** 1-800-441-2841 or www.racescan.com on the Web.

- **Racing Electronics:** 1-800-272-7111 or www.racingelectronics.com on the Web.

- **Racing Radios:** 1-800-669-1522.

If you buy or rent a scanner, be sure to get a frequency list, which has a bunch of numbers on it, each coinciding with a team, a NASCAR official, or a radio broadcast. Usually they are three numbers, followed by a decimal which is followed by even more numbers — such as 484.3400. If you're programming your scanner on your own, you have to input all those numbers into the scanner and assign them another number. For example, you can program my frequency under the number 6 on your scanner, because I drive the No. 6 Ford. So, when you tune to Channel 6 on your scanner, my frequency pops up and you can listen to me chat with my crew. Keep in mind that teams change their frequencies from time to time, so you have to get updated frequency lists to stay on top of the action.

After you get your scanner and input the frequencies, you're ready to listen in. There are a few different techniques to listening to a race on a scanner. You can listen to the radio broadcast, then tune into teams' frequencies from time to time. Or you can put your scanner on scan mode, so it stops at a frequency only when there is communication going on. Or you can listen to one team only, keeping your scanner tuned to the same frequency all day. Whatever way you choose to use your scanner, it's bound to make things more interesting for you. You can hear a crew chief tell a driver when to make a pit stop. You can hear a driver complain about his car. You even can hear a driver's reaction just after he gets into an accident.

When using a scanner, keep in mind that conversations between a team and a driver may not be appropriate for children. Sometimes, especially after something has gone wrong, harsh words — even curses and other derogatory comments — are exchanged. It doesn't happen all the time, but it does happen. Even the most clean-cut teams can become potty-mouthed after a wreck.

Leaving with Souvenirs

It's hard to miss all the souvenir trailers lined up at the racetrack. The trailers are colorful and are always in a conspicuous area, such as just outside the main entrance. If you have time before or after a race, you can mill around the souvenir area and pick up remembrances from the race such as a bumper sticker, T-shirt, or cap. (For more on souvenirs, turn to Chapter 2.) But if you really want a unique souvenir, you have to look a bit harder.

Sometimes, you'll stumble upon someone selling racing tires that were used in an actual NASCAR race. They go for anywhere from $10 to $60. Why would you want a racing tire? Well, it certainly would be a conversation piece sitting smack in the middle of your living room. Many fans lay the tires on their sides and put a sheet of glass on top of them, which makes good coffee tables or end tables. Some fans put them in their yards, fill them with dirt and plant flowers in them. Whatever their use, they are unusual souvenirs from a race.

Fans with infield passes or garage passes always comb the infield for trinkets after an event is over. They're looking for anything they can get their hands on: used tires, pieces of mangled sheet metal from a car that wrecked, or even lug nuts that flew off of a car during a pit stop. If you plan to do this, make sure the item you take is something that a team is leaving behind — otherwise, you can be arrested for stealing. So ask a team if you can take it before you go walking off with an entire hood or a used tire. Otherwise, you may be embarrassed when a security guard grabs you and makes you take the piece of equipment back to its owner. Sometimes, though, teams leave their used tires behind (without wheels) — near their pit stall or in the garage. Those are free for your taking because they're not going to use them again.

You always see fans hovering around stacks of *unused* tires after a race. They look around all sneaky-like, and then try to roll a tire or two back to their vehicles. Taking a used tire is one thing, taking an unused tire is something altogether different. Unused tires cost between $350 and $400 each, and Goodyear wants them back. So, don't try it — buy a used one instead. They are cheap and at least have some character to them, because they've been used in an actual race.

Chapter 15

Tracking NASCAR Events

Most NASCAR fans are lucky to attend one or two races a year. The rest of the time, you have to rely on TV, radio, newspapers, and Web sites to keep you apprised of what's going on. Luckily, plenty of media outlets cover NASCAR races, NASCAR drivers, and the goings-on in the sport. In fact, NASCAR's growth has attracted much attention in the news, so it's difficult to get away from it, even if you wanted to. So, if you're an enterprising individual and want to find out all you can about the sport, you can know even more than some of the drivers do.

You can also join fan clubs or hop onto their Internet sites to catch up on the latest news about drivers. In this chapter, I give you all the details you need to immerse yourself in the sport — even if you can't make it to all of the races.

Watching on TV

When you can't go to races, watching them on TV isn't a bad alternative. Even though you're missing the loud roars of the engines and the smell of rubber on the track, in general, you get to see a lot more than the fans at the event.

In any given NASCAR race, you find TV cameras set up throughout the track. Here are some views you'll get watching an event on TV, which gives you the most complete account of what goes on during a race:

- ✔ **Cars racing down the frontstretch, backstretch, and through all the turns.**

- ✔ **Cars zooming by the grandstands:** Sometimes in a blur of color; other times so that you can recognize which car is which, all captured by cameras placed near the outer edge of the track.

- ✔ **Fans cheering in the grandstands up close, and also a view of the fans in the grandstands taken by cameras in a blimp or helicopter above the speedway.**

- ✔ **Groups of cars coming through the turns, but shot from the ground up:** Those cameras are positioned at ground level in the infield.

- ✔ **Interior shots of cars:** Several cars have in-car cameras set up inside them during each race. This gives viewers at home a close look at drivers while they're in their race cars, including what a driver sees when he swerves to miss an accident — or when he gets into an accident himself. It shows you how violent a crash can be for a driver, too. Upon impact, you see the whole car shake and hear the loud thud. At home, you know a driver is involved in a bad accident when the in-car camera goes dead and all you see is static.

- ✔ **Great views of what's behind and in front of cars, through small cameras mounted to the front and back bumpers of several cars:** These cameras are especially helpful when there's an accident on the track because they give you an up-close view of how the wreck started or who started it.

- ✔ **All the action when cars turn down pit road for pit stops:** You'll see pit crew members crouched on the pit wall, waiting for their car to come down pit road. You also see, from all different angles, the pit crew servicing the car.

MARK SAYS

Ringside seats

Not only do you get many different angles from TV cameras during a broadcast, but you also get to see any confrontations. The first flag-to-flag telecast was of the 1979 Daytona 500, and it was a doozy. Richard Petty won the event, but the highlight of the afternoon was when Donnie and Bobby Allison got into a brawl with Cale Yarborough on the backstretch after Donnie and Cale crashed while battling for the lead on the last lap. The nation could see all the action — live and in color — but the fans in the grandstands on the frontstretch missed the whole thing.

TV cameras don't only capture the action on the track — they bring you all the action off the track, too. When drivers take their cars into the garage during a race — after blowing an engine or getting into a crash — the TV cameras follow. That's when you, as a home-viewer, can see more than the people in the grandstands do. You see the driver get out of his car, most likely all red-faced and huffy about falling out of the race, and then you hear his explanation of why he's in the garage and not on the track. Also, you get to see the car, perhaps crushed or banged up. It's a look into the garage that you don't get if you bought tickets to the race.

Getting insight

During every televised race, you see a few commentators describing what's going on during the race, and those commentators are helpful if you're a NASCAR novice. They sit way above the racetrack in a booth, so that they can see all or most of the track. They also have monitors close at hand so they see instant replays of a pass, an accident, or a pit stop — and they describe it to you while you're sitting at home watching the same thing. Commentators give you all the information you'd ever want — and more — including the statistics of teams, drivers, crew chiefs, and the history of the track itself. If a car stalls on the track, they tell you why. If a tire rolls off a car and down pit road, they tell you how it happened. The commentators don't do all the work, though — reporters are running from pit to pit asking crew chiefs and team members for information. If a tire on a car goes flat, for example, the pit reporter reports live from that driver's pit, shows the flat tire and describes what has happened.

NASCAR races are televised differently than football games or basketball games because commentators can talk to the pit crews while the event is going on. Sometimes the commentators even have negotiated with a driver to talk to him via a radio during caution periods. You don't see sideline reporters in football interviewing the coach in the middle of the fourth quarter. And you certainly don't hear reporters chatting with the quarterback between plays.

TV racing broadcasts

Different networks broadcast different races, so check local TV listings to track down an event. You can find NASCAR races on the major networks: ABC, CBS, NBC, and (in 2001) FOX. You also can tune into them on cable stations such as ESPN and ESPN2, The Nashville Network (TNN), and TBS Superstation. Each network has different commentators and pit reporters, but all-in-all, the coverage is informative and interesting.

All races are broadcast live. Most NASCAR Winston Cup Series races are on Sunday afternoon, but a handful are run on Saturdays or Saturday nights.

Starting in 2001, races will be broadcast on FOX and NBC-TBS only, with FOX broadcasting the first 18 races of the season, while NBC and TBS split the rest of the races. FOX and NBC will alternate coverage of the Daytona 500.

Daily and weekly shows

If you can't get enough NASCAR on weekends, plenty of networks have daily and weekly NASCAR shows — so you can inundate yourself with information. These shows give you breaking news, driver interviews, race reviews, technical information, and almost everything you'd ever want to know in a 30- to 60-minute segment.

Here are some of the TV shows that feature NASCAR:

- **RPM 2Nite on ESPN2:** This show airs at 7 p.m. Monday through Friday during racing season. It reports on all types of auto racing, but covering NASCAR is one of its fortes. The show is similar to a nightly news show, but auto racing is the only topic of conversation. ESPN does a great job at following NASCAR and has some of the best commentators and reporters in the TV business. The network also has other shows on NASCAR and auto racing, such as NASCAR 2Day about a half hour before a race begins and RPM 2Day on weekends.

- **Inside NASCAR on The Nashville Network (TNN):** Inside NASCAR is an hour-long show on every weekend. Two-time NASCAR Winston Cup Series champion Ned Jarrett hosts the show, which features driver interviews and panel conversations about different NASCAR divisions. TNN also airs a show called Raceday at 11 a.m. on Sundays.

- **NASCAR Garage on TNN:** This 30-minute weekend show delves into the technical side of the sport. Usually, you see a driver, mechanic, or car owner describing a part of the car or engine and explaining how it works.

- **This Week in NASCAR on Fox Sports/Speedvision:** This is a weekly show that reports on the goings-on in NASCAR's main divisions.

- **Inside Winston Cup Racing on Fox Sports/Speedvision:** A commentator and group of drivers talk about NASCAR Winston Cup Series racing every week, delving into the previous race and news from the circuit.

Radio Broadcasts

Radio provides great play-by-play descriptions of races. In fact, they're so good that some people watch races on TV, but turn down the sound so that they can listen to the radio broadcast instead of the television broadcast. Radio reporters are everywhere on race day: above the track, watching the entire race and providing analysis; in the pits, talking to crew chiefs and crew members during the race; in the garage, interviewing drivers that have fallen out of the race; even in various turns of the racetrack, so that they can give play-by-play commentary without missing a thing. (If an accident happens in turn 3 of a big racetrack, the commentators in the press box may not be able to see it, so the reporter in turn 3 chimes in and provides the details.) Radio reporters stick around after the race, too. After TV reporters interview a driver in Victory Lane, the radio reporters get to talk to him next, and many times that interview is broadcast throughout the grandstands.

Racing radio networks

When you're listening to a race broadcast, you'll hear one of the following networks. To find out which radio station in your area carries the race, call one of the following networks for a list of their affiliate stations:

- ✔ Motor Racing Network (MRN) is based in Daytona Beach, Florida, and owned by International Speedway Corporation. ISC is the company that owns Daytona International Speedway, as well as many other speedways in NASCAR racing, so you can hear MRN broadcasts at all ISC tracks and at races held at several other NASCAR tracks as well. They broadcast the Daytona 500, the Southern 500 at Darlington Raceway, and the Winston 500 at Talladega Superspeedway, among other races during the year. Write, call, or surf for information and the radio network affiliates near you: MRN, 1801 W. International Speedway Blvd., Daytona Beach, FL 32114; phone 904-947-6400; Web site `www.mrnnet.com`.

- ✔ Performance Racing Network (PRN) is based in Concord, North Carolina, and owned by Speedway Motorsports Inc. SMI is the company that owns Lowe's Motor Speedway, among other tracks hosting NASCAR races. They broadcast the Coca-Cola 600 at Lowe's Motor Speedway, the Goody's 500 at Bristol Motor Speedway, and the NAPA 500 at Atlanta Motor Speedway, among other races. Write or call for information or affiliates: PRN, P.O. Box 600, Concord, NC 28026-0600; phone 704-455-3228; Web site `www.raceshop/com/prn.html`.

- ✔ The Indianapolis Motor Speedway (IMS) Radio Network broadcasts all races from Indianapolis Motor Speedway, including the Brickyard 400. Write or call for information: 500 Brickyard Plaza, Indianapolis, IN 46222; phone 317-481-0060.

Radio racing shows

Just as TV does, radio stations broadcast daily and weekly NASCAR shows throughout the week during racing season. They range from several-minute, newsy segments to hour-long call-in shows. Here are some you can listen in on, including their phone numbers so you can find radio affiliates in your area:

- ✔ NASCAR Garage, featured during NASCAR races, provides listeners with professional car-care tips.

- ✔ NASCAR Live airs once a week for 50 weeks a year and is broadcast from its 380 radio affiliates across the nation. Eli Gold, who has a different guest from the NASCAR world every week, hosts the show on Tuesday nights between 7 and 8 p.m. (eastern time). He interviews his guest, then takes calls from people who phone in with questions. You can phone toll-free 800-2-NASCAR from anywhere in the continental United States to get on the show and get answers to what's been bugging you.

- ✔ NASCAR Now is a weekly radio program that focuses on the NASCAR Craftsman Truck Series.

- ✔ NASCAR Today is hosted by Joe Moore and provides daily NASCAR updates at 4:45 p.m. on weekdays. It lasts about five minutes, so it's a quick and easy way to get NASCAR news.

- ✔ NASCAR USA is a show that counts down the top country songs of the week. It's aired on Sundays and has driver interviews squeezed between songs. Check your local radio stations for air times.

Following NASCAR in Print

Many newspapers and magazines cover NASCAR racing, but the depth of the coverage varies. Some newspapers, for example, only run stories on races and who won them. Others may run features throughout the week leading up to a race and report on breaking news as it happens. Some magazines run a NASCAR story only once every three weeks, while other magazines are entirely devoted to the sport.

If you want to get a subscription to a newspaper or magazine that covers NASCAR regularly, here are some you can choose from:

- ✔ *Inside NASCAR* is a monthly magazine with features on drivers, team owners, crew members, and their families. It's full of color and off-beat stories. Phone 888-722-3527.

- ✔ *NASCAR Racing for Teens* is a bi-monthly magazine geared toward younger NASCAR fans, particularly those ages 12 to 18. It has driver interviews, features, technical facts, and columns on racing. Phone 800-443-3020.

- *NASCAR Preview and Press Guide* is a magazine that comes out once a year, profiling drivers and providing statistics of drivers in every NASCAR division. It also has a section devoted to NASCAR's tracks. Phone 800-747-9287.

- *NASCAR Winston Cup Illustrated* is a monthly magazine with features, commentary, and profiles of people in NASCAR racing. Phone 800-883-7323.

- *NASCAR Winston Cup Scene* is a weekly newspaper published in tabloid form, which covers the NASCAR Winston Cup Series, NASCAR Busch Series, and NASCAR Craftsman Truck Series circuits. If you want to get all the lowdown in NASCAR, including which jackman's wife just had a baby (see Chapter 6 for more on the role of the jackman), this paper is for you. Phone 800-883-7323.

Staying in Touch with Your Favorite Driver

You can find ways to keep tabs on your favorite driver besides going to every race or watching every NASCAR TV program: Log onto the Internet and go to a driver's Web site to find out his schedule for the week or his statistics; join a driver's fan club to get official fan club gear or just to show your support; or send souvenirs to the driver at his race shop where he will autograph them and send them back to you. It's all part of how fans stay close to NASCAR drivers and how NASCAR drivers stay linked to their fans, even though drivers travel to different racetracks — and sometimes different parts of the country — every weekend.

Driver Web sites

It's easy to keep up with your favorite driver if you have access to the Internet. Most drivers have their own Web sites that are chock full of information, so, if you hop onto a search engine such as Yahoo! or Excite and type in the driver's name, the driver's Web site will pop up if he has one. The sites have biographical information, statistics, photographs, race schedules, and personal appearance schedules (meaning you can find out where a driver will sign autographs, then be there to meet him in person). Not every driver has a Web site, but as the Internet becomes more popular — and as NASCAR becomes more popular — expect every driver and team to jump onto the Information Superhighway.

Driver fan clubs

If you can't get enough of your favorite driver just by watching him race, then you may want to join his fan club. Fan clubs are groups of people who ardently support a driver and want to show that support by banding together. Membership fees ranges from $8 to $25, depending on the driver and the perks you get for being in the club. Most clubs provide you with an ID card, a signed postcard, and a discount card to buy your driver's souvenirs at the racetrack. Some even send you a personalized card, signed by the driver, on your birthday and during the holidays. Many clubs have meetings where fans can get together and discuss their driver, or just talk shop.

If you're doing an Internet search for a driver fan club, remember many of the sites are unofficial sites. While those are fine to look up, keep in mind a driver's official site is the only one that will guarantee the posted information is correct. When you go to the Web site, it will say "official" somewhere on it, meaning it's the real one set up by a driver or his company.

Here's where you can write or call to join your favorite driver's fan club:

- **Bobby Allison:** Bobby Allison Racing Team Club, 6616 Walmsley Blvd., Richmond, VA 23224

- **John Andretti:** John Andretti Fan Club, P.O. Box 2104, Davidson, NC 28036; Web site www.jafanpage.com or www.pettyracing.com/andretti

- **Johnny Benson:** Johnny Benson Fan Club, 3102 Bird St. NE, Grand Rapids, MI, 49505; Web site www.johnnybenson-fanclub.com

- **Rich Bickle:** Rich Bickle Fan Club, 7365 Elwood Dr., Charlotte, NC, 28227

- **Dave Blaney:** Dave Blaney Fan Club, P.O. Box 470142, Tulsa, OK, 74147-0142

- **Brett Bodine:** Brett Bodine Fan Club, 304 Performance Rd., Mooresville, NC 28115; Web site www.brettbodine.com

- **Geoffrey Bodine:** Geoffrey Bodine Fan Club, P.O. Box 1790, Monroe, NC, 28111-1790

- **Todd Bodine:** Todd Bodine Fan Club, P.O. Box 2427, Cornelius, NC, 28031

- **Jeff Burton:** Jeff Burton Fan Club, P.O. Box 1160, Halifax, VA, 24558; Web site www.jeffburton.com

- **Ward Burton:** Ward Burton Fan Club, 3475 Myer Lee Dr. NE, Winston-Salem, NC 27101; Web site www.billdavisracing.com

- **Stacy Compton:** Stacy Compton Fan Club, P.O. Box 637, Hurt, VA 24563

- **Derrike Cope:** Derrike Cope Fan Club, Web site www.derrikecope.com

- **Ricky Craven:** Ricky Craven Fan Club, P.O. Box 472, Concord, NC, 28026

✔ **Wally Dallenbach Jr.:** Wally Dallenbach Fan Club, Web site www
.wallydallenbach.net

✔ **Mike Dillon:** Mike Dillon Fan Club, P.O. Box 30414, Winston-Salem, NC,
27130

✔ **Dale Earnhardt:** CLUB E, 4707 E. Baseline Rd., Phoenix, AZ 85040; phone
888-33-CLUB-E; Web site www.earnhardtfan.com

✔ **Dale Earnhardt Jr:** Club E Jr., 4707 E. Baseline Rd., Phoenix, AZ 85040;
phone 877-CLUB-E-JR; Web site www.dalejr.com

✔ **Bill Elliott:** Bill Elliott Fan Club, P.O. Box 248, Dawsonville, GA 30534

✔ **Tim Fedewa:** Tim Fedewa Fan Club, P.O. Box 428, Terrell, N.C. 28682

✔ **Jeff Gordon:** Jeff Gordon National Fan Club, P.O. Box 515, Williams, AZ
86046-0515; phone 520-635-5333; Web site www.jeffgordon.com

✔ **David Green:** David Green Fan Club, P.O. Box 4821, Archdale, NC
27263-4821

✔ **Mark Green:** Mark Green Fan Club, P.O. Box 5735, Concord, NC 28207

✔ **Steve Grissom:** Steve Grissom Fan Club, P.O. Box 989, Statesville, NC
28687-0989

✔ **Bobby Hillin:** Bobby Hillin Fan Club, 110 Knob Hill Rd., Mooresville, NC
28115

✔ **Lance Hooper:** Lance Hooper Fan Club, P.O. Box 903323, Palmdale, CA
93590-3323

✔ **Ron Hornaday:** Ron Hornaday Fan Club, P.O. Box 870, Kannapolis, NC
28082-0870

✔ **Ernie Irvan:** Ernie Irvan Fan Club, 703 Performance Rd., Mooresville, NC
28115; phone 704-663-3263

✔ **Dale Jarrett:** Dale Jarrett Fan Club, 4707 E. Baseline Rd., Phoenix, AZ
85040; phone 888-DALE-JARRETT; Web site www.dalejarrettonline
.com

✔ **Jason Keller:** Jason Keller Fan Club, P.O. Box 14748, Greenville, SC 29610.

✔ **Bobby Labonte:** Bobby Labonte Fan Club, 4707 E. Baseline Rd., Phoenix,
AZ 85040; phone 877-4-BOBBY-L; Web site www.bobbylabontefan.com

✔ **Terry Labonte:** Terry Labonte Fan Club, P.O. Box 843, Trinity, NC 27370;
Web site www.kelloggsracing.com

✔ **Randy LaJoie:** Randy LaJoie Fan Club, P.O. Box 3478, Westport, CT 06880

✔ **Kevin Lepage:** Kevin Lepage Fan Club, 159 Bevan Dr., Mooresville, NC,
28115

✔ **Chad Little:** Chad Little Fan Club, P.O. Box 562323, Charlotte, NC 28256;
phone 704-662-9700; Web site www.chadlittle.com

- ✔ **Sterling Marlin:** Sterling Marlin Fan Club, 1116 W. 7th St., Suite 62, Columbia, TN 38401

- ✔ **Mark Martin:** Mark Martin Fan Club, P.O. Box 68, Ash Flat, AR 72513; phone 870-994-7422; Web site www.roushracing.com

- ✔ **Rick Mast:** Rick Mast Fan Club, Rt. 6, Box 224-A, Lexington, VA 24450

- ✔ **Jeremy Mayfield:** Jeremy Mayfield Fan Club, P.O. Box 2365, Cornelius, NC 28031

- ✔ **Ted Musgrave:** Ted Musgrave Fan Club, P.O. Box 1089, Liberty, NC 27298

- ✔ **Jerry Nadeau:** Jerry Nadeau Fan Club, P.O. Box 1358, Harrisburg, NC 28075; phone 704-455-8180; Web site www.jerry-nadeau.com

- ✔ **NASCAR:** NASCAR Fan Club, 4707 E. Baseline Rd., Phoenix, AZ 85040; phone 888-533-1200; Web site www.nascarfans.com

- ✔ **Joe Nemechek:** Joe Nemechek Fan Club, P.O. Box 1131, Mooresville, NC 28115; phone 800-81-RACE-CLUB; Web site www.joenemechek.com

- ✔ **Steve Park:** Steve Park Fan Club, P.O. Box 172, East Northport, NY 11731-0172; Web site www.steve-park.com

- ✔ **Kyle Petty:** Kyle Petty Fan Club, 135 Longfield Dr., Mooresville, NC 28115; Web site www.pettypage.com or www.pettyracing.com

- ✔ **Richard Petty:** Richard Petty Fan Club, 1028 East 22nd St., Kannapolis, NC 28083; Web site www.pettypage.com or www.pettyracing.com

- ✔ **Robert Pressley:** Robert Pressley Fan Club, P.O. Box 46361, Washington DC 20050-6361

- ✔ **Ricky Rudd:** Ricky Rudd Fan Club, P.O. Box 7586, Richmond, VA 23231; Web site www.rickyrudd.com

- ✔ **Elliott and Hermie Sadler:** Web site www.sadlerfanclub.com

- ✔ **Andy Santerre:** Andy Santerre Fan Club, Attention: Sue Santerre, P.O. Box 994, Harrisburg, NC 28075-0994; phone 704-455-1447

- ✔ **Elton Sawyer:** Patty Moise/Elton Sawyer Fan Club, P.O. Box 77919, Greensboro, NC 27417

- ✔ **Ken Schrader:** Ken Schrader Fan Club, P.O. Box 1227, Kannapolis, NC 28082; phone 704-786-8493; Web site www.schraderracing.com

- ✔ **Mike Skinner:** Mike Skinner Fan Club, Web site www.rcracing.com

- ✔ **Jimmy Spencer:** Jimmy Spencer Fan Club, P.O. Box 1626, Mooresville, NC 28115.

- ✔ **Jack Sprague:** Jack Sprague Fan Club, 280 Hwy 29 S., Suite 120 Box 173, Concord, NC 28027

- ✔ **Tony Stewart:** Tony Stewart Fan Club, 5777 W. 74th St., Indianapolis, IN 46278; phone 800-867-6067; Web site www.tonystewart.com

- ✔ **Hut Stricklin:** Hut Stricklin Fan Club, P.O. Box 1028, Calera, AL 35040

- ✔ **Dick Trickle:** Dick Trickle Fan Club, 5415 Vesuvius-Furnace Rd., Iron Station, NC 28080

- ✔ **Kenny Wallace:** Kenny Wallace Fan Club, P.O. Box 3050, Concord, NC 28025

- ✔ **Mike Wallace:** Mike Wallace Fan Club, 224 Rolling Hill Rd., Suite 9A, Mooresville, NC 28115

- ✔ **Rusty Wallace:** Rusty Wallace Fan Club, 4707 E. Baseline Rd., Phoenix, AZ 85040; phone 877-RUSTY-WALLACE; Web site `www.rustywallace.com`

- ✔ **Darrell Waltrip:** Darrell Waltrip Fan Club, P.O. Box 381, Harrisburg, NC 28075; Web site `www.dw17.com`

- ✔ **Michael Waltrip:** Michael Waltrip Fan Club, P.O. Box 339, Sherrills Ford, NC 28673

Race shop addresses

If you'd like to get a souvenir autographed by a driver or a crew member, send it to that driver's or crew member's race shop with return postage. Usually, the race shop has a room just for souvenirs, where a driver goes to sign all types of T-shirts, die-cast cars, posters, and other trinkets. It may take them awhile to send your souvenir back to you, maybe six months to a year if it's Jeff Gordon or Dale Earnhardt, so don't get impatient. They're signing as fast as they can!

Here are addresses for some of the bigger race shops. Just address your package to the driver, care of the race shop, and it will get to him eventually:

- ✔ Brett Bodine Racing, 304 Performance Rd., Mooresville, NC 28115

- ✔ Dale Earnhardt Inc., 1675 Coddle Creek Hwy., Mooresville, NC 28115

- ✔ Penske-Kranefuss Racing, 163 Rolling Hills Rd., Mooresville, NC 28117

- ✔ Penske Racing South, 136 Knob Hill Rd., Moorseville, NC 28117-6847

- ✔ Bessey Motorsports, 11881 Vance Davis Dr., Charlotte, NC 28269

- ✔ Travis Carter Enterprises, 2668 Peachtree Rd., Statesville, NC 28625

- ✔ Richard Childress Racing, P.O. Box 1189, 236 Industrial Dr., Welcome, NC 27374

- ✔ Bill Davis Racing, 301 Old Thomasville Rd., High Point, NC 27260

- ✔ Donlavey Racing, 5011 Old Midlothian Pike, Richmond, VA 23224

- ✔ Bill Elliott Racing, P.O. Box 7048, Statesville, NC 28687

- Joe Gibbs Racing, 13415 Reese Blvd., Huntersville, NC 28078

- Larry Hedrick Motorsports, P.O. Box 511, Statesville, NC 28687

- Hendrick Motorsports, Papa Joe Hendrick Blvd., P.O. Box 9, Harrisburg, NC 28075

- Irvan-Simo Racing, 703 Performance Rd., Mooresville, NC 28115

- Jasper Motorsports, 110 Knob Hill Rd., Mooresville, NC 28117

- LJ Racing, 129 Bevan Dr., Mooresville, NC 28115

- Mattei Motorsports, 6007 Victory Lane, Harrisburg, NC 28075

- Marcis Auto Racing, P.O. Box 645, Skyland, NC 28776

- MB2 Motorsports, 185 McKenzie Rd., Mooresville, NC 28115

- Butch Mock Motorsports, 217 Rolling Hills Rd., Mooresville, NC 28117

- Melling Racing, 2004 Pitts School Rd., Concord, NC 28027

- MidWest Transit Racing, 4909 Stough Rd., Concord, NC 28027

- Morgan-McClure Motorsports, 26502 Newbanks Rd., Abington, VA 24210

- Andy Petree Racing, P.O. Box 325, East Flat Rock, NC 28726

- Petty Enterprises, 311 Branson Mill Rd., Randleman, NC 27317

- Roush Racing, 122 Knob Hill Rd., Mooresville, NC 28117

- Rudd Performance Motorsports, P.O. Box 3185, 292 Rolling Hills Rd., Mooresville, NC 28117

- SBIII Motorsports, 103 Center Lane, Huntersville, NC 28078

- Team SABCO, 114 Meadow Hill Circle, Mooresville, NC 28117

- Tyler Jet Motorsports, 6780 Hudspeth Rd., P.O. Box 910, Harrisburg, NC 28075

- Wood Brothers Racing, 21 Performance Dr., Stuart, VA 24171-4000

- Yarborough Motorsports, 4200 Stough Rd., Concord, NC 28027

- Robert Yates Racing, 6510 Hudspeth Rd., Harrisburg, NC 28075

Part V
The Part of Tens

The 5th Wave   By Rich Tennant

In this part . . .

This part gives you tidbits of information about some of the greatest racers and the greatest races in NASCAR — my unsolicited opinion on a few important subjects. You find out who I think are NASCAR's greatest drivers and future stars, and which NASCAR races I think are the best, from a fan's standpoint of course. (This is why I list super-speedway races, which most drivers dread.) If you're in a rush to digest as much NASCAR information in the least amount of time, this part is the perfect place for you to turn.

Chapter 16

The Greatest NASCAR Drivers of All Time

. . . .

In This Chapter

▶ Reviewing my pick of NASCAR's legendary drivers

▶ Looking at the stellar statistics of great drivers

. . . .

Some drivers win races but only a few — those with special talent, charisma, and personalities you just can't forget — become legends. These drivers have left an indelible mark on the sport of stock-car racing, and while they may not be the drivers you cheer for, they are the ones who garner your respect.

The greatest NASCAR drivers of all time can be argued until the end of the next millennium, but here are the ones — in alphabetical order — that I think are the best. Some have won championships. Some have won a lot of races. Some have shown unparalleled determination. I've raced against a lot of them, so I've gotten to know their driving styles and personalities firsthand. Because of that, I'm convinced that they're some of the best drivers ever.

Bobby Allison

In his 25 years of NASCAR Winston Cup Series racing, Bobby Allison was fearless. And, from time to time, he was reckless. But that in-your-face driving style and unmistakable talent was the reason he was one of the most successful drivers in NASCAR history. He won the 1983 NASCAR Winston Cup Series championship, and 84 races in his career, tying him with Darrell Waltrip for third on the all-time wins list.

The most memorable moment of his career came when he won the 1988 Daytona 500 — his third Daytona 500 win — and his son, the late Davey Allison, finished second. The two celebrated together in Victory Lane, with son proud of dad, and dad proud of son. Bobby retired in 1988, but still attends many races.

Dale Earnhardt

Ask any NASCAR driver, and they'll tell you that Dale Earnhardt was the one person they didn't want to see in their rear-view mirrors, especially during the final laps of a race. You see, there's a reason he was called the Intimidator. It's not just because he didn't exude warmth. It's because he was the quintessential bully on the racetrack, driving rough enough and fast enough to win 74 NASCAR Winston Cup Series races (through the 1999 season). That ranks the driver from rural North Carolina sixth on the all-time wins list. But the number of championships Earnhardt won overshadows his race victories. He won seven championships since he started racing at NASCAR's highest level in 1975, tying him with Richard Petty for the most NASCAR Winston Cup Series championships in history. He also won more than $30 million in his career to rank first on NASCAR's money list. While Earnhardt won on nearly every NASCAR track, his forte was on superspeedways where legend has it, he could "see" air coming off the cars around him, and thus navigate through the air better than anyone (see Chapter 9 for more on this phenomenon). Still, no matter what track he was racing on, his competition couldn't help but sweat when they saw his legendary No. 3 Chevy coming up on them, because they knew the temperament and the talent of the man who was driving it.

Jeff Gordon

When Jeff Gordon came into NASCAR Winston Cup Series racing in 1992, everybody thought he was going to make it big and become the next greatest NASCAR driver of the century. Everybody was right.

In 1995, Gordon won the first of three NASCAR Winston Cup Series championships, winning it when he was just 24 to become the youngest champion in NASCAR's modern era, which dates back to 1972. After that immediate success, Gordon quickly was dubbed "Wonder Boy" and booed at nearly every racetrack on the circuit. Why? Perhaps because he won too much, too early. Perhaps because he grew up in California, then moved to Indiana to race, so he wasn't a Southerner or a good ol' boy like Earnhardt or Bill Elliott. Perhaps because he becomes more and more unstoppable as the years go on. Gordon won back-to-back NASCAR Winston Cup Series titles in 1997 and 1998, but 1998 was his best season yet, during which he won 13 races to tie Richard Petty's modern-era record for wins in a season. He also won a record $9.3 million in prize money. The scary part is, he's not retiring any time soon and has many more years to break records, win races, and clinch championships. That's good for the fans — bad for his competition.

Alan Kulwicki

Even though Alan Kulwicki won only five NASCAR Winston Cup Series races in his career, he still was good enough to win the 1992 NASCAR Winston Cup Series championship. And he made an impact on the sport that no statistics could measure, as one of the first competitors to treat the sport as a science. Kulwicki grew up in Wisconsin, driving in the American Speed Association in the Midwestern United States before moving south to try his hand at NASCAR racing. But Kulwicki was different than most drivers. He had a college degree in engineering and used the physics and math that he learned in school to set up his race car. At first, people laughed when he showed up at races with a briefcase filled with numbers and calculations — but now briefcases have become part of the mandatory gear for crew chiefs and the team members who work on the setup of a car. Also, Kulwicki was determined to be his own car owner and make it to the top the hard way. He did just that, winning the 1992 championship while winning only two races that year. Kulwicki wasn't able to defend his title the next season, however, because he died in a plane crash.

David Pearson

No one wanted to mess with David Pearson when he was driving on the circuit. He was just the kind of quiet, cool, confident guy you didn't want to make angry — and people called him the "Silver Fox" because of his sly, cunning style. Perhaps that's why Pearson, who is retired from the sport, won 105 races in his NASCAR Winston Cup Series career. He ranks second on the all-time wins list.

Pearson was a versatile driver who did well on superspeedways, intermediate tracks, short tracks, and road courses. He won nearly everywhere, so much so that Richard Petty still insists Pearson is the best driver in NASCAR history. Pearson won three NASCAR Winston Cup Series championships — in 1966, 1968, and 1969, but continued to drive until 1986 before retiring. Even in his final years as a racer, though, he was still a daunting sight on the track for his opponents. Not that he tried to be — that's just the way he was. He made racing and winning look easy.

Richard Petty

Richard Petty isn't called stock-car racing's King for nothing. He won a record 200 races in his 35-year career, nearly twice as many as anyone else. He won a record seven NASCAR Winston Cup Series championships. He won a record seven Daytona 500s. He also won a shocking 27 of 49 races in 1967, including ten in a row. But more important than all that, Petty, who retired from driving in 1992 and is now a NASCAR car owner, won the adoration of the fans.

Petty wasn't just a successful driver. He was the sport's public relations director, signing autographs for hours, talking to fans, posing for pictures, and selling stock-car racing — which started out as a southern, backwoods sport — to modern America. For example, when he won the 200th race of his career, President Ronald Reagan just happened to be at the track to congratulate him. Of course, their meeting made all the papers. So it's no wonder Petty has become a sports icon and a fan favorite with his trademark cowboy hat, dark sunglasses, and wide smile. He's part of racing's most famous family — which started out with his father, Lee Petty, who won three championships and the inaugural Daytona 500. Richard Petty's son, Kyle, races in the NASCAR Winston Cup Series. His grandson, Adam, is currently on his way up through the racing ranks (see Chapter 18). But it'll be nearly impossible for anyone to top what Petty did in the sport — and what he did *for* the sport.

Rusty Wallace

In an age when most drivers just hop into their cars and head for the racetrack, Rusty Wallace is old-school. He still gets under the car to check things out. He still gets his hands dirty. He still tells the crew chief exactly what to do with the car, instead of just saying, "it's loose" or "it's tight." That's what has made him so good over the years — and so successful. Wallace grew up racing on short tracks in the midwestern U.S., where he built his own cars, raced his own cars, then repaired his own cars afterward. That's where he learned the ins and outs of a race car and how to tweak it to ride just the way he wanted it.

When he began his NASCAR Winston Cup Series career in 1980, he took that knowledge of cars with him — and it translated into stardom right away. In his very first race in the series that year in Atlanta, the bushy-headed redhead finished second to Dale Earnhardt and immediately earned the respect of his competitors. Now Wallace is one of the most successful and popular drivers in NASCAR history. He has won 49 races (through the 1999 season), as well as the 1989 championship. And, if need be, he could build his own cars and drive them, too!

Darrell Waltrip

The moment Darrell Waltrip began NASCAR Winston Cup Series racing in 1972, the sport was energized. Back then he was a fast-talker with a quick wit and not a pinch of humility. His personality grew even more outrageous every time he won a race. In fact, he earned the nickname "Jaws" for talking so much and boasting about his accomplishments. Fans either loved him or hated him with a passion because of his brashness. The thing is, Waltrip wasn't totally out of line when he boasted about himself — because he backed up his words with success on the track. He has won 84 races in his NASCAR Winston Cup Series career, which ties him for third on the all-time wins list. He also has won three championships along the way.

Waltrip has mellowed over the years, but he still loves to drive a race car — and he still loves to gab. Even now as he is on the verge of retirement, Waltrip can still trash-talk with the best of them. That skill won't be useless, though, even after Waltrip stops driving at the end of the 2000 season. He moonlights as a TV commentator and plans to do that full-time after his driving career is over. No doubt he'll be as successful, colorful, and entertaining as a commentator as he is as a driver.

Cale Yarborough

Cale Yarborough may be small in stature, but that didn't stop him from driving like an oversized linebacker. The three-time NASCAR Winston Cup Series champion never thought twice about pushing himself or his cars to the limit, especially when he was teamed up with legendary car owner Junior Johnson — who didn't have any limits himself. Yarborough, who retired as a driver in 1988 and owns a NASCAR team now, was a spitfire even before getting into a race car, claiming to have wrestled snakes and alligators — and even insisting he got hit by lightning when he was young. If you believe all his tales, Yarborough was a tough character even before he became one of the best NASCAR drivers in history. He won 83 races to put himself fifth on NASCAR's all-time wins list. That includes three Daytona 500s, which he won in 1977, 1983, and 1984. For a while, though, Yarborough defected from the stock-car ranks to go Indy-car racing. He raced Indy cars in 1971 and '72, then headed back to what he knew best. And that was winning.

Chapter 17

Ten Can't-Miss Races of the Year

In This Chapter

▶ Listing the NASCAR Winston Cup Series races that you shouldn't miss

▶ Finding out why certain races are so special

*E*ven though you may want to see every NASCAR race, it's okay to admit you don't have the time or the means to watch 34 NASCAR Winston Cup Series races each year. Because you probably can't catch them all, however, this chapter outlines some of the most exciting, hair-raising, or historically important races that you just shouldn't miss.

Fans and drivers have their own favorite races, but these are some of the ones on everybody's list. Sure, it's all subjective, but these races consistently provide action. Check out Chapter 13 for a full description of each track.

Daytona 500

The Daytona 500, held in February, is NASCAR's Super Bowl — the most revered and most heralded race of the year. Some of the most famous drivers have won it, including Richard Petty (seven times!), Bobby Allison, Cale Yarborough, and even Indy car legends Mario Andretti and A. J. Foyt. Unlike the Super Bowl, though, the Daytona 500 is the season opener instead of the season finale. That's what makes it so special. Teams spend almost the entire off-season preparing for this one race, and come to Daytona in February thinking they can win that year's championship. It's where hopes are born each year. If you have a good finish at Daytona, it sets a tone for your entire season, so emotions — and speeds — run high throughout the afternoon.

Watching the Daytona 500 not only gives you high speeds, plenty of thrills, and multi-car accidents galore — it also gives you a preview of who may race strong during the upcoming season.

Coca-Cola 600

The Coca-Cola 600, formerly known as the World 600, is held the Sunday before Memorial Day at Lowe's Motor Speedway and is NASCAR's longest event. With 600 miles of racing, it's NASCAR's version of a marathon, so fans have to be tenacious to watch the entire race, flag to flag. At the start in late afternoon, it isn't history's most exciting race — but give 43 cranky, hot, exhausted, and win-hungry drivers 50 laps to go at night, under the stars, and watch things get really interesting. Drivers, crews, and cars are tested in this endurance race where only the competitors with the most stamina and the cars with the sturdiest parts finish up front.

Pepsi 400 at Daytona

Races at superspeedways are naturally fun to watch because the cars run so fast and so close together. What makes them even more fun is when a race is held at night under the lights at Daytona International Speedway. The Pepsi 400, formerly called the Firecracker 400, is held the Saturday of the Fourth of July weekend and is the only NASCAR Winston Cup Series night race held at a track longer than 1.5 miles. It was moved from daytime to night in 1998 after track officials spent $5 million to install lights around the huge 2.5-mile superspeedway. Not only is the race cooler to watch for spectators because it's no longer held in the sweltering midday heat of Central Florida — but it's also one of the year's most heart-pounding and spectacular events. To top that, the post-race fireworks show is awe-inspiring.

Brickyard 400

Indy car purists said hell would freeze over before stock cars raced at Indianapolis Motor Speedway, the legendary home of the Indianapolis 500. Well, hell froze over for good reason. The Brickyard 400, held in the beginning of August, is one of the year's most interesting NASCAR races. With a hefty paycheck at stake for the winner, drivers take chances to get to the front.

NASCAR only goes to the 2.5-mile Brickyard once a year, which makes the event all that more special. But every time a stock-car driver goes to Victory Lane at the storied track, he makes history. Stock cars made their debut there in 1994, when Jeff Gordon won the inaugural event. Since then, the Brickyard 400 has been one of the best tickets in racing.

Goody's 500

If you want to guarantee yourself a good time, watch the night race at Bristol Motor Speedway, held every August. What could be better than 43 cars circling a tiny, high-banked, half-mile track and bumping into each other the whole way? Seeing all that at night — when sparks fly and tempers flare at the track tucked into the mountains of eastern Tennessee. It's the roughest racing you'll ever see.

Actually, both races at Bristol, even the one held during the day in April, are a must-see, but the night race is absolutely electric — as well as action-packed.

Winston 500

NASCAR has two superspeedways where cars run in packs only inches apart — the 2.66-mile Talladega Superspeedway in Alabama and the 2.5-mile Daytona International Speedway in Florida. Of those two, Talladega is bigger, and faster. It's just not a warm-and-friendly place. Both races at Talladega are sensational to watch, especially the Winston 500, which is held in October and close to the end of the season. (The other race is in April.) In the fall, the race for the championship may be hot — and the title may be won or lost at the super-big, super-daunting track because of all the accidents there. As a fan, you can't see the entire racetrack no matter where you sit in the grandstands, but seeing the swarm of cars coming off one of the turns is jaw-dropping. They race two-, three-, four-, and even five-wide at times, and you may wonder how it's possible.

Texas 500

Texas Motor Speedway hasn't been around long and hosts only one race a year, but it quickly has made a name for itself. The 1.5-mile track in Fort Worth, Texas, opened in 1997 and has been home to strange problems with the racing surface (such as when water began seeping through the track in 1998), and fast, close racing. The April race is always enthralling for one reason or another, so if you need a jolt of automatic mayhem, just tune in or buy tickets.

The Winston All-Star Race

Even though the Winston all-star race doesn't count toward the NASCAR Winston Cup Series championship, it still should be one of the races you see — even if it's just for the novelty. It's held a week before the Coca-Cola 600 at Lowe's Motor Speedway in May, but it's not at all like a normal NASCAR race. First, there's a funky, crazy way to qualify for this event: Drivers take a total of three laps, tearing onto pit road for a two-tire pit stop at the end of either the first or second lap. After their crew changes the car's tires, the driver burns rubber leaving the pits and completes his qualifying run. No, the usual pit road speeds don't count at the Winston. In fact, few of the real rules count. The race itself is a 70-lap sprint, consisting of two 30-lap segments, plus one 10-lap dash to the finish. The paycheck is huge, so drivers race like maniacs to the finish. From a fan's standpoint, what can be better than that?

Southern 500

Darlington Raceway is NASCAR's first superspeedway — it opened in 1950 — and the Southern 500 is one of NASCAR's most prized races. But winning the Labor Day classic and becoming a part of Darlington history isn't an easy task. Darlington is arguably the most unique and challenging track in NASCAR racing. Its walls seem to jump out and attack cars as the vehicles zoom through the corners. The rough racing surface chews up tires in a blink. So you can see why only the bravest, most skillful drivers make it to Victory Lane at the South Carolina track.

Cale Yarborough has the record for Southern 500 wins with five of them — but Jeff Gordon and Bobby Allison aren't far behind with four wins apiece. That alone puts them a notch above other drivers in the history book. Watching drivers as talented as those navigating this tricky track is worth the price of admission or spending part of your Labor Day weekend inside watching TV.

NAPA 500

What makes the NAPA 500 at Atlanta Motor Speedway a don't-miss race is that it's the NASCAR Winston Cup Series season finale. If it's a close race for the championship, the race may be a nail-biter for drivers and teams who are in the running for the title — as well as their fans who have to bundle up to sit in the grandstands at the perennially chilly event held in late November.

The 1997 NAPA 500 is a perfect example of how exciting the season-ending event can get. Jeff Gordon, Dale Jarrett, and I each had a chance at winning the championship before the race was over. As it turned out, Gordon won his second title — but barely, after finishing 17th when he had to finish 18th or better to win the championship. He beat out Jarrett by 14 points and me by 29, which made it the closest three-way race for the title in NASCAR history.

Chapter 18

NASCAR's Future Stars

In This Chapter

▶ Taking a look at the new crop of driving talent

▶ Reviewing the prospects of NASCAR's youngest drivers

*E*ven though some of NASCAR's most famous drivers — including NASCAR Winston Cup Series champion Bill Elliott — are nearing the end of their careers, NASCAR racing won't lack superstars in the new millennium. Look for a new crop of talented racers to inject youth, energy and pizzazz into NASCAR in the coming years.

Casey Atwood

Most drivers ease their way into NASCAR's top levels, taking years to mature as a competitor, develop their racing skills, and acclimate to the pressure-packed environment. But not Casey Atwood. He started running in the NASCAR Busch Series not long after he started shaving. (Or had he started shaving yet?) In 1998, at age 17, he became the youngest NASCAR Busch Series driver ever. Later that year, to everyone's surprise, he won the pole for a race at his home track of Nashville Speedway, and then skillfully drove to a second-place finish. He won two poles in only 13 races that year, setting himself up for a memorable first full season on the circuit. In 1999, he continued to show his potential by winning two races. His first win came at the Milwaukee Mile, where he became the youngest driver to win a race in the series' history. Expect to see his name in the record books many more times in the future because he's a natural racer.

Greg Biffle

Washington State isn't exactly the hotbed of NASCAR racing, but Greg Biffle has proven the northwestern U. S. can produce talented and determined drivers. Just like many other NASCAR drivers, Biffle started out racing on short tracks, but unlike other drivers, he won the 1996 Pacific Coast Region championship by winning a whopping 27 times in 47 starts — 57 percent of the time! After dominating like that, Biffle was hired by owner Jack Roush (who has an impeccable eye for talent) to drive in the NASCAR Craftsman Truck Series. Then, Biffle, born in 1969, won Rookie of the Year in 1998. He went on to win nine races and compete for the truck series championship in 1999 (finishing third in points). Not bad for a guy who runs a fabricating business in his hometown of Vancouver, Washington, in his spare time.

Dave Blaney

Dave Blaney may be a little older than the usual up-and-coming drivers — he was born in 1962 — but he isn't a late bloomer. It's just that he started his career driving sprint cars, which are incredibly fast, lightweight race cars without fenders. And he was darn good at it, too, making his name as one of the nation's best sprint car drivers of the 1990s. Blaney was the 1995 World of Outlaws series champion and was runner-up in that dirt-track series four times — in 1993, '94, '96, and '97. He is among several drivers, including Jeff Gordon and Tony Stewart, who have successfully made the move from open-wheel cars to stock cars. The skills those drivers developed racing sprint cars on dirt were many, but one of the most important was developing the skills to control their race cars as they slid through slippery turns. It taught them how to get their cars to respond the way they wanted them to, in any kind of racing. Blaney defected from sprint cars in 1998 and so far has gotten the knack of stock-car driving without too much trouble. His first NASCAR Winston Cup Series season is in 2000, where he'll try to build as impressive a résumé as he did in sprint cars.

Dale Earnhardt Jr.

On the track, there's no doubt that Dale Earnhardt Jr. is similar to his father and namesake, seven-time NASCAR Winston Cup Series champion Dale Earnhardt. The two are winners — both confident, aggressive drivers who know how to get to the front. But they're not exactly the same, considering the elder Earnhardt is known for his rough driving and his son is known to be more courteous. What the two definitely have in common, however, are their racing genes. Earnhardt Jr.'s grandfather and Earnhardt's father, Ralph, was a NASCAR Late Model Sportsman (now the NASCAR Busch Series) champion in 1956. Still, no one expected Earnhardt Jr. to wow the racing world when he ran his first full season in the NASCAR Busch Series in 1998, when he was 24. But he proved everyone wrong by winning the championship — and seven races — during that season, and winning the championship again in 1999. His first win came at Texas Motor Speedway in just his 16th career NASCAR Busch Series start. Now everyone wants to find out what sort of impact he'll make on the NASCAR Winston Cup Series series in 2000, when he will vie for rookie of the year.

Give Earnhardt Jr. a few years and he'll be mature enough to do anything. His dad won a series championship one year after he won rookie of the year, so "Little E," as Earnhardt Jr. is called, will try to follow suit. Still, off the track, Little E isn't a carbon copy of his father. He is a younger, hipper Earnhardt — one who bleaches his hair, loves rock 'n' roll and alternative music, and is already bringing a whole new breed of fans into NASCAR. Those fans will have plenty to cheer about.

Matt Kenseth

Matt Kenseth, a Wisconsin native who migrated to the south to pursue his racing dreams, is a little older (he was born in 1972) than some of the newer drivers, and his driving shows it. He's patient, smooth, and smart with his moves. He doesn't get too excited when things go badly; he doesn't get too excited when things go well. That even temper will get him far in the sport, but his mentor and future car owner — me! — will get him even farther. I took on Kenseth as an apprentice and am now his personal adviser and private tutor on how to get the car just right, win races, and succeed in the sport. Kenseth will run for rookie of the year in 2000 for a team that I partly own with my car owner, Jack Roush. I know I'm a little biased, but there's no doubt Kenseth has the guidance, equipment, personnel, and talent to be one of the most successful new drivers in NASCAR's top series.

Elliott Sadler

You won't find a more affable, likeable guy in the NASCAR Winston Cup Series garage than Elliott Sadler. But just because Sadler walks around with a smile while humming his favorite country tunes doesn't mean he's not serious about racing. While Tony Stewart overshadowed him in their quests for a rookie of the year title in 1999, Sadler had a solid first year in NASCAR Winston Cup Series. He wasn't at all discouraged by Stewart's unusually stellar rookie performance — and it's that positive attitude that will help him in racing, where seasons can be as unpredictable as a derailed roller coaster.

He developed that upbeat demeanor while growing up in Emporia, Va., a rural town not far from South Boston Speedway (the same speedway where NASCAR Winston Cup Series racers Ward and Jeff Burton first made their names in the sport). Sadler won the 1995 Late Model Stock championship at that track before making his NASCAR Busch Series debut there that same year. He was only 21. Just two years later, he found himself in the NASCAR Winston Cup Series racing for the legendary Wood Brothers team. Soon, he'll find himself making a lasting impact on the sport.

Tony Stewart

It looks as if Tony Stewart didn't make a bad decision when he moved from Indy cars to stock cars. Even though he won the 1997 Indy Racing League championship, Stewart wanted to race in NASCAR, so he packed up and headed for the NASCAR Winston Cup Series full-time in 1999. That's when he made history, becoming the first rookie to win a race since the late Davey Allison did so in 1987. Stewart also finished the season as one of only three rookies in NASCAR history to finish in the top five in points (finishing fourth) — and the first rookie to do so since 1966.

Even though Stewart was a humble rookie, he didn't hide his fiery personality on or off the track — and that's what has made him one of NASCAR's most popular drivers. He showed his passion for racing when he drove in the Indianapolis 500 in May 1999, then jetted to Charlotte, N.C., to race in the Coca-Cola 600 later that day. It showed his versatility, just when he won titles in three different United States Auto Club series divisions in 1995, becoming the first driver ever to do so. After garnering those credentials during his career — as well as glowing statistics in his rookie NASCAR Winston Cup Series season when he was 28 — Stewart has proven he will be one of the most-heralded NASCAR drivers of the decade.

Appendix A

NASCAR Jargon

· ·

Aerodynamics

Race car aerodynamics is the way air flows over the surfaces of a car, over and under the body or through the engine and radiator. It also includes the wake of turbulent air left behind a car as it travels.

Air dam

An air dam is an extension on the front bumper that blocks air as it hits the front of a car, keeping too much of the air from flowing under the vehicle and reducing the car's speed. It plays a big role in the aerodynamics of a car, keeping the front end stable.

Appearance

When a driver makes an appearance, he shows up to sign posters, programs, and trading cards for fans or employees at supermarket grand openings, auto shows, conventions, car dealerships, fairgrounds, and auto stores.

Associate sponsor

Associate sponsors are companies that sponsor racing teams. They pay less money and, in turn, get less exposure on the car or the uniform than the primary sponsors do.

Autograph card

An autograph card is a sheet of heavy-duty paper with a driver's picture on the front and his vital statistics on the back. They are free for fans and used for souvenirs or for autographs.

Backstretch

The straight section of the track located on the opposite side of the track of the start/finish line. On an oval track, it is between the second and third turns.

Banking

The angle of a racetrack's racing surface.

Battling for position

When two cars are racing each other for the same place — whether first place or 20th.

Being on the lead lap

A driver has completed the same number of laps as the leader.

Bite

See *wedge*.

Blocking

A driver positions his car to keep the driver behind him from passing him.

Blowing an engine

A driver won't finish the race because his engine failed beyond immediate repair.

Camber

The amount that a tire is tilted from vertical so the tire can touch more of the racing surface.

Champion's provisional

The champion's provisional is the last provisional given out for a race. Former series champions are eligible for it if they don't make the race based on their qualifying laps and if they are high enough in points. The champion's provisional is the 43rd starting spot in a race, meaning the driver must start last. See also *provisional entry*.

Car chief

Person who works closely with the crew chief in figuring out setups for the car. The person who, along with the rest of the crew, physically makes changes.

Carburetor

The part of the engine where air and fuel mix in an internal combustion engine.

Carburetor restrictor plate

A thin metal plate with four holes that restricts the flow of air into an engine's carburetor, thus reducing horsepower and speed. Used only at Daytona and Talladega — NASCAR's two superspeedways.

Catch can man

The catch can man stands behind the car on the left side and holds a special container at the end of the car to collect gas that overflows from the gas tank.

Caution flag

A yellow flag that's used to indicate trouble on the racetrack, including oil or debris on the racing surface. It signals drivers to slow down and follow a pace car around the track.

Chassis

The steel frame of a car.

Chassis dynamometer

Machines that measure the amount of power translated from the wheels to the ground.

Check valve

A safety valve that prevents fuel spills if the car turns over.

Competition Performance Index (CPI)

A formula that evaluates driver performance in the NASCAR Weekly Racing Series, including average finish, number of wins, driver attendance, and the average number of cars in the field.

Compression ratio

The volume of a cylinder compared to the volume it compresses to when the piston is fully extended. The higher the compression, the more horsepower.

Contingency programs

Bonus money given by companies whose products a driver uses or whose decals a driver runs on his car.

Crew chief

A crew chief is the leader of the race team who oversees employees and handles the building and fine-tuning of a race car. He's responsible for deciding which changes to make to the race car throughout race weekend and what race strategies to use on race day.

Dash cars

Dash cars are sub-compact cars that are scaled-down NASCAR Winston Cup Series cars.

Deck lid

The rear trunk lid.

Displacement

The size of an engine measured in cubic inches. A NASCAR Winston Cup Series car's engine can't be larger than 358 cubic inches.

Downforce

The air pressure and downward force that pushes a car onto the track, causing it to stick on the racing surface. It keeps cars from losing traction at high speeds, especially going through the turns.

Drafting

Drivers race in single file and share air flow among them. Cars cut through the air much faster together than they do separately — the first car creates a vacuum that actually pulls the car behind it.

Drag

Drag is the aerodynamic force of resistance that hinders a race car as it moves through air. It's caused by air flowing beneath the car and lifting it higher in the air, as well as air flowing through the cooling system, ducts in the body, friction between a car's body, and open windows. Air travels into these openings instead of smoothly sliding over the car. With less drag, a car can accelerate faster, especially at higher speeds, because the car needs less horsepower to move forward through the air.

Engine builder

Team member in charge of building engines and coaching people to build engines nearly from scratch. His goal is to make it as lightweight — but still as durable — as possible. The engine builder is in charge of the engine assemblers, who actually put the engine together.

Engine specialist

Team member in charge of preparing the engines at the race shop, and then taking care of and tuning them after they get to the racetrack. Also called *engine tuner.*

Engine tuner

See *engine specialist.*

Fabricator

Team member who puts sheet metal on the car's frame and molds it to the shape of the car, creating the body or outside shell of the car.

Five-point seat belts

Five belts that come together at the center of a driver's chest. Each of the belts passes through a steel guide that is welded onto the car's frame: One belt goes over a driver's left shoulder, one goes over his right shoulder, another comes from the left side of the seat, one comes from the right side of the seat, and still another goes between a driver's legs. They're all latched on at a single point, where a quick-release buckle locks them into place.

Flagman

The NASCAR official who is perched over the racetrack, just above the start/finish line. The flagman signals to the drivers by waving different-colored flags that mean different things.

Flags

- **Green:** The race is started.
- **Yellow:** Caution — all drivers must slow down.
- **Red:** All drivers must stop.
- **Black:** The driver at whom the black flag is waved must get off the track.
- **White:** The lead car has one lap to go.
- **Checkered:** The winning car has crossed the finish line.

Frontstretch

The straight section of racetrack between the first and last turns.

Fuel cell

The fancy word for gas tank.

Garage pass

A permit that lets a fan behind the scenes during a race weekend, obtained through the racetrack or through NASCAR, and reserved for people who know someone who works in the sport (at the racetrack, as a sponsor, on a team, and so on). Only a few tracks sell garage passes to the general public. Also called a *pit pass*.

Gas-and-go

A quick pit stop where a car gets only gas — but no new tires.

Gas man

Pit crew member who steps over the pit wall carrying a 90-pound, 11-gallon can of gas, and then fills the gas tank. When the first can empties, he usually gets a second can from the second gas man (who doesn't go over the wall), and fills the tank with that gas as well.

General mechanics

Crew members who help the car chief set up the car, build shocks back in the trailer, rework the body of a car after a driver crashes it into the wall, and so on. They're not specialized.

Getting hung out to dry

Racing slang that means a driver has lost the draft and is losing positions by the split second. To remedy the situation, the driver must get back in line with other cars where the aerodynamics are much more conducive to going fast.

Going behind the wall

A car is too damaged to be fixed on pit road, so the team brings it to the garage.

Handling

How a car responds on the track. A car's handling is determined by how it was built (including its suspension, tires, aerodynamics, and body style) and how it is prepared for the race.

Hanging a body

Sizing sheet metal, cutting sheet metal, and then molding it onto a car's frame to form the shell of a car.

Happy Hour

The final hour of practice before an event, usually held in the late afternoon the day before the race.

Hat dance

When a race winner puts on dozens of baseball caps with sponsors logos on them in Victory Lane. Each time a driver puts the cap on, the photographers snap photos to send or sell to the sponsor involved.

Head protectors

Protection built into a driver's seat to keep his head from moving to the left or right during an accident.

Hitting points

When a driver talks about "hitting their points" or "hitting their marks" on the racetrack, he's referring to the fastest route around the track that he has mapped out in his head.

Horsepower

A unit of measurement representing how much power an engine generates.

Hospitality

Pre-scheduled meeting that drivers hold with a group of employees or guests from one of their sponsors.

Inspections

The process NASCAR officials go through to approve cars to race, qualify, and practice.

Intermediate track

Tracks more than one mile long, excluding superspeedways. See also *short track, superspeedway.*

Jackman

Pit crew member who positions the jack under a specific spot on each side of the car, pumps the handle of the jack one or two times so that it lifts the car off the ground enough for the tire changers to change the tires, and then drops the jack and lowers the car.

Lapped traffic

Cars that aren't on the lead lap. Many times, these cars are considerably slower than the leaders.

Licensee

The licensee is the person or entity who sells NASCAR goods and must pay royalty payments to the licensor (who gives the rights to sell the goods) at pre-arranged times.

Licensor

The licensor is the person or entity who gives the rights to sell NASCAR or race team goods, receiving royalty payments from the licensee (who sells the goods) in return.

Loose

A car is termed *loose* when a driver goes through a turn and the rear of his car starts to fishtail, making the driver feel as if he's losing control of the car and about to spin out. The rear tires aren't sticking well to the track and providing enough traction. This is also called *oversteer.* See also *tight.*

Mph

Miles per hour.

Modern era
Period in NASCAR history that began in 1972.

Motor mounts
Where the motor sits in relation to the body of the car.

Motorhome lot
Where drivers and owners parks their motorhomes during race weekend.

Motorhome Racing Outreach (MRO)
Organization that provides religious services, a daycare for team members' children, and organizes events for drivers and their families at the track.

NASCAR
NASCAR stands for the National Association for Stock Car Auto Racing, the organization that governs and makes rules for NASCAR racing.

NASCAR Busch Series, Grand National Division
A different series than the NASCAR Winston Cup Series, where many drivers begin their professional racing careers. Drivers train themselves and hone their driving skills before moving up to NASCAR Winston Cup Series. Some drivers stay in this league because there's less pressure to perform.

NASCAR Craftsman Truck Series
The NASCAR Craftsman Truck Series is the newest NASCAR series, featuring souped-up pickup trucks.

NASCAR Winston Cup Series
The NASCAR Winston Cup Series is NASCAR's top series.

One-groove racetrack
A racetrack with just a single path around it where cars stick to the track and handle well. If a driver gets out of that path, he could be on a portion of the track where there's not enough grip to keep his car stable — and that means he could end up in the wall. Some tracks have more than one groove — a high groove and a low groove, meaning cars can run side-by-side or two-wide around the track. Some tracks have no grooves because cars race easily on any part of the track.

Over the wall guys
The seven crew members who jump over the pit wall to service a car when it pulls onto pit road. See also *pit crew*.

Owner

The owner of the entire team. He or she has a financial stake in the race team, and therefore has final say in hiring everyone who works on the team, from the driver to the crew chief to everyone who prepares the cars for racing. The owner must also secure a sponsor to help pay the bills.

Paint scheme

The way a car is painted and decorated.

Panhard bar

See *track bar*.

Pit boxes

Pit areas, delineated with yellow lines, for the 43 cars in the race to use during pit stops.

Pit crew

A maximum of seven people who are allowed to go over the pit wall and service a car during a pit stop. See also *over the wall guys*.

Pit pass

See *garage pass*.

Pit road

A separate road inside a racetrack that usually runs parallel to a track's frontstretch. It's where cars go when they need gas, tires, or repairs.

Pit stall

Where teams watch the race and keep their equipment — separated from the pit box by the pit wall.

Pit stop

When a car pulls off the racetrack and travels down pit road where his crew services his car.

Pit wall

The cement wall separating the pit box from the pit stalls.

Pit window

An estimate of when the crew thinks the driver will need to make a pit stop to refuel.

Pole winner (pole sitter)

Driver who records the fastest lap during qualifying and gets rewarded by starting the race from the inside of the two-car front row. The outside pole winner is the driver who had the second-fastest lap during qualifying. He starts the race from the outside of the front row.

Primary sponsor

Companies that pay large sums of money to put their names on the car hoods, which is the best place to advertise because fans see them so well.

Provisional entry

Guaranteed spot in a race, given to drivers who qualify poorly during the weekend and who are high enough in points. See also past *champion's provisional.*

Racing show

Television show in which races, qualifying, and practices are dissected, and everyone from the driver to the car owner to the guy that puts gas in the car is interviewed.

Radio frequency scanner

See *scanner.*

Real money

The money that a team actually gets after winning a race. Most teams aren't eligible for all of the award money because they aren't affiliated with all of the companies that provide financial awards to the race winner.

Rear spoiler

Metal blade that runs the width of the car atop the back of its trunk. It regulates air as it flows over a car and helps push the back end of the car into the track, which gives the car more traction and better handling.

Relief driver

A driver who replaces the original driver due to injury or illness.

Revolutions per minute (rpm)

How fast an engine is turning and how hard it's working. See also *tachometer.*

Right off the truck

A driver usually says his car was great "right off the truck" when his car runs well in the first practice without any tweaking.

Road courses

Racetracks with complex configurations of left and right turns at varying angles. The track may have elevation changes as well. Sears Point Raceway and Watkins Glen International are the only two NASCAR road courses.

Roll bars

The part of the car's frame that protects the driver because it is made of strong tubing with a minimum thickness — like a tubular cage.

Roll cage

The protective frame of steel surrounding a driver. It keeps the driver safe during an accident because it protects him from the impact of another car or of a wall if the car flips over. The roll cage consists of roll bars, which are made from steel tubing.

Roof flaps

Rectangular pieces of metal attached to the roof of a car that are designed to lie flat when the car is moving forward, but pop into the air when a car spins backwards or sideways, helping to keep a car from becoming airborne.

Rookie of the year

NASCAR awards rookie of the year honors to the first-year driver whose best 15 finishes are higher than any other first-year driver.

Rounds of wedge

Putting rounds of wedge into a car means a crew member is adjusting the handling by changing the pressure on the rear springs.

Rubber

A piece of rubber that's placed between the coils of a spring to increase tension and taken out to decrease tension. This changes how a car handles.

Running wide open

When drivers depress the accelerator all the way to the ground.

Saving tires

A driver takes it easy through the turns and doesn't run the car too hard, so his tires don't wear out too early.

Scanners

Walkman-sized instruments that pick up radio waves in the immediate area. They allow you to listen in on conversations between drivers and their crews during practice, qualifying, and races.

Scuffs

Tires that have been on the car during practice, used for only one or two laps. See also *sticker tires*.

Setup

The way a car is prepared for qualifying and a race, including the suspension package, weight distribution, and engine tuning.

Shock absorbers

Hydraulic cylinders attached to the car's wheel that make the car ride smoother over bumps.

Shock dynamometer

Machine that pumps the shock absorber up and down as if it were in a real car.

Short track

Racetracks shorter than one mile in length, where aerodynamics and horsepower aren't particularly important in winning the race. Bristol Motor Speedway, Martinsville Speedway, and Richmond International Raceway are the three NASCAR short tracks. See also *intermediate track, superspeedway*.

Show car

Former real race car that was taken out of the rotation for being too old, suffering irreparable damage, or just not being suited to the driver.

Show-car driver

A driver whose job is to drive a show car all over the country, bringing the car to stores, fairs, and driver appearances.

Spoiler

See *rear spoiler*.

Sponsors

The companies that pay for the right to have their names on cars and team uniforms.

Spotter

Team member who watches a race from on top of the grandstands or press box. His job is to be the driver's second set of eyes, telling the driver where to go on the racetrack to avoid an accident or when to pass another car.

Standing on time

Standing on time means a driver isn't going to participate in second-round qualifying. Instead, the driver hopes the time that he recorded during the first-round qualifying will be fast enough to make the field.

Sticker tires

New tires that still have the manufacturer's sticker on them. See also *scuffs*.

Stop-and-go penalty

When a driver must come down pit road, stop in his pit box for a moment, and then drive down pit road to the racetrack.

Superspeedway

An oval track that's two and a half or more miles long where NASCAR requires cars to use a carburetor restrictor plate. See also *intermediate track, short track.*

Suspension

The system of springs, shock absorbers, sway bars, and so on, directly connected to the wheels or the axles, that affects the handling of a race car.

Sway bars

Parts that alter the amount a car rolls to one side or the other through the turns.

Tachometer

The instrument used to measure the number of revolutions per minute. Drivers use it to determine how fast they are going. See also *revolutions per minute.*

Taking air off a spoiler

Instead of the air flowing onto the lead car's spoiler and pressing the car's rear-end into the track, it flows off and onto the second car's front end. That leaves the lead car with little rear-end downforce and causes it to become unstable and wiggle out of control, especially going through turns. See also *rear spoiler.*

Taping a car off

A crew places tape over the grill of the car in order to keep air from entering the radiator and slowing the car down. Done only during qualifying.

Team hauler

The place where the team hangs out when they're not working on their car. It's a large semi truck that is a team's base during a race weekend. It's a place to eat and hold meetings at the racetrack — some even take naps in the forward lounge.

Team manager

Team member who serves as the owner's representative in the shop, overseeing everything including ordering equipment, hiring personnel, and organizing test sessions.

Tearing down

When cars are torn down, teams take apart their engines, but tear downs also can include whatever NASCAR officials want. The winning team goes through a thorough tear down, meaning it will take apart the engine, the suspension, the power train, or whatever else officials want to check out.

Tech

NASCAR lingo for technical inspection. See also *inspection*.

Telemetry

Telemetry is a series of sensors attached to various parts of the car. Those sensors transmit information such as miles per gallon, revolutions per minute, and transmission gear selection to a remote computer. It's illegal for teams to use during official NASCAR events.

Templates

Individual pieces of metal that conform to the body of a car. They are blueprints of each car make, used to ensure that cars conform to NASCAR specifications.

Tight

When the front tires don't turn well through the turns because the front tires are losing traction before the rear tires are. When a car is tight, it also means it's *pushing* — and if a driver isn't careful, he'll end up zooming right into the wall. See also *loose*.

Tire carriers

Pit crew member who hands the tires to the tire changers and takes the used tires away.

Tire changers

Pit crew member who changes tires — one changes the front tires, another changes the rear tires.

Tire management

A driver keeps from pushing his car too hard so his tires last longer.

Tire specialist

Team member who changes the air pressure, measures the wear, and monitors the temperature of the tires that teams use during practice, qualifying, and races.

Track bar

The part of the rear suspension that's attached to the frame on one side and to the rear axle on the other. It keeps the car's rear tires centered within the car's body. Also called the *Panhard bar*.

Transponder

A transmitter that teams affix to the bottom of their cars to monitor lap times around a track.

Tri-oval

A modified oval racetrack with an extra turn to it, albeit a slight turn, instead of just four turns. Usually that turn is located mid-way down the *frontstretch*, which is the section of a racetrack between the last turn and the first turn.

Trunk lid

The rear deck lid.

Victory Lane

A roped-off or fenced-in area located in the infield where drivers, crews, owners, sponsors, and their families celebrate a victory.

Wet

A car that's filled with the maximum amounts of fuel, oil, and water.

Wheelbase

The distance between the axles on the same side of the car.

Wind tunnel

A tunnel that shoots wind at a car from all different angles. It's used to research how a car cuts through air as it moves forward.

Window nets

Screens made of a nylon mesh material that cover the driver's side window. They keep the driver's arms and head in the car in the event of an accident.

Winston "No Bull 5" program

An incentive program run by Winston, the NASCAR Winston Cup Series sponsor. Drivers become eligible for the $1 million prize by finishing in the top five at one of five "No Bull 5" races, and then winning the next "No Bull 5" race.

Appendix B

NASCAR Statistics

The NASCAR Winston Cup Series champions from 1949 to 1999 are as follows:

Year	Driver	No.	Car Owner	Car Type	Wins	Poles
1949	Red Byron	22	Raymond Parks	Oldsmobile	2	1
1950	Bill Rexford	60	Julian Buesink	Oldsmobile	1	0
1951	Herb Thomas	92	Herb Thomas	Hudson	7	4
1952	Tim Flock	91	Ted Chester	Hudson	8	4
1953	Herb Thomas	92	Herb Thomas	Hudson	11	10
1954	*	92	Herb Thomas	Hudson	12	8
1954	Lee Petty	42	*	Chrysler	7	3
1955	Tim Flock	300	Carl Kiekhaefer	Chrysler	18	19
1956	Buck Baker	300B	Carl Kiekhaefer	Chrysler	14	12
1957	Buck Baker	87	Buck Baker	Chevrolet	10	5
1958	Lee Petty	42	Petty Enterprises	Oldsmobile	7	4
1959	Lee Petty	42	Petty Enterprises	Plymouth	10	2
1960	Rex White	4	White-Clements	Chevrolet	6	3
1961	Ned Jarrett	11	W.G. Holloway Jr.	Chevrolet	1	4
1962	Joe Weatherly	8	Bud Moore	Pontiac	9	6
1963	*	21	Wood Brothers	Ford	3	5
1963	Joe Weatherly	8	*	Mercury	3	6
1964	Richard Petty	43	Petty Enterprises	Plymouth	9	8
1965	Ned Jarrett	11	Bondy Long	Ford	13	9
1966	David Pearson	6	Cotton Owens	Dodge	14	7

(continued)

Year	Driver	No.	Car Owner	Car Type	Wins	Poles
1967	Richard Petty	43	Petty Enterprises	Plymouth	27	18
1968	David Pearson	17	Holman-Moody	Ford	16	12
1969	David Pearson	17	Holman-Moody	Ford	11	14
1970	Bobby Isaac	71	Nord Krauskopf	Dodge	11	13
1971	Richard Petty	43	Petty Enterprises	Plymouth	21	9
1972	Richard Petty	43	Petty Enterprises	Plymouth	8	3
1973	Benny Parsons	72	L.G. DeWitt	Chevrolet	1	0
1974	Richard Petty	43	Petty Enterprises	Dodge	10	7
1975	Richard Petty	43	Petty Enterprises	Dodge	13	3
1976	Cale Yarborough	11	Junior Johnson	Chevrolet	9	2
1977	Cale Yarborough	11	Junior Johnson	Chevrolet	9	3
1978	Cale Yarborough	11	Junior Johnson	Oldsmobile	10	8
1979	Richard Petty	43	Petty Enterprises	Chevrolet	5	1
1980	Dale Earnhardt	2	Rod Osterlund	Chevrolet	5	0
1981	Darrell Waltrip	11	Junior Johnson	Buick	12	11
1982	Darrell Waltrip	11	Junior Johnson	Buick	12	7
1983	Bobby Allison	22	Bill Gardner	Buick	6	0
1984	Terry Labonte	44	Billy Hagan	Chevrolet	2	2
1985	Darrell Waltrip	11	Junior Johnson	Chevrolet	3	4
1986	Dale Earnhardt	3	Richard Childress	Chevrolet	5	1
1987	Dale Earnhardt	3	Richard Childress	Chevrolet	11	1
1988	Bill Elliott	9	Harry Melling	Ford	6	6
1989	Rusty Wallace	27	Raymond Beadle	Pontiac	6	4
1990	Dale Earnhardt	3	Richard Childress	Chevrolet	9	4
1991	Dale Earnhardt	3	Richard Childress	Chevrolet	4	0
1992	Alan Kulwicki	7	Alan Kulwicki	Ford	2	6
1993	Dale Earnhardt	3	Richard Childress	Chevrolet	6	2
1994	Dale Earnhardt	3	Richard Childress	Chevrolet	4	2
1995	Jeff Gordon	24	Rick Hendrick	Chevrolet	7	8

Year	Driver	No.	Car Owner	Car Type	Wins	Poles
1996	Terry Labonte	5	Rick Hendrick	Chevrolet	2	4
1997	Jeff Gordon	24	Rick Hendrick	Chevrolet	10	1
1998	Jeff Gordon	24	Rick Hendrick	Chevrolet	13	7
1999	Dale Jarrett	88	Robert Yates	Ford	4	0

*Various drivers or owners

The all-time NASCAR Winston Cup Series race winners from 1949 to 1999 are as follows:

Rank	Driver	Number of Wins
1.	Richard Petty*	200
2.	David Pearson*	105
3. (tie)	Bobby Allison*	84
	Darrell Waltrip	84
5.	Cale Yarborough*	83
6.	Dale Earnhardt#	74
7.	Lee Petty*	55
8. (tie)	Ned Jarrett*	50
	Junior Johnson*	50
10. (tie)	Jeff Gordon	49
	Rusty Wallace	49
12.	Herb Thomas*	48
13.	Buck Baker*	46
14. (tie)	Bill Elliott	40
	Tim Flock#	40
16.	Bobby Isaac#	37
17.	Fireball Roberts#	32
18.	Mark Martin	31
19. (tie)	Fred Lorenzen*	26

(continued)

Rank	Driver	Number of Wins
	Rex White*	26
21.	Jim Paschal*	25
22.	Joe Weatherly#	24
23.	Dale Jarrett	22
24. (tie)	Benny Parsons*	21
	Jack Smith*	21
	Terry Labonte	21
27. (tie)	Ricky Rudd	20
	Speedy Thompson#	20
29. (tie)	Buddy Baker*	19
	Davey Allison#	19
	Fonty Flock#	19
32. (tie)	Geoffrey Bodine	18
	Harry Gant*	18
	Neil Bonnett#	18
35. (tie)	Marvin Panch*	17
	Curtis Turner#	17
37.	Ernie Irvan*	15
38. (tie)	Dick Hutcherson*	14
	Lee Roy Yarborough#	14
40. (tie)	Tim Richmond#	13
	Dick Rathmann*	13
42.	Bobby Labonte	12
43.	Jeff Burton	11
44.	Donnie Allison*	10
45. (tie)	Cotton Owens*	9
	Paul Goldsmith*	9
47.	Kyle Petty	8
48. (tie)	Jim Reed*	7

Rank	Driver	Number of Wins
	A. J. Foyt*	7
	Bob Welborn#	7
	Darel Dieringer#	7
	Marshall Teague#	7
53.	Sterling Marlin	6
54. (tie)	Dave Marcis	5
	Ralph Moody*	5
	Dan Gurney*	5
	Alan Kulwicki#	5
58. (tie)	Ken Schrader	4
	Morgan Shepherd	4
	Hershel McGriff*	4
	Glen Wood*	4
	Lloyd Dane*	4
	Charlie Glotzbach*	4
	Pete Hamilton*	4
	Nelson Stacy#	4
	Bob Flock#	4
	Eddie Gray#	4
	Billy Wade#	4
	Eddie Pagan#	4
70. (tie)	Bobby Hamilton	3
	Parnelli Jones*	3
	Frank Mundy*	3
	Tiny Lund#	3
	Bill Blair#	3
	Dick Linder#	3
	Tony Stewart	3

(continued)

Rank	Driver	Number of Wins
77. (tie)	John Andretti	2
	Derrike Cope	2
	Jimmy Spencer	2
	Bobby Johns*	2
	Al Keller#	2
	Elmo Langley#	2
	Danny Letner*	2
	Billy Myers#	2
	Jimmy Pardue#	2
	Tom Pistone*	2
	Marvin Porter*	2
	Gober Sosebee#	2
	Gwyn Staley#	2
	Emanuel Zervakis*	2
	Red Byron#	2
	Johnny Beauchamp#	2
	Ray Elder*	2
	James Hylton*	2
95. (tie)	Richard Brickhouse*	1
	Brett Bodine	1
	Ward Burton	1
	Bobby Hillin Jr.	1
	Jeremy Mayfield	1
	Joe Nemecheck	1
	Phil Parsons	1
	Greg Sacks	1
	Lake Speed	1
	Dick Brooks*	1
	Bob Burdick*	1

Rank	Driver	Number of Wins
95. (tie)(continued)	Marvin Burke*	1
	June Cleveland*	1
	Jim Cook*	1
	Bobby Courtwright#	1
	Mark Donohue#	1
	Joe Eubanks#	1
	Lou Figaro#	1
	Jimmy Florian*	1
	Larry Frank*	1
	Danny Graves*	1
	Royce Hagerty	1
	Jim Hurtubise#	1
	Joe Lee Johnson*	1
	John Kieper*	1
	Harold Kite#	1
	Paul Lewis*	1
	Johnny Mantz#	1
	Sam McQuagg*	1
	Lloyd Moore*	1
	Norm Nelson*	1
	Bill Norton*	1
	Dick Passwater*	1
	Lennie Pond*	1
	Bill Rexford#	1
	Jody Ridley*	1
	Shorty Rollins*	1
	Jim Roper*	1
	Earl Ross*	1

(continued)

Rank	Driver	Number of Wins
95. (tie)(continued)	John Rostek*	1
	Johnny Rutherford*	1
	Leon Sales*	1
	Frankie Schneider*	1
	Wendell Scott#	1
	Buddy Shuman#	1
	John Soares Jr.*	1
	Chuck Stevenson*	1
	Donald Thomas#	1
	Tommy Thompson*	1
	Art Watts*	1
	Danny Weinberg*	1
	Jack White*	1
	Mario Andretti*	1
	Earl Balmer*	1
	Bill Amick#	1
	Ron Bouchard*	1
	Johnny Allen*	1
	Neil Cole*	1

*Retired
#Deceased

Appendix C
Race Car Numbers

Look for the following race car numbers to locate your favorite drivers during a race:

Car Number	Driver
1	Steve Park
2	Rusty Wallace
4	Bobby Hamilton
5	Terry Labonte
6	Mark Martin
7	Michael Waltrip
8	Dale Earnhardt Jr.
11	Brett Bodine
12	Jeremy Mayfield
13	Robby Gordon
14	Mike Bliss
15	Derrike Cope
16	Kevin Lepage
17	Matt Kenseth
18	Bobby Labonte
20	Tony Stewart
21	Elliott Sadler
22	Ward Burton
23	Jimmy Spencer
24	Jeff Gordon

Car Number	Driver
25	Jerry Nadeau
28	Ricky Rudd
31	Mike Skinner
32	Scott Pruett
33	Joe Nemechek
36	Ken Schrader
40	Sterling Marlin
43	John Andretti
44	Kyle Petty
45	Johnny Benson
55	Kenny Wallace
60	Geoffrey Bodine
66	Darrell Waltrip
71	Dave Marcis
75	Wally Dallenbach Jr.
77	Robert Pressley
88	Dale Jarrett
93	Dave Blaney
94	Bill Elliott
97	Chad Little
99	Jeff Burton
00	Buckshot Jones

Index

• *N* •

• *O* •

• *P* •

• Q •

• R •

Before each event, many drivers gather with family, friends, and a minister to pray that the race will be a safe one.

Teammates like Mark Martin and Jeff Burton exchange information about their cars and give advice to each other throughout the season.

Steven Rose - Motorsports Memories

David Schenk

Roush Racing teammates Mark Martin and Jeff Burton give each other tips on how to go faster — but only before the race begins. After the green flag drops, it's every driver for himself.

Most drivers bring their families to the track, but only the winning driver gets to bring them to Victory Lane. After winning the Bud Shootout at Daytona International Speedway in 1999, Mark Martin celebrated with his wife, Arlene, and son, Matt.

Drivers become accustomed to talking to the media throughout race weekend, even minutes before beginning the race.

Victory Lane ceremonies are emotional and joyous, but they can be kitschy, at times, too. Here, Mark Martin poses with Wayne Newton and two showgirls after winning the 1998 Las Vegas 400.

Sometimes, Victory Lane ceremonies are rowdier than others. When Mark Martin won the 1998 Winston All-Star event, he and his crew went wild. Jeff Gordon had dominated the race, but ran out of gas to give Martin the surprise win.

After a driver wins, his crew usually escorts the car into Victory Lane, where photographers, TV and radio reporters, sponsors, and family await the celebration.

Driving with injuries is part of the racing business. Even with a broken wrist, broken ribs, and a broken kneecap that required surgery, Mark Martin didn't miss a single race in 1999. Here, crew members help him into his car.

Some accidents look worse than they really are. Even though a car's sheet metal is crushed and torn off, teams make cosmetic repairs and send the driver back into the race.

Teams don't pack up and go home after their driver crashes the car. They hurry to repair the car so that their driver can return to the racetrack and gain precious points for the championship.

NASCAR racing can get ugly when cars running side-by-side at full speed get together and tangle. Even the slightest miscalculation by a driver can send cars spinning into an accident.

Drivers don't want to waste time, so they often peel out of the pit box while their pit crew gives them a friendly shove in the right direction.

Pit crew members leap over the wall and into their pit box even before their car comes to a full stop.

Steven Rose – Motorsports Memories

The pit crew runs around the car carrying tires, air guns, jacks, or gas cans. While rushing to finish, the pit crew tries to perform their duties meticulously because one mistake can cost their driver the race.

Steven Rose – Motorsports Memories

As soon as the driver pulls his car into the garage during practice, the crew huddles around the window to get the driver's input. The crew then makes the discussed adjustments before the car returns to the track.

Steven Rose – Motorsports Memories

Mark Martin and team owner, Jack Roush, have been together at Roush Racing since the beginning of their NASCAR Winston Cup Series careers, which began in 1988. It's easy to pick out Roush in a crowd because he always wears his trademark straw hat.

Communication is the most important element in a successful driver/crew chief relationship. Mark Martin and Jimmy Fennig understand each other so well that often just a handful of words suffices. When Mark says the car is a "little loose," Jimmy knows exactly what changes to make to the car.

NASCAR fans often show their support by wearing T-shirts or hats bearing their favorite driver's name and number. They also bring banners and flags into the stands to help cheer on their driver.

NASCAR drivers pride themselves at being accessible to fans, stopping to sign autographs and chat at the racetrack as much as they can.